BOURBON STREET BLACK

Danny Barker. Photographed by Jack V. Buerkle.

Bourbon Street Black

THE NEW ORLEANS BLACK JAZZMAN

Jack V. Buerkle and Danny Barker

New York OXFORD UNIVERSITY PRESS 1973

To the people of Bourbon Street Black.
May their future be as brilliant
as their past and present.

Preface

SOMETIME AROUND 1897, the Charles "Buddy" Bolden band began filling the dance halls and streets of New Orleans with a new kind of music. Instead of following the notes on sheet music like they were a railroad track, Buddy made his cornet an extension of his emotions. To this rough Negro barber, popular melodies were only points of embarkation for funky, hip-swinging improvisation. Some twenty years later this new music would be called *jazz*. Many years after that it would be recognized as America's unique contribution to the arts.

In the early days of the development of jazz, Bolden was an apt personification of the music: earthy, undisiciplined, and moving with an abandon as if there would be no tomorrow. Buddy's days as a musician would, indeed, be few. By 1907 he had developed a severe mental illness and was committed to a state hospital where, twenty years later, he died alone and almost unnoticed. But jazz continued to develop and spread its exciting rhythms and tonalities throughout the world. It grew as a music of the people and was early castigated by middle class moralizers as an agent of the Devil. Saloons, night clubs, brothels, barrel-houses, bistros, and some Negro dance halls became its principal sites. Almost from the beginning, those who played it and those who listened were branded as deviant. Though jazz is frequently played in concert halls today, and its practitioners have gained considerable in prestige, the words "jazz musician" still bring an image of a deviant stereotype to many who ponder them. But, do we really know very much about jazzmen as persons? To what extent have history and circumstance given them distinctive individual and group characteristics? This book is our attempt to answer those questions as they apply to New Orleans black musicians.

Where other works about jazzmen have used history, fiction, biography, autobiography, criticism, or musicology, we have studied a community of musicians and have utilized the methods of sociology, ethnography, and social history. *Bourbon Street Black*—this community of musicians, their families, friends, and followers—is almost one hundred years old. How has the heritage of Bolden, Kid Ory, Alphonse Picou, Freddie Keppard, King Oliver, Jelly Roll Morton, and Louis Armstrong affected these people? What do they remember of their childhood in New Orleans? What is their family life like today? How do they spend their leisure time? What do they think of the music business, "squares," race relations, God, and themselves?

While *Bourbon Street Black* is a scientific study of the style of life of a people, we have endeavoured to capture the humanity in this setting. The text is permeated with quotes by the musicians that we feel are an accurate representation of our statistical results. Footnotes are intended mainly for those who wish more information or technical certification. Many theoretical and technical issues that were a part of the overall project are not dealt with here, but will appear in professional behavioral science and musical journals. To the best of our knowledge, though, none of these are contradictory to those reported here. The appendix gives an overview of our method of procedure for readers who may wish to know how we collected and analyzed the data.

A few years ago, Buerkle (a sociologist and former musician) was visiting New Orleans for the first time. Part of his mission was to locate a prominent New Orleans jazzman, Danny Barker, who had come home after many years of playing in the North. Barker had been a long-time guitarist and banjo player with Cab Calloway. He had worked with Jelly Roll Morton and Sidney Bechet. Buerkle had thought of telephoning Barker requesting an opportunity to meet him, but then decided a visit to the New Orleans Jazz Museum would be the more appropriate first approach. There a man greeted him and Buerkle said, "I'm looking for Danny Barker, the world's greatest banjo player. Can you help me?" The man smiled and said, "Speakin' to ya!" With these words this book began.

Acknowledgments

THE STEPS TAKEN to produce this book were complex and required the generous efforts and involvement of many persons and organizations. We cannot possibly note all persons who should be thanked, but following are a few who played important roles in the development of this work.

In New Orleans, our greatest debt is to all those musicians, members of Local 496, who consented to tell us about their lives. Among that group, Louis Cottrell and Alvin Alcorn, President and Vice President of Local 496, American Federation of Musicians, gave valuable assistance in our preparation of Chapter 5, "The Local." Olivia Charlot, former secretary of the Local, assisted in contacting many of those we had chosen to interview. Others especially helpful in our efforts were Sam Alcorn, Louis Barbarin, Clifford Brown, Wallace Davenport, Clyde Kerr, Sr., Cary Lavigne, Isaac "Snookum" Russell, and Clement Tervalon. We wish to thank Mrs. Paul Barbarin for allowing us to include the lyrics of her late husband's song, "The Second Line," as the introduction to Chapter 4. Sociological colleague Paul Roman (Tulane) was especially helpful to the project. A. Grayson Clark of Heritage Hall (formerly Dixieland Hall) gave us considerable insight into the "club and hall scene" in New Orleans. The New Orleans Jazz Museum graciously contributed the jazz funeral photograph for our collection. We would also like to thank Floyd Levin for use of his photograph of the Fairview Baptist Church Christian Band.

In Philadelphia, Temple University gave both encouragement and financial support for our work. Special thanks are due the Research and Study Leave Committee of the Faculty Senate, and the Computing Center. Eleanor Marshall gave strong encouragement from the project's beginning. She typed much of the rough and final drafts, and commented at length on the manuscript. Sociological colleagues David Berger, Rosalie Cohen, Eleanor Engram DeAlmeida, Robert Kleiner, Robert Stebbins (Memorial University of Newfoundland), and Holger Stub all gave valuable advice concerning our work. Dean George W. Johnson of Liberal Arts was a constant source of support. Gerald McGoneghy assisted in the construction of the interview schedule and the codes and completed a number of the interviews. Jim Wilson assisted in the computer analysis, and Linda Wood, of the Music Department of the Free Library of Philadelphia helped in solving several problems associated with song copyrights. Joe Witcher, vice president and editor of the F. A. Davis Publishing Co. and his editorial assistant, Jody Scranton, gave important editorial advice, and encouragement.

Much of the credit for whatever lasting value this work will have should go to Sheldon Meyer, executive editor, Oxford University Press. His insights into editorial problems, and the jazz scene have been invaluable. Harriet Serenkin, our assistant editor at Oxford, gave many insights and manifested considerable patience with the sometimes over-possessive authors.

We are obliged to several music publishers who were very helpful by giving permission to quote the lyrics of the songs we used as supportive material: The Anne-Rachel Music Corporation for "Cow-Cow" Davenport's "Mama Don't Allow It"; The Duchess Music Corporation for Paul Barbarin's "The Second Line"; Folkways Music Publishers, Inc. for "When the Saint's Go Marching In," new words and music arrangement by Paul Campbell; and, the Edward B. Marks Music Corporation for Arthur Herzog's and Billie Holiday's "God Bless the Child."

We wish to thank the following authors, editors, and book publishers for their permission to use these materials: From *Mister Jelly Roll*, by Alan Lomax. Copyright © 1950 by Duell, Sloan and Pearce, pp. 83-85. Reprinted by permission of Hawthorn Books, Inc., 70 Fifth Avenue, New York, N. Y. 10011. From *The French Quarter*, by Herbert Asbury. Copyright © 1936 by Alfred A. Knopf, Inc., pp. 451-54, and reprinted with their permission. From *Satchmo: My Life in New Orleans*, by Louis Armstrong. Copyright © 1954 by Louis Armstrong. Published by Prentice-Hall, Inc., Englewood Cliffs, N. J. and reprinted with their permission. From *Young Man With A Horn*, by Dorothy Baker. Copyright © 1938 by Dorothy Baker. Published by Houghton Mifflin Company, p. 4, and reprinted with their permission. From *Treat It Gentle*, by Sidney Bechet. Published 1960 by Hill and Wang, A Division of Farrar, Straus and Giroux. pp. 217-18, and reprinted with their permission. From the journal *Arts and Society* (University of Wisconsin), "Market and Moralist Censors of a Rising Art Form: Jazz," by Richard A. Peterson, pp. 254-55, and reprinted with the permission of the managing editor. From *Hear Me Talkin' To Ya'*, edited by Nat Shapiro and Nat Hentoff. Copyright © 1955 by Nat Shapiro and Nat Hentoff. Reprinted by permission of Holt, Rinehart and Winston, Inc. George W. Cable, "The Dance in The Place Congo," from *Creoles and Cajuns: Stories of Old Louisiana*, ed. Arlin Turner. Copyright © 1959 by Arlin Turner. Published by Doubleday, Inc., pp. 369-78, and reprinted with the permission of Arlin Turner.

Our parents, Henry and Clemence Buerkle, and Moses and Rose Barker, gave us an appreciation for music and a sensitivity to the people who play it. During the years this book has been in preparation, our families have been indulgent and sustaining far beyond what might be fairly expected. Blue Lu Barker was especially helpful in matters relating to the history of jazz and the blues. Martie, Steve, and Melanie Buerkle read the manuscript at all stages of development and helped shape many aspects of style. Beyond this, they understood the compulsion that made hermit out of husband and father longer than it should have.

Contents

1

Sportin' Houses and all That Jazz

JEAN BAPTISTE LE MOYNE, SIEUR DE BIENVILLE was a patient man. He had to be, for his little band of entrepreneurs had gone up and down the river on several occasions locating town sites for Louis XIV's recent namesake, Louisiana. During these travels he commented in his log that a particular bend in the river, thirty leagues from its mouth, was "one of the most beautiful crescents of the entire river." Each time he passed the crescent, Bienville became more convinced of its value to their development program. Then he decided he would build a community in this special place. He would never know just how special it was to become.

Nouvelle Orleans

What an exquisite, sonorous name! It was registered in Paris late in 1717, and sometime in March or April 1718 Bienville rowed ashore with eighty men to begin clearing land for the settlement. Though it had the virtue of access from both the river and Lake Pontchartrain (six miles from the chosen site), the place was not exactly a paradise. It was swampy at a number of points, a haven for reptiles and mosquitoes during the summer, and a damp, cold basin in the winter. Things went slowly at first as a few primitive huts were erected. The early Vieux Carré (commonly called the

French Quarter) offered little to attract a stable population and many of its early inhabitants were French deportees of "low character." Family oriented men, unable to tolerate loneliness and vice within the new settlement, were returning home. Recognizing the threat to the colony's growth, Bienville curtailed the influx of undesirables and searched frantically for way to build stability into his little town.

Gradually, he was able to bring new populations of voluntary colonists to the area, and by the late 1720s he had encouraged the Capuchin monks, Jesuits, and Ursuline nuns to settle there. A large group of "hardy and stable" Germans were persuaded to stay and establish themselves just above the city on what is now known as the German Coast. He brought women who were eligible for marriage. They were the "Casket Girls" from the middle and upper-middle strata of French society, who got their name from the distinctive casket-shaped trunk (containing clothes and a small dowry) given them by the French government when they agreed to colonization with intent to marry. Upon arrival in New Orleans, the young women, under the supervision of the Ursuline nuns, began courtship with potential mates. With this gradual stabilizing of the "quality" of its population, the new colony became more attractive to prospective settlers.

Bienville, a French-Canadian of great strength was able to guide the fortunes of Louisiana for forty years. These were frustrating and turbulent times for him, but he saw the first arrival of the Acadians from Nova Scotia, and of the Negro slaves to ease the lives of the whites. He probably didn't realize as he left his seat of power that the first Golden Age of New Orleans was about to begin and that it would herald further arrivals from Spain, Africa, the West Indies, British America, Ireland, and Italy. Elements within the Crescent City had begun to fuse into that salmagundi of humanity that people travel thousands of miles to see today.

That Special Style

With Pierre Cavagnial de Rigaud de Vaudreuil, Marquis and Governor of Louisiana from 1743 to 1753, New Orleans underwent transformation from a struggling frontier town into a vital multidimensional community. His tenure was short, but the cultural tone that Vaudreuil emphasized, along with Latin Catholicism and a particular combination of racial and ethnic subcultures, would facilitate the creation of America's single, unique, art form—*jazz*.

Through his wife's influence, the Marquis initiated a round of banquets, balls, promenades, parades, and card parties that gave New Orleans, a distinctive élan. The Marquis' and Marquise's relish for partying fit well into the Latin Catholic's penchant for unloading any pent-up passion during pre-Lenten days. With the encouragement of Vaudreuil, celebrations literally exploded within the city for months before Carnival (Mardi Gras). It was then that Mardi Gras began to take on the rudiments of the pre-Lenten celebration we know today. By this time, the social-class structure of the colony had developed to the point where a substantial upper-middle and upper class were enthusiastic about finding new ways to offset the boredom and rigors of colony life. To make it even easier, they had acquired the requisite corps of servants. New Orleans, almost from the very beginning, was a city of pleasure. Pleasure from a Crescent City point of view meant music, dancing, parading, art, good food, and relatively open fornication: a kind of perpetual hedonic binge with *style*; a style probably unmatched to this day.

While the increasingly cosmopolitan New Orleans continued to indulge its fancies, Louisiana was undergoing great political changes. In 1762 Louis XV gave Louisiana to his cousin, Charles III of Spain. The Spanish were not exactly welcome in what was then essentially a French community, but after a few executions and imprisonment of dissenters, things settled down to mutual toleration. By 1800 Napoleon had forced Spain to cede Louisiana to France. Finally, the United States demanded that they be allowed to buy the territory from France to ensure free access to the Mississippi, and Napoleon agreed. The transfer took place on December 20, 1803.

The political shifts during the eighteenth century had not altered the fundamental tone of the city—it was still basically French. And while all the political maneuvering was occurring, other changes were taking place. The river was beginning to demonstrate its dominance in the economic life of the area with an increasingly strong symbiotic relationship developing between the Port of New Orleans, the city's bankers and merchants, and the Anglo–American plantation system which had begun to exploit its major product—cotton.

Entertainment of all kinds continued to permeate the environs. Henry Arnold Krem has commented that even by the early 1800s New Orleans was literally overrun by music stores, with over eighty businesses dealing in some form of music.[1] The patrons of the arts had been effective, too, for beginning with the first decade of the nineteenth century, New Orleans opera, was for forty years, the standard to be copied in America. One company on St. Peter Street presented 92 operas in 374 performances between 1805 and 1811. Several companies toured metropolitan communities on the East Coast and in the South between 1827 and 1845, playing most of the time to packed houses. Outdoor and indoor concerts were everywhere. In an era when dancing was a popular pastime, in New Orleans, it was a mania. The varied cultural backgrounds in the population produced a wealth of celebrations and festivities. At these, the French tendency to parade at the slightest excuse (a Napoleonic legacy) was copied by other groups, and then every holiday came replete with parade bands and martial music. It seemed that every organization had a band: secret societies; lodges; fire companies; the police, religious, and military organizations, among others.

Sin had also become highly organized, and in some cases institutionalized. For the lower orders of society there were the standard, and relatively uninspiring, whorehouses. These "cat-houses" had become much more plentiful with the advent of in-creased Mississippi River traffic from the North. Down the stream they came! Flatboats, barges, rafts, and dugouts. The "Kaintucks" (Americans from places like Kentucky or Tennes-see) of every shape and size of backwoods hick you could imag-ine; all braving the treachery of the pirates, Indians, the varmints, and not least of all, the river. Assuming they did not get stabbed while in a brothel, it was probable they would be "rolled" before moving a block away afterwards. Still, they beat their way back up the river for another load (sometimes they walked), got their cargo, and headed back toward the big city for more adventure.

Some men stand out above the others in matters of ingenuity. One such individual was Auguste Tessier. An astute observer of the social climate of the city in the early part of the nineteenth century, he noted that it had been difficult for a number of upper-class men to carry on a hallowed tradition of their fore-bears—the mistress. Mistresses were hard to come by in North America. Not just any whore would do. The lady had to be re-fined as well as beautiful and sensuous. He arranged to have de-serving young ladies and eligible men brought together under the most proper circumstances—the *Bals du Cordon Bleu* (The Quad-roon Balls). The finest octoroons (one-eighth Negro) in all New Orleans were recruited for the dances where they were to make their choice of patron. The balls became so popular they were scheduled for eight to twelve times a month. Once the sponsor had made his choice, the lady was usually provided with servants and a nice house that became the love nest. A number of these houses were located on Rampart Street. The balls continued until the 1860s when the fine young men were called to war.

The Creative Admixture

More than 100 years before the Civil War, an action had been taken in the French colony that would foster another condition for the creation of jazz—the *Code Noir*. This Black Code of 1724 regulated the interaction between the growing number of slaves and their owners. It provided for the manumission, or freeing, of slaves with the consent of the owner. Miscegenation, resulting from liaisons of female slaves and their white owners had occurred widely. Because they had developed strong emotional relationships in these unions many owners began either to free the women and their children outright, or to provide for their release in their will. As free persons, the women were able to own property, and in a large number of instances were given bequests which were substantial. This was the introduction of the *Creole of Color* into New Orleans life.

By 1830, some of these *gens de couleur* had arrived at such a degree of wealth as to own cotton and sugar plantations with numerous slaves. They educated their children, as they had been educated, in France. Those who chose to remain there, attained, many of them, distinction in scientific and literary circles. In New Orleans they became musicians, merchants, and money and real estate brokers. The humbler classes were mechanics; they monopolized the trade of shoemakers; a trade for which, even to this day, they have a special vocation; they were barbers, tailors, carpenters, upholsterers. They were notably successful hunters and supplied the city with game. As tailors, they were almost exclusively patronized by the *elite*, so much so that the Legoasters', the Dumas', the Clovis', the Lacroix', acquired individually fortunes of several hundred thousands of dollars. . . . At the Orleans theatre they attended their mothers, wives, and sisters in the second tier reserved exclusively for them, and where no white person of either sex would have been permitted to intrude.[2]

Also, their craftsmen built many of the lovely homes and churches in the city. The bulk of the cast-iron lace adorning many of the older homes is their creation. A distinguished Philharmonic Society bore their imprint, and they organized musicales at an impressive rate. This freedom of movement of the Creole of Color, at least its extent, was unprecedented on the North American continent for persons of partial African heritage. This peculiarity arose primarily as a result of the Latin-oriented and relatively tolerant Spanish and French rule. By the beginning of the nineteenth century, the Creoles occupied a position very near the top of the social order of the city and though excluded from certain areas of white interaction, they had created their own social units, equal to and often vastly superior to all others in the community.

On April 12, 1861, the situation changed drastically with the start of the Civil War which brought to an end the political and economic influence of the Creoles of Color in New Orleans. Events transpired that culminated in the disenfranchisement of the colored Creoles, the destruction of their vast economic holdings, and the introduction of a newly enforced racial segregation. The Louisiana Legislative Code No. 111 designated that anyone of any African ancestry was Negro. This was irony supreme. A war that was supposed to clip the shackles from the black man had indirectly led to a new restricted class of Negroes. The change was devastating for the Creole of Color; it required the laborious task of creating a new self-image. With the imposition of the Code, Creole businessmen lost large numbers of their local white customers, and real estate brokers were eased out of their property. Cultural organizations requiring financial support were dissolved. The Philharmonic Society and the musicales discontinued. Creole artisans were soon completely out of the skilled trades, but some small craftsmen and shopkeepers were able to keep operating on a minimal basis, their customers being the penniless Negroes and almost equally indigent Creoles. In many instances, what had once been an avocation or a hobby became the basis for a new and usually precarious occupation. Money brokers became laborers, and merchants were transformed into musicians.

Now it was necessary to play music in order to earn money— the best way to do this being to join a band or orchestra. Because the whole city was organization minded, social events requiring the services of musicians were frequent. Creoles and blacks had begun to form their own marching bands by the 1860s, and Rudi Blesh stated that there were no fewer than thirteen of their bands represented at the funeral of President Garfield in 1881.[3] These bands usually had no more than twelve men, who at first played primarily martial music modeled after the Napoleonic era as well as music popular to the day and place. Because of the extraordinary development of classical music and opera, many musicians were able to get placed in the professional orchestras. For a long time, though, most of the paying jobs in music came from the Negro community. The Creoles of Color and darker complexioned Negroes formed a multitude of voluntary associations (lodges, clubs, etc.), and these often became the principal customers who hired the band to play music to celebrate success and to assuage death. Music, though, was not a full-time occupation for them as most supplemented their musical earnings with a wide variety of menial occupations.

The Creoles of Color, making their adjustment to new occupations, tried to capitalize on their educational background and training whenever possible. This worked reasonably well for a time, especially in the area of music; and then it came—a new sound—a new rhythm—disturbing, yet intriguing, played by the black man, newly disgorged from his plantation bondage. He had settled in the rough Uptown section of the city (above Canal Street) and was forcing the refined, Downtown Creole of Color to respond to his new ideas of how to play music. The Creole violinist, Paul Dominguez, in reflecting on this problem, said to Alan Lomax:

You see, we Downtown people, we try to be intelligent. Everybody learn a trade, like my daddy was a cigarmaker and so was I. . . . We try to bar jail. . . . Uptown, cross Canal [street] yonder, they *used* to jail. . . . There's a vast difference here in this town. Uptown folk all ruffians, cut up in the face and live on the river. All they know is—get out on the levee and truck cotton—be longshoremen, screwmen. And me, I ain't never been on the river a *day in my life.* . . . See, us Downtown people, we didn't think so much of this Uptown jazz until we couldn't make a living otherwise . . . they made a fiddler out of a violinist—me, I'm talking about. A fiddler is *not* a violinist, but a violinist *can* be a fiddler. If I wanted to make a living, I had to be rowdy like the other group. I had to jazz it or rag it or any other damn thing. . . . Bolden cause all that. He cause all these younger Creoles, men like Bechet and Keppard to have a different style altogether from the old heads like Tio and Perez. I don't know how they do it. But goddam, they'll do it. Can't tell you what's there on the paper, but just play the hell out of it.[4]

Such was the moan of an old man reflecting on what had become of a once golden Creole world. Dominguez's reaction to the intrusion of the black man into his musical scene was something from which he never really quite recovered. It should not, though, be taken as a typical response of the Downtown Creole to the new music. As Dominguez mentioned, many of them went wild about it and studied it to the point where their names are among the all-time "greats" of the jazz world. In general, though, the reaction of the non-musical segment of Creole society was, in the beginning, lukewarm to negative. It was simply one more detraction from their former way of life—a dream they had seen slip out of their hands.

Down Home Blues

Badoum! Badoum! Badoum! The drummers' signal went flying over the low roofs of the Vieux Carré from the clearing on the edge of town. The place—Congo Square. It was 1835, a Sunday afternoon. They came in groups of two and three at first, but within half an hour the field was a patchwork of color and sound. There were pantaloons, cotton shirts, petticoats, and the *tignon* accompanying the jingle of ankle bells. Whether or not they had come to that place via Haiti or Santo Domingo, you could see in their faces the Mandingoes from the Gambia River, the Cotocolies, Iboes and Awassas, the Senegalese from Cape Verde, the Socoes and Popoes. They chattered and sang as they waited for it to begin. George Washington Cable, the South's first significant postbellum author, describes what happens next:

In stolen hours of night or the basking hour of noon the black man contrived to fashion these rude instruments and others. The drum-

mers . . . bestrode the drums; the other musicians sat around them
in an arc, cross-legged on the ground. One important instrument was
a gourd partly filled with pebbles or grains of corn, flourished vio-
lently at the end of a staff with one hand and beaten upon the palm
of the other. Other performers rang triangles, and others twanged
from the Jew's-harps an astonishing amount of sound. Another instrument was the jawbone of some ox, horse or mule, and a key
rattled rhythmically along its weather-beaten teeth. . . . But the
grand instrument at last, the first violin, as one might say, was the
banjo. It had but four strings, not six: beware of the dictionary. . . .
To all this there was sometimes added a Pan's pipe of but three
reeds, made from single joints of the common brake cane, and called
by English-speaking Negroes "the quill." One may even at this day
hear the black lad, sauntering home at sunset behind a few cows
that he had found near the edge of the canebrake whence he has
also cut his three quills, blowing and hooting, over and over. . . .
There was entertaining variety. Where? In the endless dance! There
was constant, exhilarating novelty—endless invention—in the turn-
ing, bowing, arm swinging, posturing and leaping of the dancers.
Moreover, the music of the Congo Plains was not tamed to mere
monotone. Monotone became subordinate to many striking qualities.
The strain was wild. Its contact with French taste gave it often great
tenderness and sentiment. It grew in fervor, and rose and sank, and
rose again, with the play of emotion in the singers and dancers. . . .
The women's voices rise to a tremulous intensity. Among the chorus
of Franc-Congo singing girls is one of extra good voice, who thrusts
in, now and again, an *improvisation*. This girl here, so tall and
straight, is a Yaloff. You see it in her almost Hindoo features, and
hear it in the plaintive melody of her voice. Now the chorus is more
piercing than ever. The women clap their hands in time, or standing
with arms akimbo, receive the faint courtesies and head liftings the
low bows of the men, who deliver them swinging this way and that.
. . . Will they dance to that measure? Wait! A sudden frenzy seizes
the musicians. The measure quickens, the swaying, attitudinizing
crowd starts into extra activity, the female voices grow sharp and
staccato, and suddenly the dance is the furious *Bamboula*. . . . The
ecstasy rises to madness; one—two—three of the dancers fall—blou-
coutoum! boum!—and are dragged out by arms and legs from under
the tumultous feet of crowding newcomers. The musicians know no
fatigue; still the dance rages on:

Quand patate la cuite na va mangé li![5]

This was their "free" day, these slaves and bond servants. They were reveling in another of the currents that would feed the new jazz. The dances in Congo Square were encouraged by the whites to allow slaves to release tension, and to discourage Voodoo (Vodun). Certainly there must have been some tension release in the dances, but their effect did little to discourage the Voodoo practices! The bulk of activities at Congo Square involved Voodoo, with the music, dancing, and other performances being a cover for its practice. The whites were simply insensitive to its presence. New Orleans and much of the West Indies were, of course, predominantly Catholic, and their slaves had been proselytized into Catholicism. What had not been realized was that the Negroes readily absorbed the Catholic Saints because they reinforced and duplicated their own older (in their sense) African gods. The two religions existed in harmony (at least from the black perspective) side by side. The whites were never really able to control Voodoo fully, and it went on playing its part in the New Orleans black man's music. The dances at Congo Square went on until the Civil War, were disbanded during the War, and resumed until 1885, when authorities terminated them because they were "disruptive."

He was only seventeen years old when they stopped the revelry at Congo Square, but he had seen enough. He was the young man Paul Dominguez was to raise hell about over sixty-five years later—Charles "Buddy" Bolden, King Bolden, or Buddy the King. He was a barber by trade and had played in brass bands for funerals, Carnival, picnics and dozens of kinds of events. In the summer of 1894 he got up in front of a crowd at Globe Hall and turned his cornet into an extension of his very soul as he wailed a blues number. His playing had some of the Congo Square ease and flavor, but it was something more, something new. Buddy played practically everywhere in the New Orleans black world, but he concentrated on Lincoln and Johnson Parks. They say when he pointed that cornet toward town on a quiet night, you could hear him seven and one-half miles away. That was his way of advertising that there was a dance that night. Danny Barker[6] says the distance his horn would "carry" has to do with both the acoustics of the New Orleans area and its swampy land surface. There was a lot of ragtime in what Buddy did; ragtime and the new music fused in those beginning days. Since he made no records, what we know about his style is based on the memory of those who saw him. Louis Armstrong, commenting on hearing Bolden's playing, said it had a crude, rough sound compared to later players.

Bolden was a rough Uptown Baptist Negro who lived life as though there were no tomorrow. His time was short. A life of long hours, booze, and the "chicks," caught up with him in 1907 when he was thirty-eight years old. One day, after months of scrapping with the men in his band, he fell behind in a parade, murmuring to himself. When they took him to East Louisiana State Hospital that afternoon, he was diagnosed as a paranoid schizophrenic. He died alone in that hospital in 1931 and remains in the minds of jazz appreciators and musicians the first clear and distinguishable link to the new form of music.

Even before Bolden was committed, this new music had begun to spread throughout New Orleans. The brass bands that had partially fed it were being fed *by* it. A new kind of bounce was leaping out of the rhythm sections and cornets. It was a kind of syncopation, but something new you couldn't get out of "note music."

Both the Civil War and the Spanish American War had dumped large numbers of used musical instruments into pawn shops when military and naval bands dissolved in New Orleans. A fascinating thing occurred. The Uptown blacks, fresh off the plantation, gradually gained possession of many of these European musical instruments. They really didn't have anyone to teach them or, especially to *tell them the official limits of these horns,* so they just blew them in their own way. The tonalities, linked with their African rhythms, were combined to produce Buddy Bolden's sound. They just played like they felt and sang.

At the turn of the century, the most popular music in America was ragtime. A Negro with European classical training, Scott Joplin, was making America jump to his "Maple Leaf Rag." This was not a New Orleans movement, but it had its effect there on the new music as elements of ragtime entered into jazz. "Muskrat Ramble" and "That's a Plenty," both rags, were both a part of the early jazzman's repertoire. It's worth noting here, too, that the ragtime pianist became prominent playing, first ragtime, then jazz, in New Orleans' brothels. Actually, in this setting, these men became the highest paid musicians in the city. Several other musical currents were merging to produce the new jazz as spirituals, the blues, and the songs of minstrelsy had their impact.

In the late 1800s the musicians were playing for practically nothing, but their talents were used intensively. Alphonse Picou, for instance, spoke of playing almost continuously over a three day period as he moved from job to job. He said, "sometimes my clarinet seemed to weigh a thousand pounds."[7] Things were difficult for all the "colored," but Picou remembered some of the brighter times when he reminisced, "those were the happy days, man, happy days . . . buy a keg of beer for one dollar and a bag full of food for another and have a *cowein*." Music for picnics was a big thing. There were resorts like Milneburg on Lake Pontchartrain (inspiration for the jazz standard "Milneburg Joys"), Washington Park on Carollton Avenue, and later, West End. There were, obviously, different kinds of markets for music. Danny Barker described this to Whitney Balliett:

All these musicians played for different types of people. In fact, there was a caste system within the Negroes themselves. The Catholics like Creole music, which was refined, and the Protestants were closer to the blues shouting and spirituals and screaming to the skies and the Lord. All the bands had a particular section of society where they entertained—high yellers mulattoes, *comme il faut*, or blue bloods—and particular halls where they played.[8]

The social pressure to participate in music organizations was intense, and everyone wanted to be the best instrumentalist and in the best outfit. However, as the "dark" bands from Uptown became more numerous, the competition was even greater, and "cutting" contests between Uptown and Downtown bands occurred at almost every opportunity. If you won a cutting contest, group or individual, it meant by audience reaction you were the "greatest." The competition served to heighten the popularity of the groups even more. Individual bandsmen became "stars," and the parading black brass bands always had their "second line." The second line was, and is, a socializing device for the black youth of New Orleans. Being a "second liner" is exciting. You're where the action is right behind the band as they swing down the streets. You can strut, dance, and whirl your umbrella to the tempo of "Bourbon Street Parade," or "High Society." Just name any black jazz "great" who came out of the Crescent City, and he's paid his dues to the second line.

When a young child from either Uptown or Downtown showed *any* tendency toward musical talent, he received music lessons. It didn't matter if they were "note" lessons, or just straight "blowin' down home style." The child had the right to learn! Freddie Keppard, who followed Bolden in prominence, took lessons on accordion, mandolin, and violin before settling, at sixteen, on the cornet. Bunk Johnson commented about his own beginning:

When I was seven years I started taking music lessons. After one year, I was doing so good that Prof. Wallace he then told me to tell my mother to come over to the school because he would like very much to have a good talk with her. I did just as he told me and my mother went over to the school and seen him. He told her that he could make a real cornetist out of me if she would get me a cornet just good enough to take lessons on and when I became good on the old one she could get me a real cheap brass cornet. Now me and my old cornet, when my mother got it, nite and day I puffed on it and when I did get the slite of it, Oh boy, I really went.[9]

Zutty Singleton's first inspiration came from an uncle, Louis Armstrong was befriended by a man in Waif's School who gave him his first cornet lessons, and Sidney Bechet began taking lessons from George Baquet when he was six. "Bechet's father was a shoemaker, but he was a friend to musicians; he felt and appreciated music deeply; he sang and was an excellent dancer and played a little trumpet. There were always instruments around the house, and most of his five sons and two daughters played them."[10]

It was all working—all the parts were falling into place! The city had always been a festive, parading, music-loving town. Its Latin, French–Spanish Catholic atmosphere had unknowingly ministered to the black population in such a way as to preserve a strong African influence in its music. Finally, the events of the Civil War and their aftereffects, were creating an uneasy symbiosis between the Creole of Color with his mastery of European music methods, and the burning soul of the black African. Economic necessity was fusing these highly dissimilar peoples into interaction that would result in the creation of *jazz*. Jazz was, in a real sense, born of the street bands of New Orleans, and partially reared in the brothels of Storyville, the Crescent City's legendary red-light district.

Red Means Go Man, Go!

BE IT ORDAINED, by the Common Council of the City of New Orleans, that Section I, of Ordinance 13,032 C.S., be and the same is hereby amended as follows: From and after the first of October, 1897, it shall be unlawful for any prostitute or woman notoriously abandoned to lewdness, to occupy, inhabit, live or sleep in any house, room or closet, situated without the following limits, viz: From the South side of Customhouse Street to the North side of St. Louis Street, and from the lower or wood side of North Basin Street to the lower or wood side of Robertson Street: 2nd—And from the upper side of Perdido Street to the lower side of Gravier Street, and from the river side of Franklin Street to the lower or wood side of Locust Street, provided that nothing herein shall be so construed as to authorize any lewd woman to occupy a house, room or a closet in any portion of the city. It shall be unlawful to open, operate, or carry on any cabaret, concert-saloon or place where can can, clodoche or similar female dancing or sensational performances are shown, without the following limits, viz: from the lower side of N. Basin Street to the lower side of N. Robertson Street, and from the South side of Customhouse Street to the North side of St. Louis Street.

It had the scent of bourbon, fresh linen, and body powder; this had been the case for some time, but things had gone out of control. Alderman Sidney Story conceived of Section I of Ordinance 13,032 C.S. to enable the political establishment of New Orleans to contain all the whores within a thirty-eight block area. This action had become necessary because the respectable women, clergy, and other moralizers had badgered the city fathers for almost half a century, and they felt they must finally deal with the problem.

Phil Johnson[11] points out that by 1850 New Orleans had become a city of 125,000 "and was probably the prostitution capitol of America," with the income from whores only second to that of the Port of New Orleans. By 1857, prostitution had become a "visable nuisance" (sic), and a taxation and licensing procedure was set forth for the bawds and "house mothers." Incensed by this, the madams sued the city and the tax was held to be unconstitutional. When the "lower" element of the city heard about this, they held a party (with an erotic parade) that is still remembered. This was a victory signal for vice interests, and for over thirty years prostitution and its allied sins grew at an exponential rate. With growth came the fancy sporting houses. Though they were first concentrated on South Basin Street, they later spread throughout much of the town. The growth continued for almost thirty-five years before harassed and alarmed city officials had to choose either a course of abolition or containment. Containment was the avenue taken, and thus Alderman Story's creation of 1897—*Storyville*.

Though estimates vary, there were probably between 1500 and 2200 registered prostitutes within the District's confines at its height. The major agent of social control in this principality was

Tom Anderson, part-time state representative who, as repayment for past favors to other politicians, was given unofficial managerial control over what some called Anderson County. He ran a cabaret-restaurant that doubled as a clearing house for a number of the brothels. Though there is some evidence to the contrary, most accounts portray his reign as one of a relatively safe, businesslike atmosphere in much of the District.

There were approximately thirty-five fancy houses, managed by distinctive and often elegant madams like Lulu White (the Queen of them all), Josie Arlington, Willie V. Piazza, Bertha Weinthal, and Gypsy Shaeffer. The elegant sporting houses were well-run businesses, frequently involving hundreds of thousands of dollars of capital investment, often from respected landowners and merchants.

From an upper-class perspective these top houses often were a combination of the best and worst in taste. Lulu White, for example, specialized in octoroons of "great beauty," attired in the latest Paris fashions. Her establishment was both refined and gaudy. It contained the latest in interior design and comfort for the guests. *The Blue Book,* a then current catalog of whores in Storyville and published regularly by the enterprising Tom Anderson, said this about Lulu's place: "It is the only one [house] where you can get three shots for your money—the shot upstairs, the shot downstairs, and the shot in the room . . ." [sic].

While some legitimate enterprises were conducted in the area, Storyville was primarily a collage of cabarets, whorehouses, cafes, cribs, honky-tonks, houses of assignation, "dance-schools," gambling joints, and clip-joints, all devoted to fleecing the adventurous sensualist of his money.

All this required music, and lots of it. Restaurants and cabarets like Peter Lala's, Tom Anderson's Arlington Annex, and Billy Phillips' 101 Ranch preferred tunes like the new bold and brassy stomps or blues. The more genteel houses used the comparatively muted polyphony of a string trio, or the ragtime pianists who could evoke a profitable sentimentality from their often prosper-

ous customers. By creating the District, the Aldermen had sired
a phenomenon whose birth marked an explosion of opportunity
for the eager musicians.

The 1890s had been an especially tough period for middle-
class and poor people in the Crescent City. The younger Creoles
of Color, whose parents had struggled for almost two generations,
reached out for economic stability wherever they could find it.
Storyville was *there*. For most, the pay was small, but anything
was a gain. Young Creoles like Sidney Bechet often worked the
District without their proud relatives' knowledge, because, for
many Creoles of Color, playing in Storyville meant a loss of status
within their own community. Jelly Roll Morton's grandmother
kicked him out of the house when he was fifteen for playing in
Storyville. She loved music, but said people who played in such
places were bums, and she didn't want him to be a bad influence
on his sisters. Many of the "dark" Negroes, though, "didn't give
a damn" if it was a whorehouse they were playing in. They had
an opportunity to play the music they loved and get paid for doing it.

Storyville legitimated a "marriage" between the black and tan
musicians—one that had begun in the Uptown–Downtown cutting (carving) contests of the brass bands in the streets and at
picnics. As they spent more time together in the District, the
blacks and Creoles of Color learned from each other playing in
the house bands of cabarets, dancing schools, barrel houses and
bistros. Each liked what the other was doing and in time their
musical products came to be one. The style was growing distinct
from ragtime, and even from the black man's earlier roots; it had
become a true amalgam.

Storyville kept a dozen or more bands going every night. Holding forth in the "Abadie Cabaret" was Joe Oliver (Louis Armstrong's mentor). Joe was later to be known as King Oliver, and
would captivate Chicago with his Creole Jazz Band. By now,
Freddie Keppard was going strong at Pete Lala's cafe. Somewhat
later, Emanuel Perez, Pop Foster, George Baquet, and Sidney

Bechet would be there. It was principally at Lala's that the musicians gathered after work to socialize and exchange musical ideas.

Jazz had come alive—it had made the final transformation to a distinct identity. It need not have received that final catalytic boost in these surroundings, but it did. While Storyville nurtured jazz and its players, it contributed to an image that was to brand the music, and the man, as deviant.

2

Interlude

THE UNITED STATES had just entered World War I, and soldiers and sailors were pouring into "good time towns" across the country. Storyville was no exception. But when four sailors were killed within the boundaries of Storyville during the early part of 1917, official Washington reacted with indignation and force. Herbert Asbury describes what happened next:

Early in August 1917, Secretary of War, Newton D. Baker, issued an order forbidding open prostitution within five miles of an Army cantonment, and a similar ruling was made by Josephus Daniels, Secretary of the Navy, respecting naval establishments. Later in the same month Bascom Johnson, representing the War and Navy Departments, visited New Orleans, inspected Storyville, and informed Mayor Martin Behrman that the orders must be obeyed. Mayor Behrman went to Washington and protested, but without success, and on September 24 and again on October 1, he was notified by Secretary Daniels that unless the red-light district was closed by the city it would be closed by the Army and the Navy. On October 2, 1917, Mayor Behrman introduced an ordinance in the City Council abolishing Storyville. The Mayor said, "Our City government has believed that the situation could be administered more easily and satisfactorily by confining it within a prescribed area. Our experience has taught us that the reasons for this are unanswerable, but the Navy Department of the federal government had decided otherwise."

The Ordinance was adopted on October 9, and provided that after midnight of November 12, 1917, it would be unlawful to operate a brothel or assignation house anywhere in New Orleans.

The exodus from Storyville had begun two weeks before November 12, but most of the prostitutes had awaited the result of Gertrude Dix's application for a restraining order. When the news of her failure spread, wagons and vans began entering the District and hauling away whatever furniture had not been sold to the swarm of second-hand dealers. As late as midnight of the twelfth, there was a stream of harlots and their servants, laden with property, leaving the segregated area.

On November 14, 1917, two days after the closing of the red-light district, the *Item* announced that the police planned to round up the male parasites of Storyville and send them into the country to help the farmers. Nothing, however, came of this extraordinary idea. The next day many leading church women and members of The Louisiana Federation of Women's Clubs held a meeting and appointed a committee to help the prostitutes. But none applied for succor. Few, in fact, needed it. They had simply moved from Storyville into various business and residential sections of New Orleans and were doing very well.[1]

The abolition of the District had hit all the jazz musicians hard. Though there is considerable evidence that most of them did not like to play in Storyville, they had come to depend upon it for a living. One piano player said about the District, "I think I played a pretty good piano, but you wouldn't have knowed it—those bastards just sat there and paid me no mind!" In most instances, the working conditions had been miserable and the pay low. But the District had drawn these young men like a magnet, and had become the largest employer of musicians within the city. They had come primarily to play the music they loved.

The music scene didn't die completely with the demise of Storyville—it simply shrunk. Danny Barker describes the situation then:

It is not true that nothing happened after Storyville closed. There were always, in New Orleans, both before and after Storyville closed, there were always so many musicians, so many great cats all the way down the line. . . . There were cats like Buddy Petit, Kid Rena, Sidney Desvigne, Sam Morgan, Hippolyte Charles, Punch Miller,

Walter Blue, Maurice Durand, Leslie Dimes, and all these guys were playing in the twenties. These people didn't care to play for regular jobs in the cabarets because they were too confining. The point I want to make is that there were still a lot of jazz musicians around in the twenties. A lot of them would play roadhouses and vaudeville shows and circuses and the riverboats and lakeboats like at Lake Ponchartrain. And also—this was during the twenties, too, as well as before—there were so many halls in New Orleans, fifteen or twenty. And each one would have some kind of affair going on. There was also always some kind of lawn party or parades going on. . . . And, as a matter of fact, some of the clubs were going in the twenties. They would have a closing, and then a quick opening, under cover, in the District. Also, bands like Lee Collins would be based in New Orleans but would be on the road for a while and play towns outside of New Orleans. Little towns in states like Mississippi, Alabama, Georgia, Florida, and Louisiana. Men like Buddy Petit, Sam Morgan, Leslie Dimes, Baptiste Brown, and Victor Spencer were some of the New Orleans musicians who would take these road trips. New Orleans, you see, was the center of bands, and, as way back as I can remember, people in that area would get their bands from New Orleans, and, in fact, they still do. They would go out on the road a week or two weeks, and the people in these small towns would keep you on option, according to the business you did and according to how you acted. New Orleans had always been looked on as a city for musicians and New Orleans being an entertainment center—all the great shows played in that city, like in the Lyric Theatre. And all the big circuses would come through New Orleans. . . . And if they needed a musician, they knew they could pick up one in New Orleans. . . . And then there are musicians who didn't want to leave New Orleans to go up North. Even though they had offers. Some cats would meet a pretty Creole girl, and she'd say she didn't want him to go on the road. So, he'd settle down in New Orleans because there were enough gigs.[2]

But those who really "made it" with national audiences moved out of New Orleans to the North and West. Even long before the District closed, the migration had begun. Tony Jackson and Jelly Roll Morton had departed, and bassist Bill Johnson had persuaded Freddie Keppard to go in 1911 with the Original Creole Band. Sidney Bechet had left New Orleans some time earlier, and King Oliver left for Chicago less than a year after the District's closing.

Louis Armstrong was just eighteen when he said goodby to "Papa Joe" Oliver as the older man got on an Illinois Central train bound for Chicago. Papa Joe had been a general sponsor and guided his progress with the cornet. On Oliver's advice, Kid Ory, who had also come to the station, agreed to hire "Little Louis" and Armstrong became an immediate success with the band. Band work still didn't give Louis a full living; though he played gigs with both Ory's and Oscar Celestin's groups, he still had to supplement his income by selling coke and coal he picked up along the levee. Armstrong's story beyond this point is typical of how jazz continued to spread up the river to Memphis, St. Louis, and points beyond such as Kansas City, Pittsburgh, and Davenport, as it had to Chicago, Los Angeles, and New York. The jazzmen were looking for more of the economic security they had begun to taste in Storyville. Armstrong's first big break came when the great pianist and calliope player, Fate Marable, offered him a job with his orchestra on the Streckfus riverboat, *Sydney*. He describes this experience in his autobiography, *Satchmo*:

When he asked me to join his orchestra I jumped at the opportunity. It meant a great advancement in my musical career because his musicians had to read music perfectly. Ory's men did not. Later on I found out that Fate Marable had just as many jazz greats as Kid Ory, and they were better men besides because they could read music and they could improvise. . . . Kid Ory's band could catch on to a tune quickly, and once they had it no one could outplay them. But I wanted to do more than fake the music all the time because there is more to music than just playing one style. I lost no time joining the orchestra on the *Sydney*. . . . I could pick up a tune fast, for my ears were trained and I could spell a little too, but not enough for Fate Marable's band.

Fate knew all this when he hired me, but he liked my tone and the way I could catch on. That was enough for him. Being a grand and experienced musician he knew that just by being around musicians who read music I would automatically learn myself. Within no time at all I was reading everything he put before me.[3]

Armstrong gained experience on the river boats and he returned to New Orleans in 1921 and the ubiquitous Tom Anderson's, "The Real Thing." He continued to build his reputation in
New Orleans, but an offer from "Papa Joe" (King) Oliver to
come to Chicago was irresistible. On August 8, 1922, he left to
join Oliver, where he soon became a greater attraction than the
older man and so was launched on his legendary career as America's leading jazz musician.

Jazz was changing as it was being played in new places. Labels
were even being attached to it like "Kansas City" style and "Chicago" style. Still, wherever it was played it was a happy, boister-
ous music with the gutsy, earthy elements of the rag, the stomp,
and a distinct African and Latin character.

America's wars had brought this country no closer to solving
its race problem. World War I, particularly, had seen a massive
influx of Negroes northward in quest of solving their economic
and social problems. Like Armstrong, masses of southern Negroes
had boarded the Illinois Central and headed for points North. But
this hadn't worked out fully as they had expected—or hoped.
They were still "niggers," and if there was work to be had, it was
"nigger" work. As their numbers increased in Chicago, Detroit,
New York, and Philadelphia, so did the incidence of conflict between their own expectations and those of the whites. They continued to be put down in everything they tried. One of the first
things they did well, especially well, was play music. Musicians
like Louis Armstrong, King Oliver, Bechet, and Jelly Roll Morton
went into the '20s and the Jazz Age, where music was to cohabit
with speakeasies, gaudy low-life dance halls, and gangsters. At
that time jazz had little chance of recognition as our only purely
American contribution to the arts. Richard Peterson points out
how middle-class morality coupled with bigotry and prejudice actually froze Negro jazz into an even more deviant mold than had
been the case in New Orleans as it came to be diffused into the
Northern cities:

In the early 1920s, jazz was well on its way to becoming a popular and widely disseminated art form. A mass audience was responsive to it and diverse promoters were quick to take advantage of the potential market. . . . Yet, this brief effervescence was stunted almost as quickly as it grew. Two major groups joined hands to put jazz in its place. One group was those in the traditional music industry such as orchestra directors, bandmasters, and music instructors. Their comments that jazz is *not* music or is at best a degenerate form were picked up and used by a much more influential group which we might call institutional moralists or moralizers. . . . These late Victorian spiritual descendants of the "know nothing" party espoused the values of the vanishing agrarian America in the face of rapid industrialization and urbanization. Just as these institutional moralists found in the cause of prohibition a means of attacking the growing power of the new urban Catholic and Eastern European immigrants, they found in the campaign against jazz a means of denigrating the Negro who had migrated North in massive numbers during World War I . . . the appeals of such moralizers against jazz struck a resonant chord in the bread-and-butter interests of a large segment of the population.

In the early part of the 1920s institutional moralizers polemicized against jazz in tones of alarm. In articles and speeches they asked, "Does Jazz Put the Sin in Syncopation?" "Is Jazz the Pilot of Disaster?" and pointed, "Jazz is a signboard on the road that was traveled by Greece and Rome." A popular play of 1922, *The National Anthem,* depicted a jazz band as the pied piper of twentieth-century sin. Jazz was identified as the direct cause of heart attacks, drunkenness, and neural deterioration, but its effect on *morals* was most often stressed. A report of the Illinois Vigilance Association directed by Reverend Phillip Yarrow, found that in 1921-1922 jazz had "caused the downfall" of one thousand girls in Chicago alone. Dr. Florence Richards, medical director of a Philadelphia high school for girls, warned that jazz "may tear to pieces our whole social fabric." These institutional critics of jazz in the 1920s pressed to outlaw jazz performances, and a number of communities did pass statutes to prohibit the playing of jazz in public places. Such statutes were enacted in Cleveland, Detroit, Kansas City, Omaha, Philadelphia, and some fifty other cities. . . . By the later part of the decade, however, there had been a shift in strategy. Jazz was still defined as a negative influence, but complete prohibition was not so often stressed. Jazz was to be kept out of the home, school, concert stage, social function, and relegated to the "den of iniquity," the night club. . . . The night club might seem the "natural" home of jazz, but it certainly was not restricted to this context in the Negro community in which jazz emerged. Jazz was played for all festive occasions from weddings to wakes. Jazz might have been presented to this new, wider audience from the concert stage, but this form of presentation which began in the cities of the North before World War I was eliminated by the institutional critics crying for containment of jazz. Jazz, like the Negro, was all right, *in its place*. This strategy of containment satisfied the moralists because it meant that jazz could be isolated from "proper" society. It satisfied the traditional music professionals because it placed the aesthetic and cultural value of jazz conspicuously below that of classical music.[4]

Peterson contends that Negroes performing jazz were especially suppressed. Their recorded versions of jazz standards were diluted, the lyrics censored and in other ways commercialized for the white middle-class public. Their own "race" records had usually been pressed by small companies or were sold, almost exclusively, to a Negro market. Only supreme dedication by musicians like Fletcher Henderson, Duke Ellington, Earl Hines, and, of course, Louis Armstrong kept this black music before the American public during the late twenties.

As the twenties ended, the nation was stunned into an inactivity that seemed to last forever. The great economic depression had hit Americans hard. The music business, no exception, was severely affected. In New Orleans, hardly anything in town was moving. The wide variety of jobs Barker had described as being characteristic of the twenties were gone—nobody had any money for entertainment. The brass bands were practically gone; only the "Eureka" made an occasional parade. The avid jazz fan could hear a few small groups playing places like "Mamie's" and "Luthjen's," but the overall scene was pretty bleak. The men hadn't forgotten how to jam; there just wasn't much call for it. A lot of the musicians could be found trying to hold things together by "keeping their lip up" in Federal projects like the E.R.A. Band, but after a couple of frustrating years, most had drifted off. The government program just hadn't accomplished its purpose—to stimulate more jobs.

Heywood Hale Broun felt miserable about the way the classic New Orleans jazz seemed to be withering away as its inventors got older. He was determined to record it, and in 1940 he came to New Orleans and rounded up Kid Rena and his brother Joe. They added Big Eye Louis Nelson, Albert Glenny, Jim Robinson, Willie Santiago, Alphonse Picou, and recorded the group on Delta records as "Kid Rena's Jazz Band." The New Orleans Revival had begun! Actually, the first old Crescent City musician to attract renewed attention on a national basis was Bunk Johnson. On a tip from Louis Armstrong, Bunk had been rediscovered by Frederic Ramsey, Jr., and William Russell in New Iberia, Louisiana. After Bunk got some new teeth (Sidney Bechet's dentist brother, Leonard, made them), he began wailing with a good deal of the old feeling. Through the late '40s and early '50s the music spread throughout much of the world, with groups being heralded as the purveyors of a new kind of freedom of expression in music.

For the average musician in New Orleans, things had picked up a bit, but not all that much. Then the old music began to find permanent temples in which to be performed. Ken Mills and Barbara Reid were the first to put a "roof over the heads" of the old musicians and their art. They rented a vacant art gallery on St. Peter Street (between Bourbon and Royal) from art dealer Larry Borenstein and organized musicians to give performances for which customers contributed a "kitty" that was divided by the musicians. They called their place "Preservation Hall." Today, when people think of the old music in the Crescent City, they almost automatically respond, "Preservation Hall." After a time, the hall was taken over by Alan and Sandra Jaffe and has since developed into an international business enterprise. In 1962, Al Clark opened Dixieland Hall on Bourbon Street, and his groups have received wide notice for the quality of their New Orleans style. Dixieland Hall has recently been renamed Heritage Hall.

By the late '60s, many of the old musicians had weathered the

invasion of rhythm and blues and rock and roll and were still
playing their music, both on and off Bourbon Street. Actually,
many of the men were capable of playing several styles of music,
thereby increasing their chances for employment. It was not at all
uncommon to see a sixty-five-year-old jazzman really "cooling" a
rhythm and blues or rock and roll number on a guitar or drums.
They learned and played just about everything they were exposed to, preferring jazz, but adjusting to any style necessary.

In the '50s and '60s, many of the younger men hit the road
with rhythm and blues, rock and roll, and contemporary jazz
units, some to become especially prominent. The city continued
to be a center for music talent, giving birth to a wide variety of
hit groups and compositions. For the black musician, New Orleans had metamorphosed even more so into a polyphony of musical currents. In any event, it was still a swinging town.

⟲⟳

The remainder of our story concentrates on the *now*. The book
will discuss the life-style of these descendants of Uptown and
Downtown—the "cats" and "chicks" who "groove" both on and
off Bourbon Street every night. Instead of focusing on what they
play as musicians, it will discuss what they're like as human beings. Where do they live in New Orleans? How do they live?
What brought them to where they are? How do they look at different aspects of the music business, like travel, audiences, and
getting along with the rest of the "cats"? How does their blackness affect their attitudes toward their music, musicians, and
white and black audiences? What are their attitudes toward
themselves, "squares," "hips," narcotics, and God? How did their
father's occupation and education affect their own station in life,
and their attitudes toward the rest of the Cosmos? Do they make
up a special kind of community; a little world all its own? If it
exists, what are its boundaries, and how does it look at people on
the "outside"?

3

Who Are These Cats?

Arrival in Mecca

As the large jet began to lower for its approach, it crossed the Alabama–Mississippi border. A quick glance to the left, and a canal leading into Lake Pontchartrain. Then, in a moment, the lake itself came up on the right. As the pilot throttled down further, the plane seemed to almost hover. There was the Mississippi with freighters and tankers anchored all around the crescent. Bienville would be dazzled; the nation's second largest port, and almost 600,000 within the city limits! Just a glance of the Vieux Carré from the final approach to the East–West runway. The metropolitan area seems to be endless. Ranch houses and shopping centers seem to be flashing by now. Over the airport fence, and then in about ten seconds, the landing.

Outside the rented car is ready and a young man has just put the luggage in the trunk and handed you the keys. Now, down the ramp to Airline–Airline Highway. It must come close to being the longest straight street in the world! Those miles between the airport and town are a city planner's nightmare. Occasionally, you notice plush residential areas one block off a highway that is skirted by motels, service stations, "quickie" hamburger emporia, a golf course, rock and roll "palaces" and veterinarians' office signs saying "OPEN–COME IN." After about a half hour's drive through Metairie, Airline becomes Tulane Avenue. At this point you have arrived in New Orleans, Louisiana, otherwise known to traditional jazz buffs as *Mecca, La.*

As Tulane spikes in toward the old center of town, passing an assortment of structures, you see impressive motor hotels complete with doormen, and parking attendants herding expensive cars. Back, just off the street, the low gray clapboard houses seem to droop into the soft soil. Then, the Court House, Charity Hospital, and finally a dead end, if you had gone that far! But, you had turned onto Basin Street and headed North to where it crosses Canal, then over Iberville. Here, there is no trace of it. Nothing remains of what was once the most celebrated red-light district in the history of the United States—Storyville. Those colorful structures are no more. No Tom Anderson's, Josie Arlington's, Lulu White's, or even Pete Lala's. In their place is a massive public housing project. You're later told that a few memorabilia do remain from the Storyville days, for the *New Orleans Jazz Museum* has some pieces like Lulu White's curbstone and some copies of the Blue Book. Now, on up the street for about six blocks to Beauregard Square. Once again maps refer to it, in parentheses, by its original name, *Congo Square*. In the days since jazz had been recognized as a prominent American music, the "city fathers" were persuaded to permit the Square's existence on their maps. Basin Street, which is easy to locate now, would have been a difficult place to find some years back. In the wake of the dissolution of Storyville, the community moralizers had obliterated it and renamed the wide street. There are still a number of not too old maps lying around the Crescent City that call it N. Saratoga Street. Now, into the Vieux Carré, and to Rue Bourbon in search of the black jazzman.[1]

He's there; you just have to look for him a bit. The street itself, much like the entire city, has been throughout its history, an admixture of currents. There is something for everyone on the Rue Bourbon. For the sensual, the barker for a "strip" show cajoles to "step in and take a look" at whatever she's uncovering this week —these temptations occur in endless variety. For the "historian" tourist, there is the old bar in which Jean Lafitte and Andrew Jackson allegedly planned the defense of New Orleans. On Rue Bourbon, gourmet and "greasy spoon" are only steps apart. Red-haired young men in striped jackets and straw hats strum banjos a la "gay nineties" for some of the college crowd, and the rest of the "squares." A little further on a five piece rock group boils away as the Fender bass sets tempo for a bikini-clad "chick" gyrating atop a small circular table.

If you look closer, there's Wallace Davenport playing an exceptional trumpet as he heads his own group in the Paddock Bar and Lounge. Davenport, an impressive musician, warm but purely professional about his music, has played with Count Basie, Lloyd Price, Lionel Hampton, and Ray Charles. He has come home to the source for a "transfusion." Together with Davenport is Clem Tervalon on trombone—a man with an easy smile, who once traveled with Lucky Millinder. In recent years he has become a recording star "tailgate" trombone man within the brass band circuit. At The Court of the Two Sisters Lounge Isaac "Snookum" Russell plays a "mean" piano and sings his "skat" songs. "Snookum," who used to tour widely with his own bands once gave a significant boost to the career of the late and highly respected trumpet man, "Fats" Navarro. Going on down the street you can find a large representation of the jazzmen alternating from night to night in Heritage Hall—names like Louis Cottrell, Sweet Emma, Papa French, Placide Adams, Waldron "Frog" Joseph, Louis Barbarin, Alvin Alcorn, Jack Willis, and many others. Just a little further at the Maison Bourbon is the George Finola group with Danny Barker. Then, around the corner on St. Peter at Preservation Hall, are Billie and De De Pierce, Cie Frazier, and the like.

But, go out of the Vieux Carré onto Claiborne Avenue, Galvez, London Avenue, Paris Avenue, and the descendants of Uptown and Downtown are playing all over town. "June" Gardner's contemporary group swings regularly at the V.I.P. Lounge of Mason's Motel. And it doesn't stop there. Brass bands still play for

Manuel Crusto, Worthia Thomas, and Danny Barker at the Maison Bourbon. Photographed by Jack V. Buerkle.

funerals, parades, conventions, lawn parties, and picnics. Big bands like Clyde Kerr's and Herbert Leary's still cut a groove through the dance halls, and "Deacon" John Moore's rock group, like others, is always pushing for that extra inch of individuality that could propel it into national recognition. Its all there—still there—this fusion of dedication, sensuality, re-creation, uniqueness, adventure, and orderliness.

For these descendants of Uptown and Downtown, the music has always been there. They can't remember when it wasn't on the scene. Virtually all of them were born in New Orleans,[2] and whatever part of the community a boy came from there were always those sympathetic eyes and ears, somewhere, constantly searching. If a boy showed the slightest trace of music potential, they shoved a horn into his hands. And, so it goes—generation after generation, making the playing and appreciation of music a central motif of their existence.[3]

Makin' the Scene

Most of the professional musicians in the Crescent City are men. Only a few women, like Dolly Adams, Blanche Thomas, Jeanette Kimball, Billie Pierce, Olivia Charlot, and Sweet Emma, have become prominent playing piano and singing with jazz bands in New Orleans. This is probably related to the music being born and nurtured in its early years in the brass bands that marched up and down the streets of the city. Marching on the street, especially with a heavy brass instrument, just wasn't considered appropriate behavior for girls. Even when the bands performed indoors and used pianos (which was and still is the most common instrument taught to girls), many of the mothers just wouldn't let the girls join them.

Walking through the Vieux Carré and sampling the sounds of traditional music, you might notice something about most of the people playing there. They aren't young. There are no comparable statistics, but it is likely that the average age of Local 496

Olivia Charlot. Photographed by Jack V. Buerkle.

members is older than that found in other cities.[4] The reason for this is probably because of a peculiarity of the Crescent City scene. Since New Orleans was the birthplace of jazz and is the principal supporter of the heritage, there is today more work in the city for the practitioners of the old music. New Orleans is one of those rare places in the western world where a person is rewarded for being older, and especially older *and* black. The average tourist wants to hear some of the old-time music, and they usually have in mind an older black man playing it. Preservation Hall, emphasizing this theme, generally requires that a musician be considered "old" before they are eligible for employment.

Not too long ago, a nationally prominent music critic lamented in his newspaper column that in a few years all the old jazzmen would be dead and the New Orleans jazz style only a memory. The assumption was based on comments he had picked up that younger men prefer to play other styles professionally. It *is* true that younger musicians begin professionally by playing what is contemporary and popular. This was true for Bolden, Keppard, and Jelly Roll Morton. Because of the tourist's expectations to see *older* musicians in New Orleans, the younger ones must "wait their turn." There is a kind of "in" saying among many of the younger jazzmen: "maybe when I get old they'll let me play in Preservation Hall!" What the visiting music critic has ignored is the steady supply of young men who are continually "coming up," absorbing the techniques of traditional jazz from both brass and inside bands. Some of the young ones concentrate on New Orleans style, while others learn to play several different kinds of popular music, including rock and progressive jazz. Until a man gets middle aged or older, he will probably perform somewhere outside the Quarter or he will decide to go on the road. Many can be found "swinging" several nights a week at places such as those on Claiborne Avenue that cater predominantly to a black clientele who prefer more contemporary jazz or rock and roll. Many of the young men who leave New Orleans do so only until they approach middle age or reach a point where travel is more burden

Happy music during Mardi Gras. Photographed by Jack V. Buerkle.

than adventure. At this point they return home to be absorbed into the traditional jazz format. They begin to take gigs on Bourbon Street as they get older. These almost invariably call for the traditional music. This is repeated so often that it has become a regular pattern, and the Vieux Carré thus maintains its reservoir of old-time jazz and the old black men to play it. Before or during the time he becomes a regular in the Quarter, the musician will have begun to find a niche somewhere in the network of brass bands and play for the funerals of the older jazzmen who have been working in halls featuring traditional music. In a few years, a "younger" old cat will play "Just A Little While To Stay Here" for him as his own brass band escorts him to the cemetery.

Sorry About That Myth, Pops!

People are weird, man! They want it all so damned simple! One look at your instrument case when you're headed for a gig in the Quarter, and they think they've got you all sized up! I guess I'm supposed to be some special kinda cat! Hell, I don't care if they gawk! Anyway, it would probably be bad for the music business if they bothered to know the truth! What they don't know is that I just punch a different clock, man!

That was a forty-seven-year-old musician who frequently works spots in the Vieux Carré. He was commenting on how people tend to think of his life-style as a garish collage, an over-romanticized stereotype. Visibly uncomfortable, he is reacting negatively to being labeled, truncated into a mold that tells little of who he believes he really is. The very nature of the stereotype, though, involves taking certain features of behavior (often the most memorable or colorful) and believing them to be typical or characteristic for all persons in similar settings. The stereotype allows nothing for individual differences but assumes everyone in the same social context (like being a musician) will behave the same way.

What is the jazzman really like? According to the stereotype in newspapers, motion pictures, and the novel, he is a flamboyant and intriguing deviant. The image depicts him as running away from home at an early age because of poor home life and a compelling need to express himself as a professional musician. He is supposed to avoid marriage, family, and living in one place any longer than it takes to exhaust all the gigs in town. The succession of dingy rooms he rents (but seldom pays for) are essentially for cohabiting with loose chicks, shaking off hangovers, and absorbing all available narcotics. He may fall in love with a "straight" chick, but it's doomed because she finally makes him choose between her and his horn. Guess who wins! Playing is all he knows—he was only in the seventh grade when he cut out for the road. What else could he do, even if he wanted to? Nothing! And, band life? It's just a receptacle to hold all the other cats—a bunch of "driven" misfits, just like him. As the band moves about, their primary contacts besides the "square" public (which they despise), are gangsters, pimps, whores, and con men. All of this takes place in their own small society which uses a special argot to declare its superiority over all, especially the "creeps" who make up the audience. Finally the "cat" is picked up by a "nark" for illegal possession of narcotics, and he is sent into "stir" for a while. When he gets out, his lip is "down" and he never quite makes the good gigs again. Down, down, he goes. Heavier doses of heroin and, finally, an overdose. As he lies alone, dying (in his rent-overdue room), only one word comes to his parched lips —the name of that sweet, pure, and "straight" chick he wanted so but could never have. Fade out. The end!

Tracing the theme is not really very difficult. Elements of it were present during the operation of Storyville, and it has followed jazz players throughout the United States as they made the music popular. The association with underworld figures produced headlines in the late 'teens and 'twenties, and soon, of course, a supply of short, but fundamentally dramatic and brilliant young lives burned on the pyres of the Jazz Age. These lives, personified by Bix Beiderbecke, were ample spur to a literary establishment of the 'twenties and 'thirties who deftly wove them into the melange of deviance they chronicled.

It is necessary, however, to understand an often ignored detail of this era. With some exceptions, there was a vast difference between the ways some Negro and white youths began their careers in jazz and popular music. To the young Negro coming out of New Orleans, joining a traveling band or one that played in the big cities of the North was a move to greener pastures—a realization of economic opportunity. People in the New Orleans Negro community were proud of "the successful young man." He left town with considerable psychological support. There may have been a lot of Jim Crow humiliation to endure, but the young jazzman was usually able to reflect, for support, on the down home warmth he had left behind. He knew he could always come home if things didn't work out away from the Crescent City. This was not so for many middle-class white boys who had yearned to become a part of the scene. A last violent argument over his becoming a "bum" (musician) ended with his storming out of his family's lives. It was mainly this disenchanted young white musician of the '20s and '30s, then, who encouraged the legend of the remote and intensely defiant jazzman, one that has become the vignette we assume to be a generalized reality.

Bourbon Street Black

The late George Lewis, an internationally prominent New Orleans clarinetist, once said about his audience: "I guess one reason I made it is because everytime I went on the stage in one of them big halls I prayed—like I always do everywhere—that God would stick with me and help me play my very best for these folks who'd been so good to me." George Lewis was a member of *Bourbon Street Black—a semicommunity in New Orleans of musicians, their relatives, peers, friends, and general supporters, whose style of life is built around the fundamental assumption that the production and nurture of music for people, in general, is good.*

While "blackness" is a major part of Bourbon Street Black, this
community is not synonymous with the black community of New

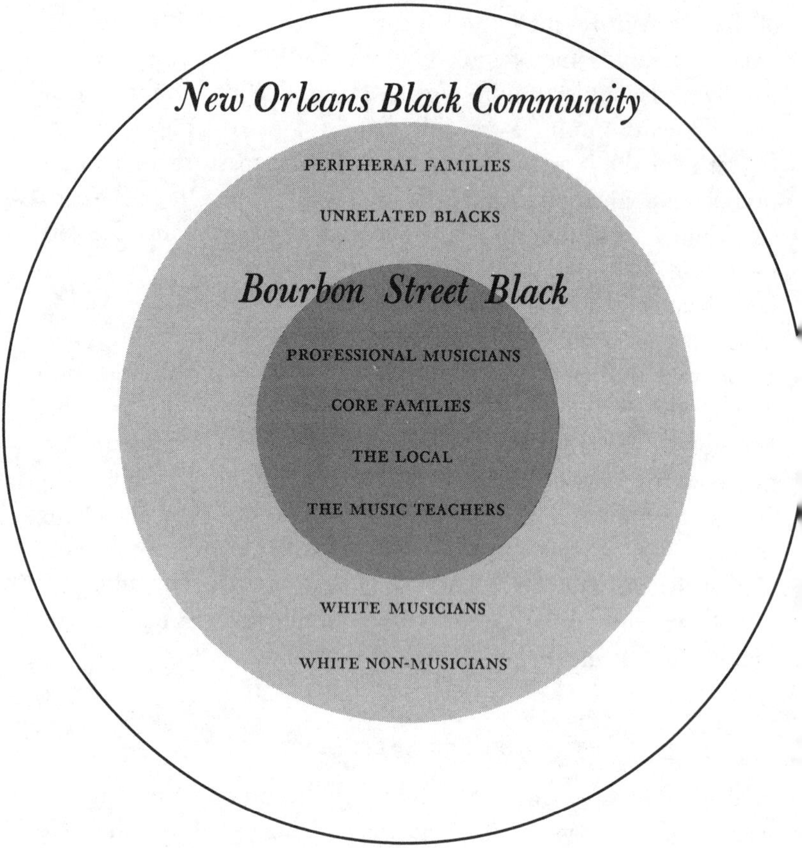

Figure 1

Orleans. It will help to think of it as a specialized semi-commu-
nity within the black community (see Fig. 1). It has a *core* where
the most intensive activity occurs and a *periphery*, which is supportive of the core.

Bourbon Street Black involves a relatively intensely shared
style of life—an interlocking network of human relationships—

emanating from a core of professional musicians, most of whom are black (Fig. 1). Also within the core of Bourbon Street Black are a few *core families* where several members of the same family are professional musicians. A number of these families have been involved in Bourbon Street Black for four or more generations and have had a major influence on the music scene.

The most recent development within the core is the Local (American Federation of Musicians, Local 496), which has in recent years become the formal spokesman for the musicians, and as such has considerable effect upon their life style and upon the music of Bourbon Street Black. Before the Local was conceived, things had been handled informally by the musicians, mainly under the leadership of the core families. The introduction of the Local had the effect of diffusing power within Bourbon Street Black—distributing it on a more formal and widespread base. The Local is now the pacesetter and has a strong influence on stability and change within the community.

This style of life has been able to persist and keep its strength from generation to generation because of one critically important group of men and women—the music teachers. From the very first days of this semicommunity, these persons have kept its core alive by being both instructor and example to emulate. All members of the core group contribute to the guidance of the style of life. They set the pattern for innovation and establish many of the norms for the rest of the community. Of course, there are great differences among the people within the core. Some are the "greatest" as musicians, some are professional, and some are not so good. Some are politically (in terms of Bourbon Street Black) more powerful than others. These latter are usually the ones who are members of long-time core families. More often than not, these people will have an important post in the Local or some other position of community prominence.

The periphery of Bourbon Street Black is composed of peripheral families, other non-musician blacks, a few white musicians, and certain white non-musicians (Fig. 1). Peripheral families are those presently involved in the scene where usually only one member is a professional musician and, unlike core families, have a history of only minimal participation in the community. Besides the peripheral families, there are a number of non-musician blacks who are involved rather strongly in the group. These are friends of the musicians and their families and are in relatively frequent contact with core members and often spend a fair amount of recreational time with the jazzmen. The remainder of the periphery is composed of a few whites—some musicians, some not. The white jazzmen involve themselves deeply in the black musical styles of New Orleans, particularly traditional jazz. Usually, to the extent that it is possible, they "live black." They frequently come to the Crescent City with the idea that by playing the old music and trying to get it "in my (their) very bones," they will have a fundamental understanding of all jazz playing. The non-musician whites are those who acquire membership because it becomes apparent to at least some in the core that they have a major emotional (and sometimes professional) commitment to the scene; some are professional writers, researchers, critics, or jazz buffs. All of the whites are in Bourbon Street Black through sponsorship, and most are somewhere in the periphery rather than in the core. Their involvement is usually not as intensive, or extensive as the black members, and it has a tendency to be transitory. Don't be misled, though. *All* persons in Bourbon Street Black have a *major* involvement with music as a life-style. Persons differ in degree of involvement, but even the least committed member is involved to a degree that is easily distinguishable from the non-member.

The closest estimate of size that we can make is that Bourbon Street Black numbers between 400 and 500 core members, with an additional 1500 to 2000 who make up the periphery. Certainly, the total number is no more than 2500 within a New Orleans black community population of approximately 270,000 persons.

The young jazzman of New Orleans thus finds himself an

integral part of a very responsive, supportive social group—Bourbon Street Black. If he is born in the general black community (outside of Bourbon Street Black), all he has to do to gain entry is to show some talent and interest. Someone will pick him up, because the jazzmen, and even people in the periphery, are always on the lookout for new "blood." Support is given to *all* those who show a commitment to music. The classical European tradition, for instance, is securely imbedded in the Creole of Color "professors" who still use classical music as a base in beginning instruction. Most of the jazzmen who hold forth in the Vieux Carré were taught European fundamentals before they picked up anything else. "Coming up" within the community, a young musician will make a choice of what way he is to go with his career. He gets much help, and usually goes with what is popular, therefore commercially marketable on a national basis (if he gets that good, or "gets the breaks"). Sometimes, though rarely, he takes the route of classical music (usually coupled with a thorough knowledge of jazz). He has become aware of the beginnings of opportunity for blacks on the classical scene. One young man, for instance, has a masters degree in music from a major university, three years advanced study in Europe, and has had major works performed by both the New Orleans and Dallas Symphonies.

Bourbon Street Black was actually created by those post-Civil War codes that told the Creole of Color he was a black man. The codes forged together people who, until that time, had no more in common than recognizable amounts of skin pigmentation beyond what was considered white. The exigencies of their situation forced these unlikely "bedfellows" to find some common ground, and it happened to be music. From that point on, they came to have more in common. By the 1870s, one of the things they had in common was no opportunity for formal education. What was available was pitiful in comparison to the most underprivileged of the whites of New Orleans. Things changed gradually but surely. From its earliest days, a basic norm of Bourbon

A neighborhood in Bourbon Street Black. Photographed by Jack V. Buerkle.

Street Black has been to "improve yourself." Of course, music has been the tested and most common route, but today education is another. Though the desire was there, many of the older musicians were unable to go very far in school.[5] The kinds of barriers that cut them short were: "My parents would have liked me to finish, but I couldn't afford it," or "I had to leave school because my parents needed the help, and I was the oldest." Radical changes in opportunity came to those who were in their late teens or early twenties during World War II. By that time, the percentage attending and finishing high school had increased considerably. Many of these took advantage of the benefits of the GI Bill of Rights, and today the core members of Bourbon Street Black have considerably more schooling than the black population in general. Actually, a greater percentage of the jazzmen have attended college than the national average for whites.[6]

Bourbon Street Black is a unique semicommunity within but not wholly of the black community of New Orleans. Members have emphasized talent and training resulting in socio-economic gain and stability that goes far beyond the rest of black New Orleans. This is not easily comprehended by the casual observer. For example, the tourist, or for that matter the average New Orleans citizen (white or even black), gets very little feeling for the community; he only sees the musician playing on the stand. Let's suppose a jazzman with a traditional band kicks off the tempo for "Mama Don't Allow It." His heel is poised as he looks at the drummer, Bam! Bam! Bam! Bam! A short piano introduction—now the rhythm is going, and then, all together—

> *Yes, Momma don' 'low no music playin' in heah'!*
> *Momma don' 'low no music playin' in heah'!*
> *Now, we don' care what Momma don' 'low!*
> *Gonna play that music anyhow!*
> *Momma don' 'low no music playin' in heah'!*[*][7]

(Then, on to a series of "ride" choruses for each of the instruments.) This is a happy, old, tongue-in-cheek standard, and actually Momma did " 'low music playin' in heah'." In fact, she
and her husband promoted all music playing and singing. Contrary to both the myth of broken home attributed to jazzmen and
blacks, most Bourbon Street Black families were, and are, intact.[8]
Watching the cats rock, sway, blast, shout, and hum, it probably
wouldn't occur to the listener that most have had long, stable mar-
riages,[9] and that they go home after the performance to a home
they usually own,[10] and have lived in for many years,[11] home to
a neighborhood they probably grew up in.

৩৩৩

One by one, the cats began to gather in the foyer just inside the
Rue St. Louis entrance to the Royal Orleans. It was a warm eve-
ning, and the uniform of the day was white shirts and cap. Across
the top of the military cap was the single word—ONWARD.
The Onward Brass Band—a proud name in Bourbon Street Black.
Years of marching for all kinds of occasions had seen people like
Oliver and Perez in its ranks. They were to move out at 7:30.
The gig involved leading a bunch of conventioneers down Royal
to the Masonic Temple on St. Charles and then inside for a few
minutes.

Three of the musicians were catching a final cigarette before
starting. "Danny and Prez here yet?" "Yeah, man—they're up
talkin' to the people about gettin' goin'." "Great, great!" Just then
Danny (Barker) and Prez (Louis Cottrell) joined them from the
upper lobby. "Let's Go!" Danny stood before them in red and
white striped jacket, "Chevalier" straw hat, and a magnificent
cane. Danny lifted the cane to the short roll of the snare drum
as it set tempo for the trumpet biting almost immediately into
"Whoopin' Blues," while Cottrell's clarinet began to lace arpegios
around the lead horn. As this was happening, Danny had stepped
off with his Grand Marshal's strut toward the upper lobby, and
the others followed. They were in full gear now. The booming

The Onward Brass Band with "second lining" conventioneers. Photographed by Jack V. Buerkle.

bass drum with Tervalon's ripping "tailgate" trombone seemed as though it would take the huge paintings off the wall. They weren't gone more than three minutes when they were back— down the stairs and outside to Rue St. Louis, followed by a mass of conventioneers, some with cocktail glasses in hand.

They paused in front of the hotel only for a moment as "Whoopin'" ground "hotter" and then moved on up to Royal. By the time they had made the turn, you could see them—*the second line*—those young black kids with their umbrellas, cavorting, jiving, prancing, and strutting. That's the way it went behind the band—all the way down Royal, across Canal, and onto St. Charles. By the time they reached the Masonic Temple, most of the conventioneers were already seated in the auditorium. Up the outside stairs single file those cats went, going at "Panama" like they were in a cutting contest. Down the hallway, and into the auditorium—the people were on their feet and cheering. They paraded around the outside aisles a couple of times and then back out into the hallway leaving behind the applause. The gig was over.

As the cats filed out the front door of the Temple, one said, "Wanta stop anyplace on the way home?" "Not me, man, I've had it. I'm bushed." "O.K."

When they got down to the street, a couple of the second liners were still hanging around. One boy, leaning on his umbrella, looked up at the first cat to get to the sidewalk, and said, "See you at the next gig." The cat smiled—"Sure son, sure."

4

Second Linin'

When you hear that beat, it's New Orleans you'll meet.
Dancing in the street, you'll see a line they call the second line.

Young and old you'll meet, dancing in the street.
Young bands, old bands, will set you prancing,
Doin' the second line![*,1]

They Said I Could

The Second Line—a traditional jazz standard depicting the antics of the boys and young men who tag along at the rear of marching brass bands in New Orleans. Youngsters so obsessed and delighted with the music emanating from the bandsmen, they gather at each event to dance and strut to the tempo as they emulate the motions of the bandsmen and the Grand Marshal.

Long before Bolden, they had followed the parades. The thing was to be near "the man," so some of it would rub off—to watch every move of the role model; how he stands, his embouchure, how he blows, breathes, struts, and laughs. "This big cat! Oh, if I can *ever* be like him!"

Second lining is not the initial spark that fires the neophyte toward a career in music but more of a middle point in the development. Some time before second line is a permitted activity

Second Liners picking up a few points on technique. Photographed by Jack V. Buerkle.

for the youngster, he has seen and heard a lot in his family and immediate milieu that moves him deeply.

Sam Alcorn recounts his first interest in music: "When I was four years old, my father used to play at the 'Gypsy Tea Room.' I followed him every night. I sneaked out. I used to follow him everywhere. Neighbors used to come up to him on the job and say 'Al, your kid is outside peekin' in the window'." Actually Alvin Alcorn was aware of his son's presence; somewhat uneasily so, because he *was* only four. But, Al was proud! Sam went on, "My grandfather was a trumpet player, my father plays trumpet, my mother plays piano, my brother plays piano, my dad's brothers all played music, and my grandmother played French horn. Man, everybody was musical!"

Throughout the Crescent City, many family traditions in music were being maintained. James Black, another young jazzman (former drummer with the Yusef Lateef Quintet), said,

Practically everybody I'm related to played; there was my mother playin' piano, my grandmother, piano, granddad, violin and guitar, my cousin, sax, and my uncle on violin and guitar. We all liked to play. When I was little, people used to like to hear me play the boogie-woogie, "Boogie Woogie Bugle Boy." They'd say, "come on and play that tune baby," and it would embarrass me, and I'd have to play the piano for my aunt and uncle.

Clyde Kerr echoed Black when he said,

Back just as far as I can remember, my father, mother, and brother played. I enjoyed hearing my father playing several instruments. And, then too, there were traveling vaudeville shows, and the movies used to bring lots of bands here, and I think that had a lot to do with it. Just to see live performances.

Throughout the generations since the blacks and Creoles were able to acquire musical instruments and form stable brass bands, there has been considerable intermarriage between those who are musically inclined. Cie' Frazier, a "star" drummer at Preservation

Hall commented: "In my family there are many musicians, inter-related. My father played guitar, my two brothers played piano. My cousins Simon, John, Eddie, Lawrence, and their father Billy Marrero, all played. Also there was my brother Sam who played drum, my two sisters Victorine and Loretta Frazier played piano, and my cousin Dave Williams, piano."

With that kind of communal encouragement, it is understandable that many began playing instruments at an early age. The average beginning was at about age fourteen; of course many began earlier.[2] Half of them became interested because parents or relatives played, and the others got their boost from the general musical environs of New Orleans; music was literally "in the air."

Some of the older men put it this way:

Oscar "Chicken" Henry

My mother bought a piano. There was a lady that taught persons at the old French Opera, and she was the one that taught me all my scales and chords and arpeggios. I was around eight or nine years old. Before I was twelve I could play all the chords on the piano. But I didn't like sittin' down on the piano stool for the simple reason the girls liked their dancin', and I didn't get to dance with the girls while I was sittin' on that stool, so I just quit playin'. Later a band was comin' down the street, and I told a friend of mine as we was standin' on the side listenin' to the band go by, I say, "Emma, I'm gonna learn how to play one of them instruments." She say, "oh, you can't do that," I say, "oh, yes I will, you'll see me, and I'll be playin," and two years and a half *after* I told her that I was in a band playin."

Albert "Papa" French

I had a Ukelele, and started with that. I graduated to banjo. My father played, two uncles, and I have a lot of cousins that play music. I just started playing myself—when I was a little kid I used to watch the wagons on the street, you know,—on Sunday the wagons would advertize the bands—not like it is now—with sound trucks—they used to have two bands, and they'd get to a corner and back up—and the best band would stick—music was in my family—I mean it was in my blood, so I had to play.

Isaac "Snookum" Russell

It was my cousins—two girls—they used to come around by my house and play on my mother's organ, and one day I just sat at the organ and played from listenin' to them, and that was it. I had always loved music—ever since the first record I heard which was an old Edison, believe it or not, the round spool type of record.

Wilfred Antoine

I was a kid when I started. I always did like music. I was about eight or ten. Started playing drum—didn't have the instrument. I used—American cheese would come in a case—and I used to get one of those cases and play a drum on that—until I got older. One of my associates—he's dead now—Sidney Bechet—Another was Buddy Petit —He started on a horn—he's dead also—We were all kids—that was way back there about 1910—and they all kept on playing their instruments till they made a career out of it. My family enjoyed it (his interest in music), but they weren't able to give it to me. Things were scarce in those days, man. Music was fifty cents a lesson. We needed fifty cents to eat—things were terrible—if you get something, it was a gift of God, that's all. People were working for almost nothing raising a family on seven dollars a week. You needed clothes and school and all that. Nobody could give you any money to go take up music.

Alvin Woods

Well, my grandmother was a musician. She used to play piano—Mary Henderson. She lived in the country. She had a brother who lived in Vacherie, Louisiana. His name was Lila. He was a Creole. A great clarinet player. I saw him a couple of times. Real early, I used to go down to the porch and just peek through a crack and get what I could from just listenin' to the records. We had one of those phonographs that you wind up. I'd play by what I heard on the records—I'd pick it up by ear—Bessie Smith. Anything I could hear, I could play. My grandmother had bought a piano for my sister. She gave my sister money to take lessons and I'd go with her, because my mother was scared durin' them times. I had a big ear when my sister was in takin' the lesson. When we went home, I'd play her lesson on the piano, and she wouldn't be able to play it. I'd play by ear—I always had a big ear. After a while, the man asked me to stop comin' with her, because I wasn't payin' for the lessons. My sister got mad and said, "you're playin' my lesson!" I had been playin' the piano I had picked up, but when I was about fifteen, I was also playin' drums. I began to have trouble with my coordination—I got confused on the piano. I went to a teacher one time, and was tryin' to play like Teddy Wilson, and I had my coordination mixed up. I had a deep mind for music, you see, I tried to carry the melody with my right hand and the passin' tone with my left hand and otherwise carry the two tones together. He gave up with me and said if I ever learned how to play the piano, I would be a good musician, because I was tryin' to be too perfect, and he didn't teach me anymore. That's how I switched to drums.

Alvin Alcorn

I was a professional when I was sixteen. I began playing with some of the old bands around here—some of the old greats. My older brother Oliver had a band and they used to rehearse at my home once in a while, and I used to go around with musicians. I got inspired by them to be a trumpet player. Louis Armstrong inspired everybody with the trumpet. So, we used to listen to Louis' recordin's. I met Louis in 1928-29 when I started playin'. But, I didn't know him before he left town. I had an urge to be a musician. My mother played an organ, my grandfather was a musician, my sister played a little piano, so I was musically inspired.

For those players who are presently middle aged, or approaching it, the theme is very similar. Modern technology was more a part of their early lives, but everything else was pretty much the same.

August Dupont

My father had one of those old time radios—oblong shaped—with a big speaker in it. I used to lie on the floor—read my funny papers— and my funny books with my head right in the speaker listenin' to the music. And the reed section was really the thing that attracted my attention. And I told my father I would really like to play an instrument. I said, "A saxophone," he said, "What kind of saxophone," and I said "I don't know what kind of sax." He said "Maybe you ought to think it over a little while longer." That was the first time I got interested. My interest in music grew, so, oh about a year later I kept buggin' him and buggin' him about a sax and he said I was too young for a sax. We had an old upright piano in the house and he was tryin' to lure me to this thing cause he played piano music, by ear. And I used to piddle around on a piano. Man, we had one of those stools that you unscrew here and adjust your height, and I used to get on it—one of those piano roll jobs, you know. But, I really wasn't interested in the piano. I'd hear a sax, Man, and it sounded so beautiful on the radio! I just wanted a sax. I didn't know what one looked like. I just wanted one. I hadn't really seen one before. That was my beginnin' in music.

Clyde Kerr

My family enjoyed seeing us perform—my brother and I—and it was quite a nice thing for them to boast about when we could play fairly well. Those things, I think, were an incentive. Their friends would compliment us. Our own friends liked it too. They thought it was unusual to be a friend to someone who could perform. It was good. Besides my father, who persisted with us, there were a lot of local musicians who influenced us. Louis Armstrong for one. I was quite young when he was doing his best work, I think, and mainly he gave me a good inspiration—to play—well. It's just the challenges I think a person would want to meet—and any field or anything he would like to do—there are some things we would like to prove to ourselves. That we can do—and you enjoy it too—the praise of others. There are some things that I guess we can see ourselves doing that become more important to us than almost anything else.

Clem Tervalon

I was eighteen years old when I picked it (the trombone) up. I've always been musically inclined. Also, I used to play the uke, sing, and tap dance when I was much younger. But, when I picked up the trombone, I was eighteen, and it was the cheapest instrument for sale—five dollars. Actually, it was my uncle, Albert Burbank, and my cousin, Homer Eugene, who influenced me most. I had always wanted to try it, and I always admired the musicians who came to town to play, besides those who were already here. We had no particular favorite kind of music at home—just liked everything.

Placide Adams

I remember that when I was seven, I was fooling around a little with the piano, but later on I switched to drums and was really after music. There was always good music around the house. You just couldn't help but get interested in it. My uncles and mother had a ball doing it. She played piano, her brother Lawrence, trumpet, and my uncle M. Minetta played all instruments. He was a teacher—an instructor. My brother plays guitar. My folks wanted me to go all the way in school, but I got to playing gigs with my mother. For a while she didn't like it too much because it was interfering with my education. But, by the time I was eighteen, I was playing professionally as a musician. New Orleans being a drummer's town with more drummers than needed, I decided to play bass, and with the help of my brother Gerald, the bassist in the family group and the influence of the late Paul Barbarin who gave me my first job playing bass, I have made a career of it, although I still can and will play drums when the job calls for it.

By the time the young jazzmen came along, things hadn't really changed that much. Like the older men, they are mainly people of their time. One young man, "Deacon" John Moore, who concentrates on trying to perfect a rock sound, said about his entry into the profession:

I was influenced by guys like Art Neville, Ferd Eaglin, and George Davis, also my family. I think musicians are born, not made. One day I just decided to play. My mother played, my grandfather (banjo), my father's uncle was a bandleader, my sisters, and brothers played. I used to sing a lot as a kid, and kind of a strange thing happened. I was singing with a little band—two singers, myself, and one other guy. During that time, everybody was trying to cut down on expenses, so they eliminated me because I couldn't play an instrument. So, I went out and said "I'm gonna have to get me a guitar or something." I was fascinated by guitar players. I used to go to dances and watch them and say, "Wow, how can he do that? Wow, that sounds so good." After I got enough confidence in myself, I went down and bought a guitar. One thing led to another, and after a while I was in the music business.

Music took up much of the young jazzmens' time as they were growing up. James Black said,

It was just there. Like my mom says, I used to always beat on walls and cans with sticks. They bought me a little set of drums. I used to practice the drums—I was really involved—I was, and I am. Like when I came home from school at three o'clock. I had a place to practice drums in a little shed out back—and all the rest of the cats would be out playin' ball and stuff. I'd be in the shed practicin'! Three o'clock till six every day till I got out of junior high school. Cats used to climb on the fence outside and listen, and yell—"play some more—play some more, Man," and encourage me. It made me proud!

The cats often began on one instrument, then switched to another. It was a common practice of Creole teachers around the turn of the century and before to force their pupils to delay final concentration on a particular musical instrument. A kid may have wanted to choose a sax, but he might have had to spend considerable time on clarinet before he got there. Sometimes, the connections between the instruments were even more remote. If a child would want to play cornet (because he had been exposed to heroes like Buddy Bolden and Freddie Keppard), the wise Creole teacher would start him on piano. In this way, the teacher could give his pupil a more comprehensive introduction to music, and thus make him a better cornet player. In many ways, the part played by the Creole teacher was critical. Certainly, not all the musicians were exposed to them, but when the experience existed, the route to becoming a professional musician became easier. But, what happened after the seductive experience with music in the family and in early childhood? How did they move further toward full participation in the core of Bourbon Street Black?

Spreadin' Out

Albert Nicholas, who grew up in New Orleans at the turn of the century, has remarked:

Sid Bechet and I didn't have any musical education at the time. We'd just sit on the curbs and experiment with different melodies. Lorenzo Tio, who had made a name with John Robichaux, the Olympia, Tuxedo, and other bands, was my idol then. When I was thirteen, I was taking lessons from him; that man really knew his music and taught me all the rudiments, and he could teach as well as he could play. I also took lessons from Big Eye Louis, another favorite of mine.

I was just like the rest of the kids—wanted to know all about that new music called jazz. I was a second-line kid. That meant I'd follow the big bands down the streets, and, Man, what thrill when Tio or George Baquet would let me carry their cases while they played! I'd walk alongside them feeling just as important as could be. I played my first street parade with Manuel Perez and his Onward Band, and that was one of my greatest thrills. All my life I wanted to participate in one of those parades.[3]

The sensation of pride and completion Albert Nicholas must have felt on that first day as a brass band member has been experienced by many young men in New Orleans. Oscar "Chicken" Henry, who was born June 8, 1888, said,

But, those bands we heard and second-lined to, was minstrel bands. Like Primrose and West; Primrose and Dockstader. The Dirtz Dixie Minstrels—R. G. Fields, Lew Dockstader. When I was a kid, I heard and saw every band that come to the city of New Orleans. And I watched the trombone players, the baritone players, and the brass players. They were the instruments I was interested in. I watched the trombone players—how they'd stand—how they'd play—how they would breathe. I watched everythin' a professional man did. I used to go to the Orpheum Theatre which was on St. Charles and watch the men in the orchestra pits rehearsin' Sophie Tucker. I was in the Orpheum Theatre when Sophie Tucker sang "Some of these Days." I studied under a man that really knew music. There was one time

he Onward Brass Band's rhythm section. (Left to right) Louis Barbarin, Chester
nes, and Placide Adams. Photographed by Jack V. Buerkle.

in my life I could take the "William Tell Overture" and just look at the key it was written in and go from the introduction down. And, when it changed key, I'd just look at the key and keep on playin'!

One of the men who came onto the scene a few years later said:

I always was musically inclined. I always used to go out listenin' to most jazz bands, to the church funerals, and the parades. I always wished I could get in a band and play like those musicians. At that time, I think they had the Excelsior Band, and the Eureka Band. Different bands. I never was too familiar with the names at that time, you know, but I would always be around to second line. When they'd leave that church, I'd make it to the cemetery and be ready to keep comin'. About that time, I was livin' in the ninth ward, and they (the bands) used to come down there. They'd leave the Street Cemetery. And, anytime I heard that big bass drum *hit*, I'd get out there! I'd go round the church; sit down there and wait till they'd bring the body out, make it to the cemetery, watch them, and as the band left, tear right down the street in the second line. I had a cousin who used to play trumpet. I used to listen to him. I always would say, "I wish I could get out there and play sumpin'—I want to get in a band," you know. Get with the rest of the musicians. It had to come out. That was the feelin' I had, and I would never have been satisfied if I didn't accomplish that. My daddy always played guitar, you know, and a little banjo. I'd sit around here at nights from time to time with daddy, and poke the fire in the old open fireplace. We had a good time. He'd get that old guitar, and he'd start singin' and jivin' sumpin' on the guitar. After I started foolin' around with the Uke, well, I'd get right in there with 'em, and he'd be playin' on the guitar, and I'd be playin' on the Uke. Oh, that helped me out! It inspired me—gave me pride. Made me feel like sumpin'. All the family loved music. They liked to sing. They *all* could sing—sing in the church choir, and just get together and sing.

The motivated and talented youth received many supportive contacts outside his family. Danny Barker remembers how it was in the twenties:

I was about fourteen when I started playing. There was such a big demand for music around New Orleans. And the musicians who could play were so celebrated. Everybody knew them, and they had respect. "There goes Mr. So and So, he's a musician," kids would whisper. So, that inspired me to play an instrument. I was also inspired by my uncle Paul (Barbarin) and Louis Armstrong. Also there were banjo players around; guitar players. Just to play in the band! There were grade (status) levels. You moved from first level to the better quality. You were inspired to play with the best. You could head toward the highest element of jazz playing. It was according to you how you moved up the brackets. You could play with nondescript bands all your career like some of the guys have always done. In New Orleans they still say who's the greatest, who's mediocre. So, you're inspired to play with the best. You keep trying to improve on your instrument. People were always telling you, "I saw you with So and So, that's nice!" Encouraging you, "You're getting somewhere, boy! You are improving"!

In those days, and before, if you were not white, music instruction was confined to the family, some relative's care, or, if you could find the money, a private teacher. There was no provision for Negroes to receive formal training in music in the public schools of New Orleans. The blacks and Creoles of Color were being denied access to city-subsidized training in something they dearly loved—music. This must have been especially discouraging for the Creole of Color for where the dark Negroes had not known formal instruction in music in earlier days, the Creoles had.

The Creoles of Color and the blacks, therefore, developed their own means to continue (in the case of the Creoles), or to begin (in the case of the blacks) formal music instruction without depending upon the whites. Even with musical instruments of poor quality they clung to and developed their mutual love for music. Both, in time, studied with the music "professor."[4]

By the twentieth century both black and Creole of Color were designated as Negro by the white man. Denial of public instruction in music (when it became available to the white) was really only symptomatic of the breach between the races, a condition that may well have accelerated the resolve of the New Orleans

Negro to excel in his music. Music, which had been an avocation, became by necessity a vocation. The Creoles' contact with the black man, which had been as minimal as possible (for there had been vast status differences), became much more extensive. Through the fusing of their talents (though not consciously so) they came to supply the New Orleans market with one of its needs (or desires)—music for hire.

Instruction continued to exist within the confines of Bourbon Street Black. Only within the past twenty years have Negro children been able to take instrumental music in the New Orleans public schools.

Josiah "Jack" Willis tells of how he experienced his first lessons, his own instrument, and playing in a band led by the first Negro hired to organize a public school band for the Negro children of New Orleans:

Professor Victor gave me lessons, but we paid for that. They had music in the schools with stuff "like music memory contests." They would play records and tell you about the different instruments. That's what the school paid for. But, if you wanted to play an instrument and be in a band, why, Professor Victor had hustled quite a few instruments on his own and we'd take lessons from him, and use the instruments he had, and then later you'd be able to buy yourself an instrument. It took me about five years to get that trumpet! I'd given a buddy of mine twenty-five cents and fifty cents till I got enough. Twenty-five dollars! Bought it on my own. He kept tabs, and so did I. I guess he got tired, Man! I know I did! With Professor Victor I had started on clarinet, and then the trombone, and then to the trumpet. But I made my first notice on the trumpet. This happened in '33 when we went to the Chicago World's Fair with the Elks. I went with Professor Victor (bandleader). Thirteen years old! First trip, Chicago. Wallace Davenport came up right after me in a Victor band, too. The cats would go to Victor, who had the best school band. It was at the Thomy Lafon School. That was the only colored school band they had in New Orleans at the time, and Professor Victor was the only colored music teacher that was getting paid to teach in the public school system here in New Orleans. And later they had a band at the Daniel School. At that time, I was influenced by Louis Armstrong. We had all his records around home, and he came down and played at Suburban Gardens! Yeah, Louis was my inspiration! It was a gas!

Even for the younger players now in their 20s and 30s, the instruction occurred much more in the communal group of family, friends, and music lovers than in the school system. In a way, the new school music program has acted to facilitate what began in the family and neighborhood. But it is really only marginal to the main base of activity. A number of church organizations, usually Protestant, also facilitated interest in group music activities, often bands.[5] Though the majority of the jazzmen are Catholics, the Catholic Church, at least in New Orleans, has not been an active supporter of jazz or any kind of church participatory music groups. It's more the formal structure of the Catholic Mass that has minimized participation in church music rather than any opposition by Church personnel. Actually, on a national basis, a number of Catholic priests are actively involved in the promotion of jazz.

Roger Dickerson, a composer and pianist, is one of the younger group who experienced familial and communal encouragement as well as public school music experience.[6] About his instructional and early group playing experiences he says,

I had a few informal lessons before I had the formal ones. They were from musicians who were friends of the family. They were irregular, but they were lessons, nonetheless. In terms of jazz, I was taught pieces. That was the way of learning. Being taught pieces to play. Showing me certain progressions, melodies, or something like that. Things that you could make something out of. I was playing in a high school marching band before I started playing in a jazz group (he plays the lower brass instruments as well as piano). When I was about fifteen, or something like that, I was playing piano within a neighborhood group. Some people would hire us—just more or less do it as a favor to our parents.

First gigs took various forms. With the older musicians they often came at later points in their youth than for those jazzmen born later, and they were usually combined with day jobs. This occurred, probably, because it took musicians born in the early part of twentieth century longer to get "freed-up" from general economic problems and musically proficient enough to "cut the book" with the local groups. Some musicians like Oscar "Chicken" Henry never made the decision to become full-time performers for very pragmatic reasons.

There was never enough money in it. At my trade I made nineteen dollars a day. It didn't make sense for me to do only music. We had a seven piece group. I could make my nineteen dollars a day, and still pick up my ten dollars at night. I'd play three or four nights a week. If the job wanted five men, well two of us were layed off. Let them five work.

Henry goes on to tell how, though he began instruction in New Orleans, he actually began work in the South Bend, Indiana, and Chicago areas as a daytime plasterer and nighttime musician:

One of my friends played when I began. It was old man Peter Davis. He taught Louis Armstrong how to play. This was in the Jones home. Davis and I were friends. We played together and played by ear. I began playin' with a group when I was thirty-one years old. It was after the first World War. One time in Chicago, I played on the same floor of a building as Louis Armstrong. This was in 1923. The first time I played for money, though, was in South Bend, Indiana. I was playin' for a man by the name of Henry Gordon. He had a band. I used to play there for money, and from there I came to Chicago. I used to see a drum in the window of a barbershop. I went in, asked the fella, "You have a band here?" and he said, "yes." I told him, "I can play a little bit, I'm a student on the trombone, and I'd like to sit in with you." He told me then to come, and I came around there Tuesday night and he put the music up there and we played it, and he invited me back, and we commenced to get some jobs. So, because the trades was down (plastering business was slow) there wasn't enough to make a livin', so I began playin' music.

This on-again, off-again pattern became evident in a number of the careers. Alvin Alcorn tells how he and his friends found

and entered jazz playing, and how his own early career was a
trade-off between temporary jobs and music:

I came into jazz from listenin' to recordings. Different things, and
listenin' to musicians playin'—and at the time I came up there was
nothin' but some great trumpet players round here, so you had your
pick of soundin' like one, listenin' to all, but tryin' to get your own
sound. Yes, I had some friends who played. We'd set our instruments
and start out. A boyfriend of mine was on saxophone; I played trumpet, one played bass, and then in a year or so, I formed a little band.
We played mostly stock music—popular music of that time. We
weren't doing jazz at that time, mostly pop tunes. I always did use
music as a main base, because when I was young, and came up, I
was classified as one of the finest musicians they had around here.
See, I had an opportunity to work with all the old musicians and
marchin' bands for parades and funerals because they hadn't heard
many of the young musicians who were playing professionally
around here. In '31 I left here with a band and went on the road.
That was music—straight music and swing music. Then, when things
died down in music, I came back here and got a job for a certain
time, and then went back out on the road again. So, every time music
used to get into a lull, I'd come back and get a little job, 'cause I always could get jobs with friends and guys with different skills.
They'd always give me work of some kind.

They came into the business in several different ways and with
various motives. Some with assurance and direction, others with
interruption and occasional trepidation. They had begun to discover that love for music often had pleasant by-products, such as
potential fame. But most of them loved to play so much that
these by-products were only adjuncts, though pleasant ones.

Wilfred Antoine

I first took up piano. I wasn't learning fast enough. It took too long
to get any techniques. I wanted somethin' faster. Nevertheless, at
that time, I didn't have the love for music I got later, and anyhow,
I wasn't exposed long enough till after World War I. On the way
back from the War, I used to watch the band on the ship, and at the

training stations. They always had music. When I came out of the
service, I went into the post office in '22. There was an old carrier
there who was a music major in high school, and we formed a brass
band in the post office. When I started there, he had taught me how
to play a tuba. I played that, and I went into the band. The band
leader's name was Robert Clark. We used to call the band the Brown
Buddies. We played around the New Orleans area, and there wasn't
much money, no union, and nothin' then.

Raymond Ancar

They had amateur night at the Palace Theatre at that time. It was
me up there; it was Roy Brown; it was Val Victor at that time playing piano. And we all was together. That's the way we started off.
I was started off singin' at the Palace Theatre. And, Sidney Desvigne
heard me, and that's where I joined Sidney Desvigne's band. And
we went all over on the *Steamer Capital,* and to St. Paul (Minne-
sota). And, I used to travel with him on the boat. Well, Sidney had
the band for quite a while till he just drifted away. And, then Joe
Phillips took the band over after Sidney, so I worked for Joe. And
then when Joe Phillips turned what he had to Houston, that's when
I formed my own group, known as the Raymond Ancar Orchestra,
featurin' Cookie Gabriel as vocalist.

Kederick Johnson (Kid Johnson)

I must have been about seventeen when I started playin' for money.
It wasn't but fifty cents a week! The man who was in charge of the
group would pay some fifty cents and some seventy-five cents. It was
accordin' to the chair you held: first, second, or third. The only
trouble we had was tough kids who couldn't play music themselves.
They would wait on us and try to beat us up and take our instruments, but they didn't win.

Olivia Charlot

When I went into music, my mother and I were staying with my
grandparents. Since my grandfather was a musician himself, he interested me in it. However, people were very biased at that time

about their kids playing different types of music. My grandmother was really against jazz. She said I'd better play 'none whatsoever'! She said I must play either church music, or the classics. My grandfather went along with her for a time. He had an old organ that he paid $450.00 for. He began teaching me on that when I was six years old. By the time I was seven years, I was coming right along. Grandfather was a Pullman porter, and I think this helped him broaden his view of life, for I can remember the first time he let me play jazz. He and my grandmother were outside one day, and while I was practicing I started to pick out an old jazz funeral tune on the organ. My grandmother called me Tutsie. Just as soon as she heard what I was playing, she called in and said, "Tutsie, don't you do that! Tutsie, don't you do that!" My grandfather said, "Olivia (my grandmother's name), let that child alone. Let her play anything she wants to play"!

I studied the classics so long until I was really interested in being a concert pianist. This was all when I was very young. I had kind of got away from jazz for awhile, but after I grew up and found out what was happening at that time, I changed my mind. There wasn't much opportunity for me as a black person to be a concert pianist. Then I really began to go back to jazz.

The first time I went out to play with a jazz band, my grandmother put up a big fuss. She said, "I think it's terrible. Those men are gonna disrespect you." I said, "Oh momma! I'm grown now"! I was married, you see, so I felt I could take care of myself. When my grandfather found out that I was going to play with a band, he was just carried away. He loved it! I guess it was partly because he had gone to New York and seen a young woman leading an orchestra there. He just stuck out his chest to know I was working with a band too, and thought it was just wonderful.

Josiah "Jack" Willis

When I was a kid, I wanted to make money. After I got that first taste of money, man, I mean that was it! We left out of New Orleans and went on a gig in Texas on the nineteenth of June 1937, and I think we played a breakfast dance. I made nineteen dollars, and they gave it all to me in "ones!" Man, that broke it up! I didn't want to go back to school anymore! That was it! Nineteen dollars in one day! Oh man, I was sold! Corpus Christi, Texas. I'll never forget it!

James Black

I didn't go into music for the money. I wasn't really thinkin' about money. It was just the joy of playin'. The satisfaction of playin' music. You don't start realizin' that you have all sorts of other problems; you have to pay rent, buy food, or think about the financial aspect of it. It was just the joy of playin'. When we played our first jobs, we'd just play for the door. We had somebody there at the door collectin' money. We didn't worry about how much he collected. We just wanted to play.

When the jazzmen began to form groups and play for a public they were moving strongly toward a decision to become professional musicians. By age sixteen, over half of them were playing regularly with groups. By age seventeen, almost two-thirds were playing for money. It should not be difficult to guess that one person represented for them, above all others, the major stimulus to a life in professional music—Louis Armstrong. While Armstrong has become a legend to Americans, and much of the world, he is semi-deified by those young blacks entering music in New Orleans. Armstrong was the personification of all they loved, hoped for, and strived to attain; the way he played (even non-trumpet players emulate his style), his success, and human warmth. Within Bourbon Street Black, he was, and is, the human being most admired. There he was! The black boy, "little Louis," who knew no unkind words for people. Little Louis who picked coal from the levee to care for his mother and sister, and later a cousin. Always a smile on his face even in adversity. The meteoric rise to success following Papa Joe to Chicago. Then, weathering the storm of the Depression and the bigoted recoil against black jazz. They see in Louis a man who could cry when he found Papa Joe sick and penniless in Savannah, Georgia that hot summer day in the late nineteen thirties.

When they decided to make music their life's work, only a few were actually discouraged by relatives or friends. A negligible number were warned that music was an undesirable avenue be-

Groovin'" begins at an early age in Bourbon Street Black. Photographed by Jack V.
uerkle.

cause the "profession and musicians had a bad name." Some were told of economic insecurities and that a second occupation would be advisable as one to "fall back on" if the music business got bad, but there were no other negative implications. They are unanimous that such talk did not make them want to quit music, and some feel the advice only made their resolve to stay in music even stronger.

Danny Barker

My grandmother. She was a hard-shell Baptist. She said, "That's no way to make a livin'. It's the Devil's music. Out all night—dissipatin'. That's no good." She was a Christian woman. She was concerned about me playin' in gamblin' houses and honkey-tonks. There were so many varied degrees of spots where music was played. So, she didn't want me to get involved with rowdy people and stayin' up all night. The old folks know what's best for you bout gettin' your rest and eatin' right. She said, "Get yourself some kind of work that's honest and respectable insteada playin' that music in them honkey-tonks and barrel houses!"

Alvin Alcorn

I used to have guys tell me, "don't do this, don't do that"—the facts of life. But, not tell me not to be a musician. They weren't tellin' me not to play, but how to live. Don't be a heavy drinker, heavy smoker, or heavy anything. Stay away from the fast life.

Roger Dickerson

No, they didn't try to discourage me. They made statements about other fields—going into other fields giving a certain amount of security. It wasn't done in a way as a deterrent to my desires, though.

Somethin' Out There

Though major civil rights legislation didn't begin to appear until the mid-fifties, occupational and educational possibilities were considerably brighter for the Negro adolescent of the 1940s than was the case in 1900 or 1910. Usually, the best an older musician could have hoped for was the possibility of getting into the family trade as a daytime buffer against the financial insecurities of a career in music. An older jazzman describes his father's work. A trade he used himself as a day job:

My father was a well-known mattress maker (reconditioner). Those days they had wool and felt mattresses, but inner-spring mattresses were in bloom too in those days. There aren't many mattress factories in New Orleans today. Most people buy new mattresses, now. Foam rubber and all. I think we only got one mattress place here. Somewhere in the ninth ward. Them days, when you cleaned a mattress, you got $1.25 for cleaning the tickin' and refreshin' it. It was $4.50 for a felt mattress.

Another commented:

I decided to go to work because I began to see I couldn't go to college. I didn't have the money, and I was sixteen or seventeen, so I decided to get a job. I couldn't depend on my stepfather to send me to school because they were indifferent about education around that time. It was mostly building trades. Most of the people we knew were in the building trades. Most of the people we knew were carpenters, bricklayers, plasterers. Builders. In those days, a youngster went and did what his father did. If his father was a painter, naturally he became a painter, because it was real easy to fall into the footsteps of a trade that was already there. If your uncle was a carpenter, they'd send you as an apprentice. Well, music was enticing, and New Orleans was slow and relaxing for a black man, and I didn't see any future in that, but I saw a future in jazz music, because Louis Armstrong came out of here. Jimmy Noone, Sidney Bechet, Jelly Roll Morton, and others had received success. That was one way to get fame, make money, and see the world while you're doin' what you like. I would have liked to have finished college. Now I wish I could have become a lawyer.

Some families found it difficult enough just to survive, and all plans for any formal education beyond the very early years had to be cancelled.

Things were kind of rough then, and my mother was having such a hard time. I went to work to help pay for things. My daddy, before he died, really wanted me to be a doctor. And, we had a little money, I imagine, from talking to my mother. But before my daddy died, he caught TB and he lived about a year. We spent all our money. All the money we had put away.

Sometimes there weren't any scholastic desires competing with music, and the boy simply dropped out of school because he wanted to play music.

Truthfully, I can say I dropped out on account of music. I started making money, and I also had to repeat a grade in school. That may have had something to do with it. My father didn't like my quitting, because he was a teacher. My aunt and uncle, they didn't say too much. I'm sorry I didn't finish, because later, I couldn't get the work I wanted. You have got to have the papers for credentials. I just dropped out like the average kid who does every day. I guess my brother wanted me to be a musician because he was one. My cousin wanted me to be one, and I wanted to be one; and I worked hard with it. I tried to improve myself with my music.

Other older musicians had interrupted their education because of war and then returned.

I paid for my high school deliverin' papers and things. I had two or three odd jobs and then I'd take music on my horn. I had a scholarship to 'Bama State College. That was during the time Erskine Hawkins was there and started a program for musicians. I was given the scholarship, but Uncle Sam was draftin' men at twenty-one years old. After the war, I went to a music school through the GI Bill of Rights, and I have a certificate in arranging, studying harmony, counterpoint, etc. I was in that course about two years.

By the late '30s, the Swing Era was in full force, and a large number of the middle-aged and young jazzmen had left the Crescent City to go on the road with the big bands—bands like Lucky Millinder, Benny Carter, Duke Ellington, Cab Calloway, Count Basie, Chick Webb, and Jimmie Lunceford. The talented and musically motivated ones who had foregone their education were quickly absorbed into this new development.

For some young Negroes, though, educational advancement had become a reality. It *was* possible for a jazzman with talent to get a music scholarship in the Negro colleges and universities. Given the ways in which prejudice and discrimination were affecting the career choices of these young men, it was not likely they would be considered eligible for aid in other academic areas.

In the late 1930s and '40s Erskine Hawkins was quick to see that many potential professional musicians were beginning to attend these colleges. One of these institutions, " 'Bama State College," or today called Alabama State University served as a supply house for Hawkins and other bandleaders and a final training ground for a number of young jazzmen on their way up in the music business. This became especially apparent when Hawkins, his flashy trumpet, and group of the colleges' music students invaded New York as the " 'Bama State Collegians." Hawkins literally decimated the music department at the university. He will probably not be recorded as a significant figure in the history of American popular music, but (aside from having the first hit recording of "Tuxedo Junction") he did start this supply house phenomenon in Negro colleges. After Hawkins' experience, it became rather commonplace for Negro bandleaders to search for new blood in the colleges. They did this because "the books their sidemen had to cut" (scores they had to read) more and more required sight reading of high proficiency. Some, at least, felt that the possibility of finding this in a college was increased. Of course, the cat had to be able to swing, too!

To some, the lure of the "road" was not the prime mover. Though they were unable to leave the enticements of music, they chose and often obtained higher education, also. One, who almost went to medical school said,

After I finished pre-med, I decided I wanted to play music. I'd be happier playing music. It took quite a bit of my time to finish pre-medicine, and I made this decision right after I finished that. I

wanted to go into music. In fact, I was playing music. Writing, composing, and doing a lot of arranging for different bands. It had been a
fight in my mind as to what decision I wanted to make regarding the
two situations all along but I finally decided I'd be happier as a musician. I don't mind going to school (summer sessions) every time I
get a chance.

This man is now an instructor of music in the public schools.
Besides composing, arranging, and leading a big band, he oper-
ates a private music studio. Another, who completed two years of
college, has coupled his career in music with one in the business
community of New Orleans:

While I was in school, I helped to pay for my education by working
in the _____ Hotel where my father was employed. When
I left school, I went right into working at the hotel, and I worked
myself from busboy to room-service manager, and then on to the sales
staff. It was a big event, in fact, I was the first Negro to receive a
supervisory position in the _____ Hotel in forty years.
There was quite a write-up in the local paper concerning my achievement.

Whatever amount of education was possible in individual
cases, parental aspirations for seeing their children through school
were high. For the most part, the parents had been realists. How
much education was it possible for a black levee worker or tradesman to give his son in 1902, 1923, or 1940? A common remark
was, "They wanted me to go as far in school as I could go."[7] It is
interesting that a large number of the parents did not try to force
their children into a specific career. They left it up to the youngster.[8] The difficulties of going on in school became very apparent
in the comment made by almost half of the jazzmen that they
simply stopped going to school at a particular point because of
economic reasons.[9]

While the younger men have acquired considerably more education because of the impact of civil rights legislation, there is no
denying that all of their lives have been formed to search out at

east one common passion—music. Few captured this possessing, scintillating élan like one younger jazzman:

I don't know how cats feel about football, but I felt it wouldn't give me the same esthetic kick music did. A cat can *dig* playin' a set. When you play sets with people you like, and who like you—like everything is harmonious—there's nothing to compare—no words to describe the feeling you have when you leave. You feel almost reverent. In the past, I've seen all these fine chicks in the joint, and they look at the musicians, and they want you to take 'em home—and many times there's a real good set goin', and the chicks look up like, "let's do somethin' "—and after the set, I walk out—I don't want to talk to nobody. Everything they say seems like it's nonsensical. It doesn't mean nothing—and, like I really can't talk to nobody when I get off a real good set. Everybody plays for their own satisfaction.

5

The Local

IT IS A BATTERED old wooden structure on North Claiborne Avenue, recently dwarfed by the massive concrete bulk of Interstate Highway 10 passing overhead. Downstairs on one side of the building, one of the hit songs of the day is being played loudly on a jukebox set for sidewalk listening. As you enter a short dark hallway on the right side, there is the barely detectable aroma of stale beer. On the door in front of you it says, American Federation of Musicians, Local 496. Inside there is a small office, no more than ten by twelve, well painted, and presenting an atmosphere of orderliness and efficiency. Two people are in the room, a light complexioned lady, probably in her late forties or early fifties and an older man. She is talking on the phone: "Yes, Charles, just drop in any time this afternoon and I'll have the contract ready. Did you say you were using five men this time? O.K., I'll be here. Bye!" After her phone conversation, she smiles and addresses a young man who just entered the room. "I'm Mrs. Charlot, can I help you?" "Yes, I guess you can. It's this job, you see. I got a call from Ray Charles last night, and he wants me to be his drummer. He heard me play when he was in town a couple of weeks ago, and now his drummer just left him. He wants me to meet him in Los Angeles in a couple of days. I've played around, but I never joined the Local, and now I've got to. What do I have to do?" She smiled again, thinking that this

The Local. Photographed by Jack V. Buerkle.

young man is really getting a break. Ray Charles! This boy must be *some* drummer! "Yes, I think we can help you. Now here's what you have to do. First, fill out this application. You'll have to talk to Mr. Cottrell and Mr. Alcorn, too. The initiation fee is $87.00, but that can be in two payments. Your dues will be eight dollars a quarter—thirty-two dollars a year. You're a lucky young man to be going with Ray Charles." "Yes Mam, I know I am!" The older man got up just as the conversation subsided for a moment. Removing the string from a box he had held in his lap, he lifted the lid and beckoned to the younger man; "Son, would you like a praeline? I make them myself." "Yes sir; thank you. I sure would"!

The Way it Works

This young jazzman is about to become a member of a brotherhood, 300,000 strong; The American Federation of Musicians. He is going to join a traveling celebrity band, and his ticket (card) will be good everywhere in the United States as he moves about. His parent Local is 496, New Orleans, Louisiana. Local 496 is a predominantly black unit with somewhat over four hundred members. Should our young man decide to settle down in another town, he can do so on a transfer basis by paying a fifty dollar fee. In fact, he can join as many locals as he wishes on this basis.

The New Orleans Local, like many others, is a microcosm of the national "Federation." It grew out of New Orleans black musicians seeking the protection of organization during the early part of the twentieth century. There had arisen a nasty and protracted series of inequities, and the musicians responded by protesting in a somewhat organized way. This attracted the attention of the Federation, and 496 was born. Historically, the function of the union has been to protect the brotherhood—the men of the union. In reality it has been dedicated to the general principle of equity for all involved. Built into the constitution, bylaws, and general rules is a basic consideration of reciprocity. These codes act as a kind of moral script in a play involving as actors, the musicians, the people who employ their services, the relevant public, and the union itself. Prerogatives and obligations are set forth with the union organization being the major watchdog or judge of the proceedings. The musicians seek better pay, better working conditions, fringe benefits, and better music. Employers and the public seek better and more dependable performances along with clear contractual arrangements concerning the performances.

The Local is operated by officials who are elected for two-year terms, and elections are set up to involve a fifty per cent turnover per annum. In reality, the officers generally serve considerably longer terms, because a large body of them continue to be re-elected. Though anyone can, theoretically, be a union official, it is generally the more seasoned, political and service oriented musician who becomes one. The major officers are president, vice-president, financial secretary—treasurer, business representative, and recording secretary. Besides the officers, there is a board of directors that meets every Tuesday. As a part of their service, the officers and board members serve on several committees, such as pension fund, credit union, wage. For new members, there is a series of indoctrination or socialization meetings to acquaint them with both the general and specific intent of the constitution and bylaws as they apply to them.

Having an extensive music heritage in New Orleans, Local 496 has a steady stream of young musicians seeking affiliation. Years of socialization by elders and peers as to the virtues of affiliation brings them to the Local's door quite rapidly after their money-making debut. Those who have played in high school and college bands often want to work professionally, so they too come in.

In New Orleans very few musicians avoid joining the union. Even for part-time musicians who depend upon the money from playing as a regular part of their income, the union becomes necessary. All the best jobs are union controlled, and the scab is forced to play in places with appreciably poorer working condi-

tions and wages. Also, he will frequently find he is cheated out
of part or maybe all of the wages agreed upon. Most of those involved in nonunion playing are neophytes—the young and the
beginners. They usually stay out of the union a year or two before they become frustrated with the vagaries of their playing
situation and go to get the "ticket." No one in the New Orleans
black music community seems to be able to fix a percentage on
working nonunion musicians, but all estimates hover around
minimal and very few.

Aside from creating better working conditions, higher wages,
and a greater assurance of getting the money earned, the union
has developed a fringe benefit package. By coming into the Local, a jazzman becomes a part of a pension fund that has death
benefits for survivors, receives union protection and surveillance
in regard to his social security deposits, and has access to the
credit union. The fringe benefits have added considerably more
stability to an occupation that has had a legendary reputation for
insecurity. Not too long ago, when a man couldn't work any
longer because of age or illness, there was little, indeed, to fall
back on. There was no pension fund, and musicians were not
eligible for social security. At this time, the Local still has no
health insurance program for its members.

The operation of each of the present fringe benefit programs
works as follows: Contributions to the pension fund are de-
posited by the leader on a job at the Local, and each man is responsible for keeping track of his own social security deposits except when he is on a steady job, for example, a member of a
"house" band. In that case, the proprietor of the establishment
would be responsible. At the same time the Local acts as the musician's agent should there be a dispute over the amount of the
deposits. Because of the "intermittent" work status of some musicians, particularly those who only intend to work part time, contributions to the pension fund need be made only when a man
works. The credit union is an optional feature; the musician who
choses to join makes deposits into a "kitty" and becomes eligible

to borrow when the need arises. In this way the member is offered a way to avoid gouging by a loan shark should he need to borrow.

The local is also a clearing house. While it does not find jobs for members nor suggest particular bands, leaders, or musicians when called by potential employers, it does supply long lists of prospects from the rosters of available personnel. This is to ensure that no discrimination or favoritism will result. It will also guide the potential employer to the type of musician or organization he is seeking. This is done in order to be certain that a club owner or hotel manager will not get a rock and roll performance when they need either "society" music or jazz. Addresses and telephone numbers of particular members are supplied upon request. This is often not necessary in a community like New Orleans, though, because most musicians, groups, leaders, etc., have calling cards identifying their music services, and the musicians tend to distribute these widely around town.

All it takes to organize a gig is an agreement from enough men to form a band, and a signed contract. The contract form, which is obtained from and registered with the union, presents a series of agreements between two parties: the band leader and the employer. The leader agrees to provide music for the employer at a designated place, on a given day, to begin and end at specified times, with intermissions of given length at specified intervals. The employer agrees to provide certain working conditions including playing time and intermission terms and a specific total amount of money to be paid the leader at an agreed upon time. The amount of money is union scale or above. Union scale is the amount of money currently due a musician for performing a specified amount of time; usually two, three, or four hours. Scale varies from city to city. The contract will specify that the leader be paid scale for all the men in the group (including himself) plus one. The leader is paid double. The logic, of course, is that he is being paid for all the effort of organization and the responsibility of making certain that the product (music) is delivered as

(Left to right) Danny Barker and Louis Cottrell. Photographed by Jack V. Buerkle.

contracted for. The employer must also pay an added percentage (currently 17 per cent) above scale as contributions to the musicians' pension fund and social security. Once the leader has been paid, he deducts the fringe benefit percentage, then pays the sidemen the remaining amount as wages. Payment can be made nightly, weekly, or on any other basis, depending upon the terms of the contract. Certainly, house bands are paid on a different schedule than groups concentrating on one-night gigs; usually weekly.

A musician in New Orleans can still work in a variety of places. The brass bands, picnics, private parties, and dances usually use union music. Even off Bourbon Street and outside the Vieux Carré, the city is permeated with hotels, cabarets, bars and lounges, many requiring musicians. Even with such great demand, though, less than fifty per cent of the members of Local 496 are classified as full-time. The Class A hotels, motor inns, and a few night clubs keep house bands and single performers. Some of the clubs hire two bands, but the size of the units has decreased over the last twenty-five years from an average of fourteen to fifteen to five or six. Of course, the jazz bands (inside bands, not marching brass bands) were always small. Though house band status usually means full-time employment, most of the gigs in New Orleans do not extend beyond three nights a week, even on Bourbon Street. Some of the musicians who are full time are able to work two gigs by playing week nights for one employer and the weekend for another. Most of the musicians, though, play two to three nights a week supplementing their primary source of income—the day job.

The Local takes the responsibility of informing the young jazzman about union rules so that he knows them well enough to protect both himself and his brothers, and can at the same time set up a professional and equitable relationship with employers. First, the Local tells him to work with only union musicians in clubs that hire *only* union musicians, and to always "work to the scale," i.e. never work for less than union scale. If there is ever any doubt of the union status of a musician, he is told to show his card; it's standard practice. In most cases this sort of thing is not necessary, particularly in the standard places such as most of those in the Vieux Carré, the better clubs, and the hotels. Everybody tends to know everybody else, and besides, the employers are scrupulous in checking on such things. Often there are several unions represented by employees in the same establishment, so no chances are taken. Thus, on such grounds, the Local and the employer are usually in total agreement. It is in the "fringe" establishments that difficulties can occur.

After working a gig for a while, a man or the members of a band might decide that their working hours are too rigid or too flexible and that they want to negotiate for a change. The men may be complaining that the intermission is too short, while the management and customers say it is too long. This type of problem is brought to the Local to mediate.

Before a group goes out on the road, the leader, or any of the men, can check the latest national unfair list at the Local, giving those potential employers in the United States who have in some way broken a Federation rule. This bulletin is brought up to date monthly. The problem is usually one of not paying a group, but it could be other things like failing to meet a number of other provisions of a contract. When a potential employer is on the list, this means that no union units are allowed to perform for that management until all grievances are cleared up to the union's satisfaction. In the case of a traveling musician, the Federation handles such matters. The jurisdiction of a particular Local extends only for a limited territory surrounding the city in which it is located. One man, commenting on the differences between travel nowadays and a few years back, said:

We used to have a hell of a time on the road. A lot of us were kids and didn't have any more sense, but aside from all the crap that used to go with Jim Crow, you never knew when some of the bastards were gonna pay you. So many of the guys used to book bands and they didn't have the capital or nothin'. These guys would just start bookin'—just gamblin' pot luck! Gamblin' with my loot! If it came out allright some of the time you'd get paid. If it didn't he'd say "sorry man, I just didn't make it." But I guess everybody was gamblin' in those days. Those were the pot luck days!

Sometimes problems out on the road go the other way. Some musician may have a contract to play a gig in Muncie, Indiana, on a cold January night. Because of the weather he is unable to show up and the next morning he sends a telegram saying the band was marooned in Columbus, and to "please accept my apologies." Apologies do not suffice, for the promoters are out $600.00 in advertising expenses, and they call the Federation office in New York and threaten to sue. The musician then has to prove he was actually marooned and he may have to make restitution to the Muncie people, in order to keep things "clean" with the Federation. In both situations matter of business are involved. The proprietor needs professional, dependable service from musicians in order to maximize his business, and the musician (though he probably views himself as an artist) recognizes also that he is in the music business. If the problem is relatively minor, it might be worked out through consultation between the two Locals involved: the parent Local and the one in whose jurisdiction the trouble occurred. Both the cases of the proprietor who doesn't pay and the musician who doesn't show are the exception rather than the rule. As the Federation has gained strength over the years, these kinds of problems have lessened considerably.

With both Federation and Local regulations placing so much responsibility in the hands of leaders, the Local does not usually interfere in matters concerning the conduct of sidemen while they are on a gig. After all, the leader is the one the employer comes looking for if there is trouble. The leader is thus free to make his own rules about conduct on the stand and the job, within limits; if he's a tyrant, word will get around and no one will work for him. Some leaders will allow no drinking on the job at all; others will allow none on the stand. Unless a sideman is in an indefinite status (which he might well be if playing with a group that does occasional one-night gigs where he can be dropped anytime), the usual contractual arrangement between leader and sideman is a reciprocal two-weeks' notice. Leaders usually will not tolerate anything that will jeopardize the employment status of the group since it is a business. One man expressed an opinion about alcohol or narcotics being taken on the job:

Man, who needs trouble? What this cat does on his own time is his bag, but I don't want to be sittin' beside him when they spot him! I gotta work! I don't *know* anybody who wants to try to work with a cat like that! It's just trouble, Man, trouble!

Union rules provide for a leader being able to file charges against a sideman and vice versa. If the case is mediated by the Local and someone is found guilty, punishments for the infringement are meted out. Sometimes it is only a light fine or suspended sentence, or it might be more severe, depending upon the nature of the infraction. When on the gig problems occur with any frequency at all in the jurisdiction of Local 496, they are handled almost always at the leader–sideman level and are infrequently dealt with by the Local.

Problems between sidemen are handled by the Local. If, for instance, one man contends that another had slandered him to the leader or the employer and caused his dismissal, the Local would investigate and might well consider the case. From its point of view, the Local must insist that the relationship between the men be a "brotherhood." They cannot knowingly tolerate what they consider to be unethical or unfair behavior between them. Another kind of problem may arise when a member may try to "move in" on another's job. Suppose someone is playing at a club on Bourbon Street and word gets around that the leader would like to replace him but hasn't because it might be "complicated" at this point. The leader has the right to drop any man with two weeks' notice by showing cause, but another sideman cannot (according to union regulations) walk up to the leader

(Left to right) Louis Barbarin and Alvin Alcorn. Photographed by Jack V. Buerkle.

and request an audition upon the hearsay that the man is replaceable. Those are, generally, the kinds of problems that arise in the operation of the Local and the way in which they are usually resolved. There is strong evidence that the Local as an educational and regulatory agency, coupled with the general professional attitude of the musicians, creates a situation where few actual disputes arise.

Myth and legend concerning the musician, particularly the jazzman, has ignored the fact that most people involved in the production of popular music in Bourbon Street Black lead highly regularized, conventional lives and just don't conform to the "Jazz Age" image.

Practically every visitor with some romantic conception (usually misconception) about the Jazz Age comes to the French Quarter looking for old, black jazzmen blasting away in a public jam session. He doesn't have to go too far to find the old, black jazzman, but he is not going to find public jam sessions. They're not permitted! The Local discontinued them some time ago for business reasons. With their absolute commitment to music wherever they can perform it with their groovin' friends, some of the cats would get carried away in the past and work all night without compensation. One prominent New Orleans jazzman remarked:

Well, public jam sessions are illegal. 496 stopped that some time ago. We found out that it was no good. It seemed like a guy would have a jam session in his club and not even have to hire musicians. The guy across the street would have hired musicians. When a set was over, some of the cats would cross the street to this other place and start blowin' for nothin'. Hell, sometimes some of them would get to groovin' so heavy they'd forget to go back for the next set. Then the guy who hired the musicians would raise hell with the Local the next day. We just cut it out. It was too much!

Some jamming goes on, but it must be a private place, like someone's house. As the old-timers tell it, there used to be a lot of jam sessions, but apparently things have toned down considerably since the Local stepped in. Now, 42 per cent of the musicians say they never jam.[1]

Old Folks

One of the unique facts of the New Orleans scene is that a premium is placed on older, black musicians. Regardless of the inaccuracy of the stereotype, many tourists walking up Bourbon Street or down St. Peter to Preservation Hall expect to hear an older black man, white shirt open at the collar, suspenders, simply cut trousers, plain black shoes, and legs crossed. He will often be envisioned methodically working his way through Alphonse Picou's solo in High Society. However, jazz was a young man's music, and the jazzmen who set the streets and halls of New Orleans "afire" in the days of Buddy Bolden, Freddie Keppard, and Chris Kelly were young men. Now the image is reversed; hot jazz is associated with old men. And although time has passed and most of the old heroes are dead, the old cats are expected to be able to recapture the golden days. Many do preserve the atmosphere of the old French Quarter, and it's these old musicians who the tourists look for when they visit New Orleans.

It's the older musicians who remember how they put the Local together almost on just the dream of getting their fair share of the scene when things were tough and fairly disorganized. Oftentimes they will just come into the Local to talk with old friends; work through tales of who won out in a particular carving contest and finding pride in asserting they had been there. An observer in this setting gets the impression of a tone that is classically oriental. In a genuine sense, the old cats are respected, indulged, and emulated. A person moving quickly into and out of New Orleans will miss that certain intergenerational "tenderness" among those in Bourbon Street Black which is focused most decidedly on the Old. When a musician gets too frail to perform regularly, he is not forgotten by the Local or his friends. The Local gives him a lifetime membership in the union with full voting rights,

Oscar "Chicken" Henry at 86. Photographed by Jack V. Buerkle.

and makes certain he receives all communications of importance from both the Federation and Local level. For the most part, too, the active members of the Local look after their fellow members when they start slowing down. When an old timer becomes noticeably absent from the scene for a while, someone will usually call on him and make arrangements to give him a little action if he wants it and can take it. Usually they do want it even if it just means watching while a band plays a gig or sitting in for someone for a set. Some even manage to get a gig now and then, sometimes as often as once a week. Like any occupation, the things that go along with retirement or semiretirement from an active life as a musician bring forth considerable nostalgia. One older and sometimes infirm jazzman spoke with considerable feeling about his present condition:

I have some friends—several—who come in their cars—it seem all the younger cats have cars—and take me down to the Quarter. With my condition I would have to get a taxi, but I don't have to—they come and take me. They bring me home too! . . . I worry about my condition. I don't think it has affected my playin', but maybe it has. I've been kind of nervous lately, 'specially when I'm alone. I have my ups and downs. Loosin' my wife a year and a half ago kinda set me back, you know. We'd been together for thirty-one years. That's a long time. *She spent eighteen years on the road with me.* Just me. That's a long time. . . . If I had a son I'd tell him to make a career out of it (music) if he could. As long as he could eat and keep it goin', then keep it goin'. I remember the time I had cheese and crackers and decided to keep goin', I loved music so well. I'd rather play music and eat crackers and cheese than eat steak and hamburgers and work as a truck driver or somethin' else. That's how much I appreciate music. One thing I don't like, though and that's to play with musicians that ain't playin' right. I'd rather not play, because it hurts me to hear it. . . . I guess I'll be alright. What I need is play—play—more play. My nerves would be better, too. I think if I could play more—if I could just play one gig a week, or somethin' like, I feels pretty good. If I don't play a gig for two weeks, I'll be down in the dumps. I just gotta start playin'. When the gigs don't come, I just start playin' here in the house to myself. All by myself.

Thinkin' About the Business

Learning about the music business has always taken time, and has usually involved some difficulties along the way. One of the functions of the Local is educational. Actually, though, formal education by the union begins *after* the new member has paid his first dues and initiation fee and begins to attend training sessions concerning the constitution, bylaws, and general rules of the Local. Whatever he would have heard about the Local prior to joining would have been, for the most part, by word of mouth, because it does not have a formal public relations program nor does it actively recruit new members. One might expect that young jazzmen growing up in Bourbon Street Black today would be more informed about getting along in the music world than were their fathers and uncles. Such is not the case.[2] It would be reasonable to expect a difference in knowledge about ways to cope, for the business is considerably more organized than it was thirty or forty years ago. Back in the old days the union was just a shadow of what it is today. The concept of "going on the road" was just getting under way about the time Papa Joe Oliver, Jelly Roll, and some of the others left the Crescent City. They went out "cold." Those who followed in a generation or so had picked up some of the stories of what could happen if one did not take care of oneself and one's money. So, some information did filter back to New Orleans about how the "big cats" were faring in Chicago, Los Angeles, and New York. By the mid-twenties, stories were coming back to town about those who had left the Crescent City only a few years back and found unprecedented success in the North, only to run into trouble because they squandered their money or led a dissipated life. Stories about the consequences of narcotics still permeate the families of Bourbon Street Black. Young people entering the music business are given *general* behavioral prescriptions about how to act in the world outside: "If you go into the music business, join the union. It will

protect you." But there were many important matters they could
only learn through experience in the business. For instance, over
80 per cent of them said they knew little or nothing about how
jobs were obtained, how much you might get paid for different
gigs (union, nonunion, class A, B, C, etc.), or about union rules
before they began playing professionally.[3] They only learned
later how to get and keep jobs, how to get along on the job with
other cats, how one became a success in the business, how necessary it was to become versatile, both in terms of music market and
in mastering several musical instruments, and how important it
was to be able to read any music put before them. They also dis-
covered that there are people in the world who will cheat you.
One man said,

When I decided to be a leader, man, I had to learn fast! I had no idea
of what was involved in making out a contract. At first, hell, I had
no idea of how much I was responsible for. I think I would have
dropped over if I'd have known what I was getting into. Man, I was
green! And one of the things a leader needs to be able to do most in
the music business is to make a decision. I guess I made out all right,
though, I'm still goin'.

Another said,

I learned that to make a living at it you have to adjust to playin' different kinds of music, not just the kind you like best. Also, I learned
how important it is to be able to read music well. If you can do this
you can make out a lot better. I developed a high respect for the
union because I think they have kept up the wages a lot better than
the musician would be able to do himself.

And one commented on the insecurities involved:

Well, playin' professionally is just like fightin' for any job. One cat
fightin' another. For every gig you go on there is some other cat tryin'
to work you out of it. It's a tough job tryin' to make a livin' in this
business, because a leader can get rid of you on just two weeks
notice. So, you're never sure of anything. That's the kinda stuff I
never knew anythin' about.

Only 12 per cent of the musicians are not actively playing in any group at this time.[4] For the most part, these men are retired, but a minority have begun to drop out of playing altogether. A particularly interesting, and perhaps unique, aspect of the New Orleans setting is the involvement of individual jazzmen in a number of different bands. Only about 20 per cent of the musicians have played in only one group for the past five years, while 30 per cent were in either two, three, or four bands during the past five years, and 17 per cent were in as many as ten bands during this period. Does this mean that the men are unstable, flighty in their employment, and unable to maintain any lasting relationship either with other jazzmen or their employers? No. Many of the men have played in basically the same organizations for much of their careers. Often what has transpired is that each of the same five or six men, though staying together as a unit, have been the leader at different times, that is, whoever got the job was the leader. In this kind of situation, a person could be technically considered a member of five or six different bands, but remain with the same group of people. By having everyone as a potential leader, though, the situation is both democratized (the leader gets double wages) and the probabilities of the band getting gigs is greatly enhanced, because each man becomes an active agent for the band as he moves about through the city.

Another facet of the "everyone can be a leader" phenomenon in New Orleans is that over 90 per cent of the musicians *have* been leaders. Of those who have been leaders, over 70 per cent said they liked it. Some of those who have led are motivated by a desire to be in a situation where they can have some control over the quality of the band. In this vein, one man said,

I like to be the leader because I've concluded that the band is only as good as the leader. If he is not the type of person who has a certain amount of continuous pushing for improvement, and watching everything to make certain a mistake is corrected, then the band doesn't improve. And, I've heard bands where the leader was satisfied just so the people didn't throw rocks at him. That would be good enough.

So, I enjoy being a leader, because I'm able to do more of what I like to do.

Others enjoy it but with qualifications like, "There are times when there are a lot of headaches. You've got to worry if all your men are going to show up, and things like that. Also, since you're always responsible, you have to go running around at intermission time, checking on things, making certain that everything is all right." Those who have led but don't like it seem to object most to the added responsibility, such as making certain the employer doesn't try to beat the band out of its money because he "had a bad night," signing contracts, and keeping track of the money that has to go back to the Local.

What do the musicians think of leaders? It is not at all surprising that a sizeable number (nearly 60 per cent) say positive things about leaders, since almost all have been involved in it themselves to some extent. Only about 6 per cent are negative, and the remainder are neutral in their opinion. The difference between the very high percentage who liked being leaders and the proportion having favorable attitudes toward other leaders is probably due to how they feel about being leaders themselves and how they feel about working under someone else.

Leadership interest extends beyond their music groups. A large number (nearly 75 per cent) said they would definitely be interested in becoming a union official in the future if they ever stopped playing music. This reflects a positive attitude toward the union and its representatives. The comments made, are almost always complimentary of union officials, even when a musician shows no desire to be one: "I wouldn't like it because most union officials are not compensated for the job they do. It is an ungrateful job, and I wouldn't take it." Most of the time, though, the members say they would like such a job because "I could encourage the guys to join the Local and stay with the union. And, it would give the younger musicians more encouragement as they are coming up." Others see it as a good job when they get older (actually many of the officials are older than the average mem-

ber) and say, "well, I couldn't do it now, but, I'd like it. I'd like
to work around musicians. Yes, I'd rather be around musicians
even if all I could do was to sell sandwiches to be around them.
It would keep me around music, because you just don't forget."
And, "I've given it some consideration. It takes a lot of work—a
lot of responsibility. I'll cross that bridge when I come to it."

One of the most serious matters confronting both the individual musician and the Local is the frailty of the craft. Neither
seem to be able to do much about it. Many bands either break
up after a time, or don't get contracts renewed by employers
causing individual musicians to be left in financial peril. Sometimes personality factors are cited as major causes in breakups,
and in other instances it's organizational matters, or changes in
the public's tastes. A younger jazzman reviewed what he considered a major factor in problems between band personnel:

From my experience some of the fellows act like you just have to have
them. A guy like that is always a potential "star," or at least thinks he
is, and naturally tries to come into his own. He can't take any direction, and wants to be special. This raises hell with the rest of the
group, and unless the leader has a strong hand, the band will probably break up.

Personality conflict, though, was not the most frequently mentioned reason given for band failures; most of the musicians cited
a group's inability to make enough money to support its members
as the greatest problem. Reasons given for economic failure often
emphasized the nature of the market. "You have to play what the
people want, or you're just not gonna get gigs. Whether you play
for a concert, or a dance, if you don't play what someone wants,
then nobody's gonna book you. Then the band business doesn't
work out—nobody gets paid." Also, bands can go out of style for
the market. This happened with the demise of "big bands" when
market conditions changed after World War II. A similar thing
happened to the contemporary jazz units after the influx of
rhythm and blues and rock and roll. Few of the jazz units adapted

to changing market tastes, and most were either wiped out within a few months or thrown into a "limping" status. Recently, some former players of contemporary jazz have made new bids for survival as musicians, by producing a new amalgam known as "jazz-rock." These changes and demands in music market conditions are outside the purview of Local 496, and through the years they have brought many Crescent City jazzmen and composers back from adopted homes like New York and Chicago to the relative security of Bourbon Street Black. An older jazzman discusses how the public and the leaders of the music business routinely affect those unable or unwilling to adapt to the current scene:

Jazz and popular music is in the hands of businessmen whose only idea is to make money. Those who make the most money know certain things about the habits and desires of the American public and they use this information in making their loot. They know the American scene—life-style—is geared and generated in all endeavours—to always wanting something new. So, they keep trying to give the public new things all the time. It's most times the same merchandise, but in a different guise, package, or presentation. All manufacturers have research, promotional, and publicity setups which are constantly peddling to the public the latest gimmick. This whole idea applies to jazz and popular music. You can see it in the short life span of composers who make it in New York. A few hit songs, and that's it. Very few composers continue at the top of the heap.

Scott Joplin and many other composers and musicians faded into the shadows—unsung but fighting and grasping at the fickle American music lovers—who will desert the current music (whatever it is) for the new thing. It's an American pattern. It's a shallowness of dedication. The "old put down." In each period of our musical history there has been this scene—the boneyard, or the graveyard—to which the artists retreat—abandoned and ignored. Scott Joplin and his contemporaries could tell many sad tales. Jelly Roll and King Oliver and their contemporaries could tell many sad tales. Charlie Parker, Fats Navarro, and their contemporaries could tell many sad tales. That boneyard, graveyard, is piled high with the bones—manuscripts—music—great music that was rejected by the people who control the music business. Each of these poor cats at one time or another got the familiar statement, "your music is dated—old hat. Haven't you got

something new, fresh like what the new musicians are writing"?
"I'm busy now. Come see me next week. I have an important meeting
in the next ten minutes." Joplin heard that statement. Jelly Roll and
Oliver heard it. Charlie Parker, Navarro. They heard it. In other
businesses workers are given a gold or silver watch and a retirement
party, but in music old artists in New York are told, "Don't call us;
we will call you." It's a statement that is poison for the person. It
slowly kills.

Almost fifty years have passed since Local 496 was formed to
improve the life chances and general security of its members. The
officers and members agree that the brotherhood has been very
much worth their effort, but many aspects of their original goal
are yet to be achieved.

Epilogue

Once every two years the families in Local 496 used to get together for a grand banquet. It usually had all the earmarks of a
sentimental journey, for the jazzmen *had* come a long way since
their earliest attempts to bring their calling up alongside the other
arts. Getting together was always gratifying, but there was something warmly poignant about these reunions. Old-timers retold
drama after drama about their part in the youth and growth of
jazz. All of this to the eager ears of the captivated neophyte,
while the ladies discussed the latest happenings in the community. There are many who remember 496 as a kind of "family"
affair. It was, by Federation standards, not a large Local.

Local 496 is not in existence anymore. Within the recent past
it amalgamated with the other Local in town, 174. The new
Local is called Musicians Mutual Protective Union, Local Number 174-496. It is located at 2401 Esplanade Avenue. Both Locals
had arisen independently over the past years under the guidance
of the American Federation of Musicians. The independent development was along racial lines, for 174 was known as the white
Local. These developments were not regional, as might be sus-

pected. They were certainly not peculiarly Southern; they were national. Until January 1971, several of the largest northern cities had dual Locals; one for black, another for white. When asked why they amalgamated in New Orleans, one brother commented:

I guess the question is why we didn't do it sooner. It used to be real strange. Many of us have always been friends across the two Locals— We grew up together. Sometimes, a big hotel would have two bands playing on the same night; one white, and the other colored. They'd be playing on one side of the hotel, and we'd be on the other. When it was all over, the money (for the union) would go back to two different Locals. Two different plants to keep going. And, besides our strength as a brotherhood was diluted. We just decided it was stupid to go on like that. 'Specially since we were friends.

First reports on how the new brotherhood is working out are encouraging. Certainly now the musicians of the Crescent City can present a united front to New Orleans. Some of the family-like warmth has been lost in the new Local setting because, if for no other reason, of the increased and necessary bureaucratization brought about by greater size. Most likely, the fate of Bourbon Street Black does not depend upon the presence of Local 496. The Local was an important institution in the organization and further implementation of black participation in a wary and sometimes belligerent market. But, times have changed, and, with that in view, 496 simply outgrew its usefulness as a distinct entity. Certainly, it will be missed, but very probably its dissolution will not affect community organization and structure perceptibly. After all, Bourbon Street Black was a reality long before the Local was conceived.

6

Of Race and Men

ON FEBRUARY 26, 1917, five young white musicians from New Orleans walked into the studios of the Victor Talking Machine Company to record two songs. The compositions, "The Livery Stable Blues" and the "Dixie Jass Band One-Step" (Victor 18255), were the first jazz records to be sold to the American public. Slightly more than a month before Nick LaRocca (cornet), Larry Shields (clarinet), Eddie Edwards (trombone), Henry Ragas (piano), and Tony Sbarbaro (drums) had opened at Reisenweber's Cabaret at Columbus Circle, New York City. They were billed as the *Original Dixieland Jazz Band–The Creators of Jazz*. Things went slowly at first, and initial reactions of the patrons and the New York press were not favorable. It was difficult to convince people that the music was for dancing, but in a couple of weeks they caught on and the ODJB was a sensation in New York.[1] Within less than a year, they were popular over the whole country, and by 1919 a successful tour to London had resulted in worldwide acclaim. Early in 1917, Nick LaRocca had become the group's general manager and major composer. The boys were working toward accumulating a large library of their own tunes, and LaRocca was credited with such compositions as the "Tiger Rag," "Livery Stable Blues," and "At The Jazz Band Ball."[2] They had worked hard, received a few breaks, and now they were on top with most people thinking of them as their promotional material had proclaimed: "the creators of jazz"—almost, but not quite everybody.

Jim Crow Blues

During 1917 Joe Oliver was still in New Orleans; Freddie Keppard had been on the road touring nationally with the Original Creole Band on the vaudeville circuit since 1913. The band was first billed as playing ragtime, but in actuality the men were playing predominantly what was to be later called jazz. A few months before the Original Dixieland Jazz Band made its recordings for Victor, Keppard was asked to put the sounds of his group on wax. He didn't do it, and several stories have arisen to explain his refusal. One of the most popular themes is that he believed that wide distribution of the New Orleans music would result in national commercialization of what he saw as a kind of Crescent City Negro folk form. Whatever the reason for the rejection of the offer, a white group (ODJB) was recorded first, and the national image of jazz music was first that of white musicians. It didn't really matter about Bolden, Oliver, Keppard, or Jelly Roll Morton. As far as most of the American public of 1917 was concerned, these men simply didn't exist as their music was being presented to an almost exclusively Negro audience. Freddie Keppard's "beat" when he was in New York in 1917 was Harlem—a pattern that was to remain for other Negro musicians for years yet to come.

Around the turn of the century in New Orleans, whites practically never worked with black organizations, and it was usually only some of the lighter Creoles of Color who were able to "pass" who worked with the white bands. Two such cases are those of Dave Perkins and Achille Baquet, Creoles of Color (considered Negro by New Orleans standards). These men worked regularly in the Jack Laine organization. Papa Jack Laine, a white, had control of several brass and inside bands from the 1890s, and had almost a monopoly in supplying the musical needs of the upper class and middle-class whites in New Orleans. Perkins and Baquet were among the best in his "stable," as were LaRocca and his colleagues before they went North.

Given the number and magnitude of celebrations and public events of note in New Orleans, it was, and is, a common practice for white and Negro brass bands to work in close proximity. White bands stayed pretty close to the standard style of European martial music and the United States Marine Band format of John Phillip Sousa. But they often marched, or stood close to the Negro bands who were playing their own swinging versions of the same music, the blues, and ragtime. Preston Jackson commenting in Shapiro and Hentoff's, *Hear Me Talkin' To Ya* about white musicians coming to Billy Phillip's 101 Club to hear Joe Oliver said, "One of the best numbers I ever heard Joe play was 'Eccentric.' He took all the breaks, imitating a rooster and a baby. He was a riot in those days, his band from 1915 to '16 to 1918 being the best in New Orleans. The LaRocca boys of the Dixieland Jazz Band used to hang around and got a lot of ideas from his gang."[3] Whether or not Preston Jackson's memory is completely accurate is relatively unimportant. There actually *was* a Bolden, a King Oliver, a Keppard, and an Alphonse Picou. Still, according to H. O. Brunn, author of *The Story of the Original Dixieland Jazz Band,* the black jazzmen never existed, or at least were irrelevant to the history of jazz.[4] The early chapters of the Brunn book deal with the ODJB members' experiences in New Orleans and particularly with the Jack Laine bands. It's as though no Negro population existed in New Orleans. The book illustrates precisely what Ralph Ellison had in mind when he wrote *The Invisible Man.*[5] Of *all* prominent New Orleans jazzmen only Louis Armstrong and Jelly Roll Morton appear in Brunn's index, and their presence in the text is utilized only to confirm the members of ODJB as the "creators of jazz." While the book describes the accomplishments of an important white jazz group, it also reflects a widespread denial in America of the black man's role in the creation and development of this music.

In early 1918, Joe Oliver left New Orleans to join Bill Johnson's band in Chicago at the Royal Garden Cafe, and within two
years he led his own group. By the summer of 1922, Armstrong
had joined him, and they were playing to full houses at Lincoln
Gardens (the old Royal Gardens). A large number of jazzmen of
Bourbon Street Black had migrated to Chicago by that time, but
attention turned toward King Oliver's Creole Jazz Band once
Armstrong arrived. They were packing them in, still only the
white bands had recorded. After a while a group of young white
Chicago jazzmen who had first been impressed by a white band,
The New Orleans Rhythm Kings, started hanging around. They
went wild over Louis! Now they are known as the Austin High
School Gang, and the nucleus contained the McPartland brothers
(Jimmie and Dick), Bud Freeman, Frankie Teschmaker, and Jim
Lannigan. Other white musicians who were to later join the
Austin High Gang or be somewhere on the Chicago scene were
Benny Goodman, George Wettling, Dave Tough, Mezz Mezz-
row, Jack Teagarden, Gene Krupa, Eddie Condon, Jess Stacy,
and Joe Sullivan. Most of these young men were to become internationally famous jazz personalities, and all were fundamentally influenced during their early musical development by the
Negro bands on the Chicago scene. Certainly, after a time, the
influence was to become mutual, but in those early days the Negro bands were imparting a "swinging" approach, a looseness,
that was new to the white musicians. Bix Beiderbecke was playing in Chicago during this period, but the earlier influences on
his style had been the ODJB, and only later was he influenced by
Negro bands such as that of King Oliver.

By 1924 a number of Negro bands had recorded, but their efforts were confined exclusively to "race" records that were disseminated to a minority (Negro) audience. Musicians such as
Clarence Williams, Bennie Moten, King Oliver, Louis Armstrong, and Sidney Bechet were recording, and if you take Negro
bands as a whole, most were playing in surroundings vastly inferior (in terms of working conditions, wages, etc.) to those of

white bands. In order for the Negro band to survive, it had to travel more frequently, and further. Often, after a long bus or train trip, there was no place to stay.

By 1922 Don Redman, a graduate of the New England Conservatory of Music, had joined the Fletcher Henderson band and together they were beginning an approach to "big band" arranging that was revolutionary.[6] Redman's arrangements contributed greatly to a Henderson band that was swinging strongly by 1926, years before the concept would be embraced by white bands. During the twenties, the most successful white bands had instituted the practice of utilizing Negro arrangers, and in one instance, Redman supplied Paul Whiteman, "The King of Jazz," with twenty arrangements for his orchestra at $100 each. Beyond his talent as an arranger, Redman was an outstanding alto saxophonist, but it would have been unthinkable to employ him as a sideman in one of the white bands of the '20s.

Benny Goodman, who pioneered in bringing Negro musicians into white bands, gained considerable momentum by doing so. Fletcher Henderson, one of these men, supplied the band with much of its "book" of arrangements for the beginning years. It was these arrangements, along with ones like Edgar Sampson's "Stompin' at the Savoy," that played a critical role in the band's ultimate success. Negro stars contributing to Goodman's success were Teddy Wilson, Cootie Williams, Lionel Hampton, and Charlie Christian. These comments are in no way intended to minimize the role played by Goodman himself in the situation. It took stamina and conviction to challenge a popular music establishment that was highly bigotted in many respects. Black men had incomparable talents to offer, and Goodman gave them exposure. The '30s and '40s saw more "mixing" of bands, but the course was never easy for either the minority member or the bands as a whole. A hostile reception by some law officer, booking agent, club owner, or the public was often the fate of the integrated band. Roy Eldridge, in Leonard Feather's *The Book of Jazz*, gives a touching account of the racial indignities he suffered from the general public when he was the only Negro member of the Gene Krupa band.[7] White groups were not the only ones to integrate. Leaders like Dizzy Gillespie, Benny Carter, Duke Ellington, and Count Basie hired white sidemen and thus risked jeopardy that ranged from commercial disaster to physical danger from an outraged public.

While the experiment in the racial integration of swing bands was going forward, other cultural patterns that would change the form of the popular music business were emerging. Perhaps for nostalgic reasons, a handful of music critics and jazz buffs became concerned with the possible extinction of New Orleans Jazz and went to the Crescent City in search of remaining practitioners of the old art. The twenties and particularly the thirties, had all but decimated the playing of New Orleans style, but several of the old luminaries were "dug out of the woodwork." By 1939 Bunk Johnson had been located in retirement in New Iberia, Louisiana, by Frederick Ramsey, Jr. and William Russell on the basis of an earlier tip from Louis Armstrong. About the same time, Heywood Hale Broun recorded the Kid Rena band. The consequent recording of both groups and Bunk Johnson's nationwide tours sparked what is now known as the New Orleans Revival. All over the United States, musicians began forming groups based on the New Orleans motif so that they might supply part of the demand for the old music. Whenever possible, instrumentation was exactly like the Crescent City groups. Bunk and a few of the other old-time New Orleans Negroes did tour, and for a time they caused considerable stir among the relatively "pure" jazz buffs and their friends. But there really were not that many jazz buffs who followed the New Orleans style; certainly not enough to financially sustain the movement by themselves on any extensive scale. Within a few months, though, numerous white groups copied the New Orleans Style as best as they could. One group, The Dukes of Dixieland, was particularly outstanding. Incidentally, they came from New Orleans. There were others. Lu Watters, who had been playing New Orleans Style on the West

Coast in the mid-thirties, formed the Yerba Buena Jazz Band, which attracted national prominence. Tommy Dorsey had the Clambake Seven; and there were the Turk Murphy and Bob Scobey groups, and the Tigertown Five coming out of Princeton University, to list only some of the more prominent ones. An important characteristic of these groups was that they were *all* white. What had begun as a revival of an essentially black art form ended up being a financial windfall for some white groups.

It becomes even more remarkable when we realize that the complete revival and its ultimate waning occurred with the belief (at least by those who thought about it) by most Americans that a group of white musicians had revived "their" music. We are able to understand this when we recall that most people had given credit for the creation of jazz some years back to either the Original Dixieland Jazz Band or Paul Whiteman. As one would expect there was a great deal of bitterness in the veteran black jazzmen as they began to notice this new chapter of their "invisibility" unfolding before them. While we recognize that the motives of the white musicians on the surface, at least, were just to get more and better gigs, a somewhat more exact explanation is that this has happened in a national culture that at least overtly professes the black man to be incapable of innovation or creation of any substance. The cultural milieu that has permitted this reaction by the white man is one that stereotypes all Negroes, making no allowances for differences of personality, creativity motivation, intelligence, or social class. It would be incomprehensible to many white Americans to think that such black musicians as the late Don Redman and Fletcher Henderson were intelligent, sensitive human beings who saw their music as an art to be nurtured with the greatest care. Through all these past years, any response by the black man to this degradation remained subterreanean, but it finally became recognizable in several ways.

The Crow Jim Syndrome

During the early forties, there were several jazzmen on the New York scene who were both young and not content to perpetuate the Swing Era. It would have been unthinkable for them to become a part of the New Orleans Revival because they saw it as Jim Crow. They wanted to create a music that was not as "pat" as the fox trot or standard jazz—a music involving massive alterations in addressing form, beat, harmony, modulations, and even the behavior of the musician while he was on the stand or off the stand. Though these musicians dressed like Madison Avenue executives, their delivery on the stand involved a seemingly relaxed slouch while they "fooled around with the beat," often seeming behind in attack, and giving the impression to some of the older jazzmen, who watched them often in disgust, that they were playing both out of tune and time. There was a coolness and freedom about the music, but it impressed many who first heard it as having been expressly composed and played with the intent of non-communication. What the musicians were playing was re-bop, be-bop, or just plain bop. But, it wasn't really all that plain. Some now contend that it was set up to be appreciated and played only by certain people, the black and the "hip."

The bop period that followed the swing era was primarily a black experience, with its central stars being Dizzy Gillespie, Kenny Clarke, Thelonious Monk, Charlie Parker, and Miles Davis. It was just getting under way with the advent of World War II, was submerged by promoters during the conflict, and reappeared for a short period after the war. Though bop's period of public exposure was short, it greatly altered the course of jazz development. The general belief was that its performers rejected the "square" society which had supported swing. No longer were performers anxious to please the public. Most jazz before this time had been seen as existing primarily for the joy and entertainment of the customer. For the professional musician (apart from the fact that he often loved it), music was a commodity to be marketed to the buyer. With bop, the jazzman was said to put his own musical experience foremost without considering whether the public appreciated it or not.

As bop developed, musicians became technically competent in it and soon introduced two variants, progressive jazz and cool jazz. For the most part, progressive jazz (epitomized by the Stan Kenton organizations) was a rather vapid attempt to Europeanize or intellectualize jazz in the big band format while retaining a vestige of bop. For a time it was commercially successful, but almost exclusively with white, middle-class, college-oriented audiences. These bands attracted few black musicians. At almost the same time, cool jazz was being explored by such white musicians as Gerry Mulligan, Lee Konitz, Shorty Rogers, and Chet Baker. Actually, though, one black musician, Miles Davis, was intimately involved in framing many of the styling characteristics of cool jazz. Davis was instrumental in the music's inception and through its middle period, but then deserted it to become involved in new forms. Cool jazz became commercially successful with the college circuit between 1950 and 1956, but almost entirely for white musicians. The black innovators had not been attracted to it and were thus undergoing grievous economic struggles. The public was attuned to the cool jazz format which was controlling the entire market from the West Coast. The black jazzmen on the East Coast continued to develop their music outside the most profitable marketplace. To make things even much more difficult, much of the potential appeal of contemporary black jazz to any substantial public was gradually being absorbed by the new rhythm and blues, and then later by rock and roll. This invasion of the commercial sector was facilitated by the antijazz taxing policies of many of the big cities and the increasing greed of jazz nightclub owners. Together they drove admission prices to a prohibitive point. By the mid-1960s, all but the heartiest, and sometimes the most commercially compromising, of jazzmen had been driven out of the field.

Though the pre-World War II integration of swing bands had brought black and white musicians emotionally closer than they had ever been, a new tension and renewed segregation began to develop between them. Not only was there the omnipresent white rejection of the black, but a new form—Crow Jim, black rejection of the white musician—became prevalent. Where relationships in the past had been at the very least cordial, they were now often strained and evasive. For the first time, at least publicly, white jazz musicians were claiming that they were being discriminated against by both black musicians and bandleaders on the one hand and by club owners on the other. The white musicians contended that they had talent that would be valuable to a black band but were denied the opportunity for jobs because they were white. They added that club owners weren't interested in them because the public expected to see only a black man playing authentic jazz. The blacks retaliated that for years they had "eaten crow" and now why should they allow a white man in when there weren't enough jobs to go around for the "soul brothers."[8] Black musicians also felt they had been exploited by the white musician who had adopted and made profits from their musical innovations while many black musicians continued to live in near poverty.

By the late 1950s this new aggressiveness had taken the form of "funky" or later "soul" jazz. No longer were the goals of the music to portray assimilation into the mainstream of white culture, but to reaffirm the positive virtues of African heritage. LeRoi Jones, the black playwright and poet, put it this way:

By the fifties this alienation was seen by many Negro musicians not only as valuable, in the face of whatever ugliness the emptiness of the "general" culture served to emphasize, but as necessary. The step from *cool* to *soul* is a form of social aggression. It is an attempt to place upon a "meaningless" social order, an order which would give value to terms of existence that were once considered not only valueless but shameful. *Cool* meant non-participation; *soul* means a new establishment. It is an attempt to reverse the social roles within the society by redefining the canons of value. In the same way the "New Negroes" of the twenties began, though quite defensively, to canonize the attributes of their "Negro-ness," so the "soul brother" means to recast the social order in his own image. White is then not "right," as the old blues had it, but a liability, since the culture of white precludes the possession of the Negro "soul."[9]

As the '60s progressed, the term Negro was dropped in favor of black. Black meant precisely what Jones was talking about and carried none of the negative historical connotations of the term Negro.

Color the Music Black

As America's Negro population became "black," a wide range of meanings developed around the new concept. The varying ideas of what constitutes black music is a good example. To some like Cannonball Adderly, it meant, "music created by and oriented to black people."[10] In several interviews, he described black music as that music which is essentially endemic to black culture. He sees it as an element of black heritage of which to be proud, and for the past few years he has used the occasion of his quintet's visit to college campuses to offer seminars taught by the members of his group:

We don't talk about black militancy or any such things . . . we never suggest there is any thing wrong with any other music. It's ironic that one of our teachers and members is Joe Zawinul, who is white and has a great concept of expressing this black oriented music —*anybody* can do it if they love it and get involved in it.

Racial orientation has nothing to do with the performance of the music. We talk about its origins and development on the basis of its blackness simply because that's the way it has to be, but we don't say that this is something peculiar to black people because *that* is ridiculous.[11]

David Baker, Director of Indiana University's Institute of Black Music, takes a similar position in describing black music and its position in the broader culture:

. . . We're talking about music written by black composers primarily, our music, played and sung by black artists, and music that is generally thought to be an indigenous part of the black culture. . . . There has never been a white innovator yet, only developers, though really that is just as important in a lot of respects. But there have been three syntheses in jazz at this point—by Louis Armstrong, Charlie Parker, and Ornette Coleman—and when you look at these three giants, the figureheads in all of jazz's brief history, these are the innovators and these musicians are black. Still, I don't think jazz is vouchsafed just to our keeping. I think that cultural, sociological, and economic conditions have made it such that it has thrived, it has grown as a part of the black culture. But this doesn't mean that there won't be, or couldn't be, significant achievements from another race.[12]

Adderly's and Baker's positions on black music are moderate ones. They are saying that black music is a distinct and unique part of black culture. Further, the fundamental innovations and syntheses in the music's development have been made by black men alone. Still, they allow that persons from other cultures or races could perform the music, or perhaps even be responsible for future innovations.

While the attitudes held by Adderly and Baker tend to de-emphasize the direct political relevance of black music, another group contends the music and the politics are intertwined. Musicians like John Coltrane, Ornette Coleman, Cecil Taylor, Archie Shepp, McCoy Tyner, Max Roach, Sun Ra have described black music as not only a unique contribution of the black man but as a tool of protest and social change.[13] Frank Kofsky, in his *Black Nationalism and the Revolution in Music,* sees these musicians as creating a new music reflective of the conditions of ghetto life where its thematic course prescribes nationalistic separatism which takes an aggressive tack.[14] To him these musicians are the vanguard of revolution for the oppressed black in America, and he cites what he considers a number of incidents where avant-garde jazz musicians have been denigrated by a white establishment (critics, club owners, etc.) who are intent in maintaining the black jazzman's subjugation.

Jazz, which is sometimes called "the music" (to remove it from its alleged sexual origins)[15] by some of the group is seen as a purely black art form. These people feel that no white, because of different cultural experiences, is capable of either creating or performing the material. From this perspective, jazz is the black man's property, and European classical music belongs to whites. Several European jazz critics, including some prominent ones in Great Britain, France, and Germany, have supported this kind of ideology by claiming on essentially *racial* grounds that only blacks can become the "true" jazz musicians. The black radicals themselves, however, ascribe the alleged differences to *cultural* factors.

The historical reasons for the black man's distrust of white society's intent and action has, to an extent, been documented in this chapter. But, what of the New Orleans Scene? We have utilized a considerable portion of this chapter thus far reviewing those social currents that have affected the black jazz musician in the national setting so that we might look at the attiudes of Bourbon Sreet Black in light of this overall context. How do the jazzmen in New Orleans view black music and racial matters?

Coolin' it in Crescent City

Like their counterparts in other sections of the country, the black musicians of New Orleans are aware of many aspects of black history and the role that their music has played in it. Whereas others may occasionally doubt that New Orleans was the exclusive "source" for jazz, they are steadfast in their conviction that they live "where it all happened." At one time or another, most of the jazzmen have traveled with bands or played in other cities for a time. They are not parochial in the sense of being unaware of general racial developments outside New Orleans and the South.[16] Also, several of them have been involved directly or indirectly in civil rights work within metropolitan New Orleans, and vigorously reject the avant-garde musician's assumption that anyone who plays traditional New Orleans jazz is, by definition, Uncle Tom.

Wallace Davenport, Curtis Mitchell, and Herman W. Niehues, Jr., at Steve Valenti's Lounge on Rue Bourbon. Photographed by Jack V. Buerkle.

Although the musicians of Bourbon Street Black are aware of
the indignities suffered by the black man at the hands of whites
over the past years in America, they react to this knowledge differently from the radical black musicians of the urban Northeast.
It would be a mistake to label their attitude as Uncle Tom. The
music scene and the general interracial cultural settings of New
York, for instance, and New Orleans are extremely different. For
many years, the music market in the Crescent City has emphasized New Orleans style jazz, or Dixieland, because that is what
the white customers (who are the music's principal consumers)
have wanted to hear. Besides this, there is a local pride in maintaining the music begun by Bolden, Keppard, and Oliver. A number of the inhabitants of Bourbon Street Black see themselves as
the keepers of a precious tradition. For the most part, the music
they play is "happy jazz" (even the various blues tunes) and is
almost devoid of political content. The intent is to please the listener—to make him happy.

The massive neighborhood turnover of the northeastern black
ghetto produces decidedly different interpersonal relationships
both *among* blacks and *with* whites. Much of Bourbon Street
Black is a relatively stable community with a good deal of security for its inhabitants. For many generations the community has
lived intimately with, and bargained with, a white community
that has never quite been "southern." Blacks and whites in New
Orleans "know" each other; they have had long-term educational
experience with each other's personality and social characteristics.
This is much less the case with the northern-ghetto black and the
white man who has contained him into innercity compounds,
where there is only fragmented contact between the two.

As a whole, the jazzmen in Bourbon Street take what can be
described as a "moderate" approach to racial matters in music. For
instance, though more chose a black as "playing the best" (a common choice was Louis Armstrong) than chose a white musician,
the difference was not great.[17] Actually, slightly more than half
of them see *no difference* between white and black music, while

the remainder see differences that hinge on such matters as black music having more soul and being less disciplined, or formal.[18] When asked whether black or white music was "better," over four-fifths responded by saying "neither." For the most part, they don't seem to prefer playing one type of music over the other.[19] All of this becomes even more vivid when we go over the transcript of some of their comments. First, some typical comments of those who *do* see a difference between black and white music. One older musician with considerable "big time" experience throughout the world as well as within the Crescent City said:

Black music has more depth, feelin', and expression to it. Blacks tell or relate more about their lives, emotions, tragedies. I don't think one is any better than the other, though. Just different bags. Oh, yeah, I like to play earthy music myself, which is jazz. I like to play music that people dance to and sing to—got no pretense—just play good music—down to earth—good, swingin' jazz music. As far as race goes, we're havin' a problem in the country. And this thing of the black militant is goin' to keep poppin' up. But generally, musicians respect somebody who can *play. First!* And you can have black militants, pink militants, any kind of militants, but when RCA Victor calls a group of musicians, or NBC or CBS calls a group of musicians to make some money—man, that militancy disappears! He's gonna make that money! If he's got any intelligence, he's gonna smother this personal bag, or this brainwashin' he has, and make this money. And he's gonna play! If the music is allright, he's gonna play. But this ethnic thing. Birds of a feather flock together— This is a squeeze play and they're tryin' to be identified—this black thing—put some importance on themselves, because they've always been looked at as if, "Oh, they're nothin'; don't pay 'em no mind," so they have to thrust forward to get some recognition, and they're smart now, and they're gonna keep pushin' whitey, cause they've learned that if you don't, whitey will say, "O.K., we'll give you that; come into my office tomorrow." They don't want to hear this business about tomorrow! They're thrusting—thrusting—thrusting, 'cause America's the "land of plenty"—whitey's got everything, so gimme some today, and don't tell me about tomorrow! So you got to do all kinds of devious means to push whitey. You know, shake his rockin' chair, or turn his car around (laugh)—stick sumpin' in his tire so he can't move—just keep him annoyed so he will see that you are *there!*

Another older musician said:

They claim that we came from Africa, and we were slaves comin'
here singin' and moanin'. Well, the white man never did moan and
groan like that. I never heard no white people doin' it. But *now* you
can hear it, cause if you go right down to Bourbon Street and see
white cats singin' the blues, you can't tell the difference. Our beat,
the old two beat is different. The rhythm is different because the
Negro does a lot of stuff with it that the white man doesn't do. But
some whites can do it. There's an English guy—Tom Jones. He's got
soul. He ain't the only one. They're imitatin' and it's good. He's got
soul. And, jazz—some of the bands—they call 'em Dixieland. They
play little pieces, and some of 'em have been listenin' to the Negro
musicians, playin' around—and they put it together. And, it was just
a little bit more organized. LaRocca. He went up there (to the
North). He wasn't no great musician. He just played a little straight
horn, and, I don't think he could read much. But, some of the guys
like Edwards, I think he was a fair musician. Larry Shields, he
couldn't read much, but he had a nice tone. Ragas was one of them.
They were a little bit organized. They got their harmonizin' voice—
they got together. And, they're the one's who put this stuff together,
but it's not the way we play it. Their stuff was more organized. We
just play. It's accordin' to how you feel. I think there is a little bit of
difference between theirs and ours. I also think there is a little bit of
difference in the different parts of the country—between Negroes.
I'll give you an idea. Down all through this way, we play with a beat,
and it's a slow thing. Snap! Snap! Snap! It's drivin', still and all, it's
like a medium tempo. You can feel it. It give you spirit. As I've experienced this—see. I've worked all up North, and they play faster,
with lots of time changes. Well, I think the climate may have somethin' to do with that. I think a lot of white musicians take pattern
after Negro musicians, and a whole lotta Negro musicians take pattern after white musicians. I think the spirit is different. If a white
man comes up (is reared) around Negroes he's gonna act like one.
He's gonna dress like them, and he's gonna have his ways, but, he's
gonna like that. I know an Italian, and he has associated mainly with
Negroes, and when he came up, he was just like 'em!

A younger jazzman, who has traveled extensively, sees these differences:

Because of things I have done along this line, this is not a very easy question for me to answer. I'll say, yes, there is a difference between black and white music. I think black music houses a different spirit. A different spirit than is expressed by whites. The kind of spirit that any music houses is an index of the culture, its developments, its own particular and unique characteristics. For example, well, we know the spirituals, gospels, New Orleans jazz, not Dixieland, that's not black music. The blues. It's an experience of black—a certain aspect of the black experience. Neither is better than the other. That kind of measurement doesn't fit. I have no choice in terms of playing black or white music. As long as the music has something in it. As long as it expresses something, then I am sure I would enjoy playing it, if I could play it.

Not all those who see differences between black and white music have the tolerance of these men. A very small minority (less than four per cent) have a negative opinion concerning white music while recognizing its difference from black music.

Yes, I think there is a difference. Very much so. Because white music is the European style classical, while black music is jazz. A white guy doesn't play jazz; he imitates it. This is true for all whites. You can't name me a white musician who has contributed anything to jazz. He has copied—he has stolen from the black musician. And any white musician you name—any white cat who believes he plays jazz, I can tell you where he stole his music from! The white musician will sit back and tell the black musician to come up with somethin', then he'll get "buddies" with the black musician to learn what he's doin'; then he copies it. I'll still play with a mixed group for money, but for kicks, I would rather play with a black group. I've turned down several chances to play with white groups just so I could stay with the blacks. I coulda made a lot more loot too, with the white bands.

Among the majority of jazzmen who really see no fundamental difference between black and white music, the following response reflects the more common attitude of the members of Bourbon Street Black toward black-white relationship:

Some say only blacks can play soul music. Well, I wouldn't say so. We all have a soul. Some of us may have a little more soul than

others. I know. I've played with some of the finest white musicians in
the city. I don't know what soul is. I can't say that I have more soul
than they have. I don't think there is any difference between black
and white music. If you're a good jazzman, you're a good jazzman.
Some guys say, "he's a good colored jazz trumpet player," or "he's a
good white jazz trumpet player." I just say he's a good jazz trumpet
player, period! I don't want somebody to single me out for anything
but the way I play the trumpet. I was born and raised here in New
Orleans. My grandmother, mother—they can tell you about years ago.
They can even tell you about Buddy Bolden. He was the first
trumpet player. Now, I had an uncle—he was a school teacher. In
those days they taught some white students. He taught them—when we
moved here to this neighborhood, it was all mixed. Most of the white
ones who rented moved out. But there was a white family that owned
the house next door who stayed. They were born in that house. I've
been here twenty-five years. We're very good neighbors. Lately, she's
been sick, and everything else. When she needs help, she'll come
over here, or my wife will go over and help her. We have helped her
to get the doctor a number of times. One time the doctor was a little
slow in gettin' to her house, so my wife called and told him off. When
he got to the neighbor's house he asked her, "who's that lady who
called me? She gave me hell for bein' so slow in gettin' here." She
said, "that's my neighbor," and he knew it was us over here, and said,
"I want to tell you, anytime anybody calls like that and raises hell
with me, you gotta damn good neighbor." It's a tie between us, you
know. We treat each other as equals. I don't know anybody better
than me. I don't care who they are! I don't care how much money
they got—how much education they have. They're no better than me.
I'm a person. I believe that and taught it to all my children. I told
them that I've played jazz all over the world and met some big people, but they're no better than me. They're not my superior. My children understand that. Now you can live almost anywhere in New
Orleans, if you've got the money.

In Bourbon Street Black the musicians are primarily dedicated
to the production of good music and tend to put other things into
the background. Their feelings about racial matters are not strong
enough to interfere with their performing across racial lines, i.e.,
playing in integrated bands. Almost four-fifths of them said that,
if an integrated band played better music, they would rather take

that route than to play in a black band not as good, musically. One of the jazzmen put it this way:

At one time they had this thing of all white and all black bands, but now it's gotten to the point where you play with musicians because musicians are musicians, white or black, pink or yellow, blue or brown or green. They have a certain feelin' and a certain personality. They're made up of certain elements of things, and you can get along with 'em whether they're white or black or green. They're musicians *while you're playin'*. Now, after you get through playin', then you come into who you want to socialize with, and who you want to speak to, but that's an American dilemma—that's an American problem. But musicians are generally musicians, when they're playin'. And the job you're playin'—you don't live with the guy. You play with him.

There is no assumption that things are completely satisfactory in racial matters with the white man, but there is a general belief that "we're workin' things out." The black musician still has a long way to go in New Orleans to participate equally with the white man in the music business. The great demand for live music in the Crescent City keeps many of the musicians working steadily, but most are still dependent on their day jobs. Still, as in New York, Philadelphia, and Boston, there is, as yet, no such thing as black entrepreneurship. To the best of our knowledge, there are no black club owners or employers along Bourbon Street or within the Vieux Carré. Though there are some exceptions, especially, on occasion in the "celebrity" groups that visit the white-owned clubs catering to middle-class "imitation" jazz, integrated bands are not common. For the most part, there are black groups and there are white groups. The tourist generally has to go to two different clubs to hear both a black man and a white man play. Part of this probably results from the fact that tourists come to town expecting to hear jazz played by musicians with a particular racial composition; nobody would expect to find old white men playing at Preservation Hall. Some of it may be because of the traditional pattern of "like working with like." Some of the jazzmen expressed the view that "it's easier that way—you can relax more." And, some of it is probably racial discrimination. Whatever the balance of these factors as they affect their lives, the men of Bourbon Street fashion the rest of their existence *after* they have attempted to solve any problems that may arise in the production of their music. Some believe that they can solve at least some of their problems through music.

ᏚᎵᎣ

Not too long ago, Paul R. Lentz of the *Downbeat* magazine staff wrote a feature article on New Orlean's Wallace Davenport that may well turn out to be prophetic:

In some circles, mention of *any* Dixieland-oriented group brings the response: "Man, that's Uncle Tom music!" . . . And that seems a shame to those who recognize the treasure still to be tapped from this long-mined mother lode. Wallace Davenport feels strongly about this dilemma and has set out to do something about it. . . . Davenport is no shuck artist or gimmick man. His stand has been taken with a great deal of thought, care, and a rare insight. . . . "I'll tell you what I've been trying to do," the trumpeter said. "Ofays and the average soul brother have been referring to Dixieland as Uncle Tom music. It has been a prostituted form of music. I'm trying to get the Uncle Tom out of Dixieland. . . . Take the average soul brother; he doesn't dig that kind of music, but since I've been doing this, they've been coming down and really digging what we're doing."[20]

7

Who Am I?

Myself. Jazz musician. American. I'm sixty. I tried to make it the best I could with what I had to work with. I had a little success here and there. I have always tried to do my best. Sometimes I've failed. That's natural. But, I got involved and went the route. I had a lot of ambition. You look back over the past and see things that went wrong, but they weren't always my fault. I could have been a much greater success, but I had limited talent. I realize that. Each person can only go so far. I have no regrets. I really tried, and this a country where success and comforts and enjoyment are generally reaped by what you put in. But, on the spiritual side, I try to do the best I can, so I have no kick. I'll leave some record behind, and someone else can evaluate that.

IT HADN'T BEEN easy for the old man. Though he finished saying what was to be said in less than three minutes, it was obvious the question had hit him hard. "Who am I? Who am I? Who am I?" Finally, he came out with it; faltering at first, but then with a sureness that betrays the question, for it had asked him to display his conception of *self*—his very being—for at least semi-public scrutiny.[1] Few of us ever go this far—take such stock of ourselves —unless we are prodded by events. Surely, most of us reflect upon certain aspects of our behavior frequently so that we can get a glimpse of how we might look to others (and ourselves). But, the attempt to open up our personalities to *sudden* and *total* self-inspection is relatively rare for each person. Even people in psychotherapy are seldom guided to ask such piercing questions of themselves all at once.

The jazzman's responses locate him—reveal his *identity*—his *self*—in a network of human relationships that have been forming, changing, and guiding him since he was born. When he was an infant, his tie to and dependence upon others took one form; as he grew older and into the roles of boy, adolescent, and then man, other patterns of interdependence emerged. Always, he has known and judged himself only within a web of relationships to others. How "good," "bad," "successful," "unsuccessful," "happy," or "sad" he is now, or has been, is realized only against a backdrop of others that he uses as a benchmark. The old musician is a lot like other old musicians, and even some younger ones. Old and young alike have been taught that excellence in music is a virtue. Each has internalized the idea of working hard as a musician, and each recognizes how competition affects the artistic and business aspects of his career. Still, each jazzman will differ from others in the way he evaluates his performance and relative success. The standards by which he measures his own progress may be such that, as he tells himself he has failed, others are reveling in a similar accomplishment.

Cuttin' the Book

Almost invariably, when you ask a man who he is, among the very first things he will tell you will be his occupation. To many of us, our occupations *are* what we are. The men and women of Bourbon Street Black are no exception. In many ways, the desire to be a musician—a jazzman in the Crescent City with the urge to spend a lifetime "groovin' "—is instilled much earlier and much more consistently in the young of Bourbon Street Black than are occupations for most other American children. Most of us are quite indecisive about what kind of work we want to do and usually settle somewhat apprehensively on a vocation during our late teens or twenties. Not so for the young cats! Theirs has not been a problem of *what* occupation, but *how* to get "movin'" in the music business. Most of the working musicians can't remember ever wanting to be in any other kind of work. From the first time they saw the cats lined up for a parade or a funeral, that special sensation about playing music has been there. They get it even now when they mount the bandstand and the beat is "kicked off." Most nonperformers, straights, and squares couldn't possibly understand the emotional conditions under which these people both choose their occupation and perform in it. Probably, the best way to emphasize how the jazzman's work is the major part of his identity is to picture him on a perpetual emotional binge, with his instrument and music as the booze. Most of the jazzmen will tell you they don't need anything but their work to "turn them on." Like a lot of other performers, when they get before the public, something happens. The jazzman becomes "high" on his music, and his love affair with his horn becomes public.

Loving your music is one thing. Finding and evaluating your place in the vast network of interrelationships devoted to its production and sustenance is another. We don't all do equally well in our work, and we usually know it. We have some idea about how others whose opinion we consider important look at our performance on the job, or in life in general. Actually, our own opinions of ourselves are made possible through the conceptions we believe others to hold of us. When a musician evaluates his own work, he is certainly taking into account what he believes others think of it. He may or may not agree with what he believes is their estimate, but it is information he uses. The self-evaluation process is continuous, and the musician is always attempting to pick up cues on how he is doing and how he might do better. The standard outlook among the musicians concerning the quality of their playing is a mood of optimism—a belief that they will get better as time passes.[2]

It's this sort of positive approach to their own ability that indicates the almost total commitment they have to the production of music. When you recognize that all these men are professional musicians and that most have relatively regular employment in music, one of the more intriguing questions about them is not who is the "greatest" but what kind of self-conviction propels the average jazzman to play each night? Jazzmen of all ages are able to maintain the conviction that they are always "gettin' better" through constant practice off the job and frequent comparisons of their own playing to other musicians, both local and national: One of the older men looks at it this way:

Music is advancin' all the time. You hear sounds. All these sounds get added to jazz, and it changes. It's forever changin'—forever growin'. You have to change with it, so you have to improve. You keep gettin' better all the time if your mind is active. And the same way, you can start goin' back down the ladder, you can also begin to start gettin' worse. It's the physical thing, ya know. You can get a little deaf, or your nervous system can start actin' up. You don't have the beat you had. That comes with age.

Another old cat said:

I get better to a certain degree. Mostly by pickin' up new tunes, and learnin' new little passages, and things like that. I'll keep on gettin' better if age don't kill me!

Another:

I still get better as a player, even now. I do this largely by constant practice on the more technical things.

A middle-aged cat:

I'm tryin' to get better all the time. I'm not satisfied with myself. I guess we're all like that. I think when you're satisfied with what you're doin', it's time to quit! You're slowin' down! Nobody in this business can afford to be satisfied. This is somethin' that goes on and on. There's somethin' new for you to try to cut every day.

Another middle-aged cat:

You always try to improve. One way to do it is to listen to old record-in's, and try to improve on them. I certainly hope to not get worse, I know that! When you play every night, you get new ideas. You always want to do something different, and do it as well as you can. If you've got an audience listenin', and they like you, sometimes they'll say, "I never heard you sound like you sounded last night! You were great!" This sort of thing makes you try more.

Finally, a young cat:

I improve every day, because I practice every day. I'm not satisfied with the way I play, because I figure if you're satisfied, progress ceases.

Most of the jazzmen believe that their playing has improved considerably since they first began professionally,[3] but fewer than half claim they are better musicians than their friends.[4] The usual response to questions asking how good they are compared to others is one that professes competence but an almost Apollonian hesitance to profess superiority to other jazzmen.

Whenever other musicians are thought to be better than themselves, the usual reasons given for the believed superiority are such things as more practice, more experience, or more frequent opportunities to perform.[5] Typical of the response that professes competence but refuses to claim supremacy is the following by one of the older men:

Well, I couldn't say exactly how good I am. I can hear myself play, but I can't say how bad or good I am compared to what the other fellow is. Some people have told me they wished they could play as good as I can. I think Louis Cottrell is better than I am, and he *plays* that instrument! He likes that instrument, and he *plays* that instrument! His father was a drummer. A theater drummer. He started playin' in the theater pit. Cottrell, himself, is like Louis Nelson. Louis Nelson is one of the best trombone players in the city of New Orleans. He and I used to sit down and play the same parts. I know Nelson has more range than I have. He's in a class with Tommy Dorsey. Tommy Dorsey was one of the best trombone players in the country. There are a lot of cats playin' trombone today, but in spite of it, I think I'm probably still pretty good, 'cause I don't have any trouble gettin' gigs. Even at my age (eighty-four)! Also, I think you've always got to get better, if you're gonna stay in the business. I think I get better all the time. If you don't try to improve yourself, there is nobody that is goin' to improve you!

Another of the older cats:

I think I'm good enough to take care of myself. I'm about average for a New Orleans musician. But the guys who are better than me got that way because of wider experience. Usually, they've been with bands that travel. Bands that have been in the limelight, where the guys you work with know more. I didn't have too much of a chance to go out with bands like that, but I went out with a few. I still get gigs, though, 'cause when I'm available, they hire me.

Another older man stated,

People compliment me a lot on my playin', but, you know, I don't know really how good I am compared to the other musicians.[6] For instance, I think George Lewis was better than I am. He was a great musician. He had, to my belief, one of the best reputations as a clarinet player. He played as well as anybody who was around here and he wasn't the type of musician that some of the fella's was that didn't have his reputation. But, he had a reputation all over the world. People still think a whole lot of his playin', and he had more people imitatin' him—playin' like him! Mostly European boys. And, some of 'em sound just like him!

Then, there is the old man who, speaking hesitatingly about his present capabilities, tries to account for things not being the way they used to be:

Well, I don't know. I don't know how good they think I am now. Sometimes I think they don't think too much of my playin' anymore, 'cause I don't get much gigs now on account of my handicap. The fellas tell me to come around when they're on a gig, so's I could watch and listen, but I don't go 'cause I can't get around easy. But, I get a few gigs once in a while. It may be that some of these cats are just better than me. Take Louis Barbarin, for instance. We have a lot of good drum players in New Orleans, and he's one of 'em. I guess I'm pretty good, though. I could play with any band, and I wouldn't make it sound bad. I'm not the best, but I wouldn't make it sound bad.

A middle-aged musician looks at it this way:

Well, it's not a braggin' point, but I think I could match anybody. To be honest, I listen to other people's stuff, and then my own, and I think I can match any of them. Even the top musicians. Some of them have had a better break in life than I've had, but they're not better. I worked with a top group for a number of years, and did a pretty good job with them. It's hard to say who's better. Many of us are professional. Some guy may have somethin' I don't have, and I have a little somethin' he doesn't have. I tell you one thing. I never heard nobody play like me but *me*! I'm very proud of that. When I was a kid, I tried to listen to Louis. They had Louis, King Oliver, and Kid Rena. Even the fella I studied with. I thought he was the greatest trumpet player who ever lived—that I ever heard in my life. . . . Beautiful! He had everythin'! Technique. Intonation. Everythin'! But, I've often said that I never wanted to play like him, or Louis, for that matter. I use some things like they had, but most of it is *me*. Even if it's not good as the other fella—somethin' of your own is a little better. Over the years, I've managed to get a little somethin' of my own. People can always say to me, "I know that's you when I hear it. I can tell your style!" So often I've heard people from all over say that about me. I used to tell my son that all the time. "Listen to everybody, but get a little somethin' of your own."

Another comments:

I'm about average, but some of the cats who play about like me are doin' alright. Some are playin' with groups with a bigger "name" than the one I'm with now, but I've played with "name" groups too. I could play with some of these groups now, but man, I'd rather be home. The only reason I think a lot of cats travel with a well known band is that they don't have families, you know, like kids and all that. So, they can branch out and go on the road.

Not all musicians feel that playing of instrumental music is their main "bag" in the music business:

I think I have a little more than most of my friends. I concentrated a little longer. I do believe I have put in a little more time, and naturally, I've gotten a little more out of it by being positively concerned with music as a whole. Actually, I spend most of my time writing (music), and I enjoy writing now more than playing. I guess this is the reason some of the men perform better than I do now. I think I rate pretty well, overall. At least, in the service, I headed up two bands.

The younger men approach the assessment of their own playing with considerably more confidence and verve than the older ones:

Honestly, I really think I'm better than most cats. There's nobody better than I am. That may sound conceited, but I just don't know of any. I improve all the time by practice, listenin', thinkin', and experiencin'. It ain't just practicin'—mechanical. Sometimes you just gotta sit and think about things you wanta do, and wanta play, and *why* you wanta do 'em, and *why* you wanta play 'em. You gotta ask yourself how these new things will affect the other people in the band. It's not just physical practice; it's also mental practice, too. Most people think you practice to get your hands fast, but you can just practice a roll if you're a drummer, and you might have the best roll in the world, but, man, if you don't know how to fit it in to other things, you're nothin'!

No, I don't think there is anybody better than I am. There are some things these other players can do that I can't do, and there are some things I can do that they can't do. One reason I never answer that question; well, take Miles Davis, for instance. There are a lot of things I can do that Miles Davis can't do. There are things Clark Terry can't do that Al Hirt can do. Some cats are better at one thing, and others at something else.

And, so it goes, this immersion in an atmosphere of individuality, hard work, competition, professional competence, pride of craftsmanship, and the love of excellence. Still, all of this is fringed with a norm of tenderness for the other cats and chicks. In Bourbon Street Black, you *are* your "brother's keeper." It's a genuinely friendly place. You don't take another man's "bread,"

Clement Tervalon at Heritage Hall. Photographed by Jack V. Buerkle.

or try to minimize his victories. You try, hope, and pray to be the greatest yourself, but you don't undercut another musician when he's "makin' it." If he makes it and you don't, you take pride in his accomplishment and wipe away your own disappointments.

Whether you are the "greatest" or just an average musician, whether you "make it" or remain in the ranks of the relatively unheralded, there is one thing you are likely to be when you "come up" in Bourbon Street Black: versatile. New Orleans is peculiar in that most of the time they will ask for jazz, but that's not always the case, so a jazzman has to be ready to supply what the customer wants. Most of the musicians consider themselves jazzmen but *all* can play some variety of styles, and practically all are competent in several styles. While one older man who has spent his career primarily with traditional jazz said, "I don't like that rock music, and I never tried to play it," his remark is rather atypical, and most of the musicians had kind and sometimes enthusiastic appraisals of what they would usually call "good rock." Most tend to feel more comfortable playing jazz, though they are able to see great value in encountering other styles as educational experiences. An older cat said:

I play jazz best, 'cause you improvise as you play, and the more you're around it, the more you get a kick out of it. But, I still can't stand to play church music. You can't do all you want with it. Every damn time I've started cuttin' up a little with church tunes, I get some preacher raisin' hell with me, so I just stay away from 'em 'cept with a brass band. We got some old church tunes there, ya know.

Another old cat looked at it this way:

You know, I can play any kind of music; jazz, rock, or symphony. But, I play jazz best. It swings, and I like to swing. But this rock and roll is somethin' different. I never was too much for that stuff. I can play it, but I just don't dig the foundation of it. I don't have that kind of feeling. I didn't come up in that time. A lot of the kids I know can really dig it, and I got a lot of respect for their ability, so there must be somethin' to it.

Makin' the Charts

The Protestant Ethic guided the development of the American nation. The message had been clear: work diligently for the Kingdom of God. Never look to the left or right; just aim straight ahead as you march unbending through a life of sinful temptations toward the goal of Heaven. Toil, sacrifice, and the knowledge of service to God were in themselves ample reward. Should fortune smile upon you in competitive enterprise, most profits were to be given and dedicated to the glory of God.

With the gradual conquest of the North American frontier and the accompanying urbanization, people's attitudes toward life in general, and themselves, in particular, became more secularized. The new version of the Ethic still included toil, sacrifice, and all the other elements necessary to get the job done, but now the principal benefactor was no longer God but one's self. One was to work toward success, a goal that was first and foremost self-oriented. For many years, books like the Horatio Alger stories showed young people how to get ahead and pointed out the material virtues of success. Making it or getting ahead became standard prerequisites for happiness.

This prescription for success was, of course, only intended to apply to whites, and the black jazzman has had to endure the knowledge that this American success formula did not in the past apply to him. But all the while he was being kept out of the mainstream of the social and economic life of the United States, the black man was "peekin' through the window" of a world of which he wasn't supposed to be a part. This strongly affected what he thought about himself and where he wanted to "go" in the world. The people of Bourbon Street Black manifest some of the results of "peekin' through the window," but reveal some unique and probably more interesting goals in life than would have been the case had they been given every opportunity to advance materialistically. They not only differ in their views as in-

dividuals, but there are some revealing intergenerational varia-
tions. Several of the old musicians spoke about success:[7]

Success means to keep pushin' yourself. To keep goin'—to a higher
cause—like to climb higher. I can't explain it, but you know what
I'm talkin' about. To keep workin'. To work hard. If you work hard,
you will be successful. When I was workin', I always worked hard!
Lots of music fellas is successful. They made it because they play
good music. Me? I've been a little bit successful, and I appreciate it
very much, but maybe I didn't push quite hard enough, or I'd gone
farther.

Another older man who has recently achieved considerable
financial success and wide acclaim said,

I think if you have a well rounded life, you have tranquility at your
home. What I mean is that you're successful if there is peace and
harmony with the people you live with and love: your family—your
wife and children. And, I don't mean moneywise, but you have to
have some money. Also, you ought to have peace with your associates—the people you have dealin's with. They have things they will
say about you, one way or the other, and there'll be ups and downs,
but you have to be able to get along with people. If you're always
comfortable, and you're always well, you never know what it is to
want. But, if you get sick, you can appreciate the good things. To a
sick person, just bein' well is success.
There's a way to a kind of success—money success, but there were
certain things I wouldn't do to get there. And I had opportunities.
Now, I don't mean legally! I mean illegally! I had opportunities.
People—they were the greatest success financially, and everything,
but there are certain things I disapprove of, and I wouldn't do them.
But there are a whole lot of people who are on top of the world and
don't care how they got there. They've done a whole lot of things
like (names prominent college founder) who set up _____
University. They say he was a big crook, but look! He did some
good! He was a thief and everything, but they say he accomplished
a lot when he made that school possible. I just couldn't cut corners
like that—no matter if I could found a school.

An equally non-materialistic approach to success was expressed
by another older musician:

I think if a person is able to do what he wants to do—sets forth his plan—says "this is what I want to do"—that's success right there. I know quite a few musicians who are successful. They're just about able to do what they want to do.

Some of the older musicians tended to emphasize material success or renown, while others saw success as a combination of several factors. One old man, living today on the edge of poverty, emphasized financial success but was actually defining as material success the possession of things most people consider everyday necessities.

Well, I never got to that point. I imagine it's a wonderful feeling when you can get what you want without headaches. Doing what you want, when you want. If you want something, you don't have to wait six months to get it. You can get it now, without headaches.

One who viewed success as a combination of factors said:

I have a friend in Chicago—he's a doctor, and is one of the greatest blood specialists in America. He started out with nothing, and made himself a millionaire. I consider myself successful with the things I have done, and the way I'm goin' along. I think I'm very successful in a line of business (music) some people call a gamble. I started out by one of my friends tellin' me why didn't I learn to play. I kept on buyin' literature (music) and studyin' and readin' and figurin' and workin' it out, and today I think I'm pretty successful.

Another commented:

As an American, to be successful means to be acclaimed, somewhat. Recognized. Have a reputation of bein' a first grade musician, in jazz, that is. And, makin' some money at it. I know so many who became successful. Sidney Bechet was one. He wrote a little tune in his last years, *Petite Fleur*, and it made him a wealthy man. There's Fats Domino, also; he's wealthy—has fifteen or sixteen gold records. That's one kind of success, but there are others. I've been successful within myself knowin' that you . . . it's not all the time *what* you play, it's the breaks you get in music. I'm considered a first rate jazz player. I've been given that rating by critics and authorities of jazz magazines. I'm not rich, but I think I'm successful.

A somewhat novel description of success was given by this older musician:

For a man to be successful, he must first have ambition. With no ambition, you can't be successful in nothin'. And, *the hardest thing to be successful at in this life is makin' love! It's the hardest!*

The musicians who are middle-aged usually see in success a variety of elements. One who has traveled extensively with road bands said,

It means reaching a certain pinnacle in life. Being successful demands respect. And, it gives one a clear mind; an easy mind. In success, the capability to earn money is a dominant factor, but also to be successful in recognition gives one a jubilant feeling. Being recognized is one thing. Having money adds to this. It gives one the feeling that you've reached a notch in life. To want success gives us the feeling that we're always on our way to a station we never quite reach.

Another said:

Success means everythin' in the world. With success you can support your family. You can do whatever you want—live good yourself. If you strive and give it everythin' you have, you're successful. A certain amount of money is involved, because you need money to live. But, I try my best, even when I play for charity. A couple of successful guys I know are Kid Ory and Louis Armstrong. They're successful because the things they do, they do so well. They get out and meet the public, and people like them. I don't know how they feel about themselves. Anyone who has ever gotten anywhere seems to want a little more. Still, I don't think any man should be satisfied, regardless of what he's doin'. I've never been a satisfied person, but I think I've done pretty well, and I expect to go much farther.

A middle-aged female musician took a somewhat different position:

To be successful is to utilize whatever you know or whatever you have learned to do as a means for making a living. That is, to be economically successful. If you're able to work at it. Make a decent living. Maintain the essentials of life. Also, though, it means to lead a respectable life. To be comfortable. Not to be rich, but maybe have a few pennies on the side. I know some successful people. They have raised their families—have decent families, and have some of the niceties of life. But, I've been successful, too, in that I've had five wonderful children. I've been able to raise them successfully. I'm able to maintain myself. I have a home and a few little things I wanted. In working all these years, I've been able to keep three-quarters of my health. I still work and am able to maintain my status in life. I'm carrying on.

One musician, still feeling the economic pressures of a growing family, put it like this:

Success is to be able to make money. To get things for my family. Things that they need. I've known quite a few cats that are successful. They're doin' alright. They look like they are happy doin' what they're doin', and they're makin' the loot! When a person can earn a livin' at any one particular thing, and not have to moonlight, that's success. That's particularly true in music, because it's a job that's hard to work steady at, year after year. I've known lots of people who are successful. For instance, Duke Ellington and Lionel Hampton. They're financial successes, but they also have people who like them, and even love them. That's bein' a big success! I guess if I'd had the promotion, I might have had a chance to be a big success, too. But, I wound up promotin' myself. And, that's hard to do.

Several of the young musicians have had wider experience in the music business than one might imagine. Over half of them have worked a year or more as sidemen in some of the top black bands and combos in the United States. As a group, they have "made the scene" and considerable money, at least for short periods. Some of them were soloists on top rated jazz records of the past few years. They have experienced the usual sense of success —material success and recognition. But the young jazzmen seem to be coming off the road and returning to the Crescent City earlier than their grandfathers, fathers, uncles, and older brothers did. When their elders came home, it was often under the pressure of economic necessity. This doesn't seem to be so much the case for the young jazzmen. Things are better now for talented black youngsters than they were twenty or thirty years ago. What often brings them back is the quest for a style of life they remembered leaving and want to continue. Consider now these young men describing success:

To be successful is to realize one's self. I have known people like this. They have achieved a kind of self-realization. A kind of self-development. I think I have been able to achieve some of that myself. I'm not successful according to the usual yardstick. But, I've managed to continue in the same direction without being distracted from what I'm trying to do.

To me success is the greatest thing in the world. It's to be able to play and express myself the way I want to. I think I am successful in life. I feel great that I have been able to accomplish a lot of things spiritually. A lot of other people haven't been able to do that.

To be at peace with yourself. Yeah! I know one cat like this. He plays trumpet. He has the right vibrations. At least he's closer to being at peace with himself than most people I know.

Success, to me, is a state of mind. To some people, it means having money and other things that go along with it. To me it means being happy at what you are doing. So, I think I am successful now just by being a musician. I'm successful just by being able to pick up my horn and play.

Among show people there are usually a number of stories as to how certain people made the big time. In Bourbon Street Black where the norms of success become a part of each man and woman's concern at an early age, the legends of "makin' it" abound. The stories herald both material and non-material success, and the particular ones championed or disseminated by a person grow out of his own orientation to success. Whether success is seen as money, recognition, or personal satisfaction and happiness, the musicians see different ways of attaining it. Some see it coming purely as a matter of chance[8] or fate—your number has been chosen. Others contend that it is influence that allows one to achieve success. Still others believe you get there primarily on your ability, plus perhaps some drive. Finally, many see it becoming possible through some combination of ability and chance. Those who see it essentially as a matter of chance say:

It's the way the ball bounces. That's what makes musicians. Performers play till they die, or they're seventy, eighty, or ninety years old, because it's the breaks you get. You're in the right place at the right time. Fate has somethin' to do with it too. Like there's an old sayin' amongst performers as to how "he" was there at the right time. It's not so much *what* he plays. He happened to be there and it was what they wanted. There are so many cases in music where two friends would have an appointment: one didn't make it, and the other one did. The man picked the one who was there—who wasn't really as good as the one who didn't show.

Success is funny. It really does hang on some of the breaks a man gets if he is to be a success as far as money goes. But, you can be a good musician, and you might never get a break. That's kind of a funny deal. Some guys that have gotten a break—man, I don't consider them too much. But, that's the way it goes.

This jazzman approached the matter primarily from the standpoint of influence:

I always did believe you have to get the breaks, as well as be good. Musicians are all made of different styles. And, some of them can play equally as well. Some can play better, and they don't get the recognition. You have to have somebody in your corner to help you. You can't do it on your own. For instance, I know a guy who was in a fine band at one time. It was a band that was equal to Duke Ellington or Cab Calloway. They couldn't get into New York to play. They played in Brooklyn. Couldn't get into New York, because they didn't have the contacts. You got to have people make way for you. Today, it's the same way. I've played in New York. I worked two years there. They split up the money they give you about four or five ways to get in there. In New York, the agencies got the business tied up. So, you gotta have the break. You gotta get with somebody who has the contacts. If you don't, you don't get anywhere.

One who saw it as primarily growing out of ability said:

A lot of a man's success depends upon the ability to want to be great. It's ability and how much you want to be a musician. It depends on how much you try, and how much you are willing to sacrifice and make yourself great. It is possible to be commercially successful without playing very well. There are some like that right here in New Orleans. I'd better not name them.

Finally, another saw it as a mixture of ability, chance, and the breaks one gets:

As far as commercial success goes, you've got to be heard. If nobody hears you, there won't be success. You have to have a break where somethin' like a big corporation comes along with lots of money to promote you and spread your name over the country. If you've got any kind of talent, man, you're made! I think stars are made—not born. You've got to have a certain amount of talent. You've got to be able to do somethin'. But, there are plenty of people who are talented. Some just never got the break, and they withered on the vine. Gettin' along is just pure luck, sometimes. Bein' in the right place at the right time. But, the main thing is you got to have somethin' to offer. Nobody's gonna hire you if you can't do nothin'. You gotta be able to do somethin', so that means it depends on your own talent too, once you get the break.

How Deep it Runs!

The demise of traditional New Orleans jazz has been often proclaimed, but still it continues and sets down deeper roots. Within Bourbon Street Black, generation after generation continue to develop a profound involvement with their heritage. Even the very young are able to observe that the music business is not just a job but a cherished way of life. They see most of the old jazzmen keeping active on gigs until they either die or are incapacitated.[9] One older man said:

I imagine I'll always play music as long as I'm able to hold an instrument. I don't know how competitive I'll be, but I'll be involved in it, and I imagine I'll have my instruments around.

(Left to right) Placide Adams, Alvin Alcorn, and Theodore Riley. Photographed by Jack V. Buerkle.

Another older musician illustrates in his comment how an aging musician may dispense with all other employment except playing music professionally:

I decided a while back that I would stay in the music business. I was traveling at the time, but things got rough, and I had to come back home and take a day job. Just recently, around '63 or '64, I decided I would do nothing else but play music, because I was gettin' too old.

Music is seen as the normal way of life. The day job is something you take when the gigs are not coming along at a sufficient rate to support you and your family. The peculiar nature of the New Orleans music market makes it possible for many of the musicians to pursue the career of their choice on a more stable basis as they approach old age. One middle-aged man who had made a lengthy statement about his love for music ended on this jocular note:

Well, I'm fifty years old, and I guess it's got to be that way, don't you think? I'll stick to music—there's not much left. Maybe I can get one of those cats who's goin' to the moon to give me some moon dust! I'll put that in my vitamins every day, and I'll be jivin' for a long time! I'll call it a moon dust pill! Maybe I could sell it!

The closely knit network of communication in Bourbon Street Black, where the musicians continuously shout the virtues of a life in the music business, produces a high yield among its youth.[10] The search for talent is intense and unremitting, and there is a strong feeling of obligation to put something back into a system that has rewarded them. Men like the following see a career in music as an aid in understanding human nature and an opportunity for a stable life:

Any youngster! Any instrument! Because it helps him. It will give him insight. On the bandstand, you dig human nature. You see different people, and you're gettin' much pleasure out of makin' people happy by playin' for them. I help kids in the neighborhood. It keeps them out of trouble and might make a career for them.

Yes, I certainly would advise a youngster to make music his career. I think it's a nice living, and not only that; it's very educational, because in your social life you meet all kinds of people the ordinary working man doesn't meet. You have more tied up in your future, because you never know who you're going to meet outside.

This lady, a long-time, highly competent Crescent City pianist, remarks about her son and his career in music:

Because it's (music) a part of him, and he's a good musician, he plays trumpet now. He's good. He has good octaves, and a lovely tone. I encourage him almost every day. I feel this music is a part of him. I think it's in him.

A father, an outstanding trumpet player with several traditional bands appearing in the Vieux Carré, comments on the possibility that his son might seek a music career:

Yes, it's a great thing! If he wants to be a musician, I'll be happy. But, he must finish school first. Then he can go to the better things like gettin' with a studio music group, and that's the best thing goin'. We couldn't make that kind of gig because of color when I first came up, but things are changin'. Now, with a good education, he could make studio work. That's about the best deal a cat can have. That's what I preach to my kid. "Stay with it if you like it, but you must have the education, too."

There was very little attempt to discourage young people from entering a music career, but when discouragement was present, the reasons given were usually economic:

Well, there are musicians from coast to coast. You find qualified musicians in other jobs all the time. There just aren't enough jobs in the profession for the musicians we have now. If they would have had enough work through the years, I wouldn't have had to go into the trades!

What is especially intriguing about these musicians is the distinctive, patterned way they approach the music public. Unlike the

fabled northern jazzmen of the '20s (and even later) who were
thought to play only for themselves, these people play a happy
music designed to please others as well as themselves. There is
a definite desire to please and to be liked by those who listen:

I wouldn't tell anyone to get out of music because it's been too good
to me, but I always advise youngsters to get some education, too. I
say, "this horn can take you anywhere you want to go, but get some
education, and you can go even farther." Music has really been good
to me and my family. I sent all my kids through college on music. I
think music is like medicine for people. It *is* medicine! It gives people somethin'. We (musicians) have our way of givin' somethin' to
the people. I remember the first time I went to Europe with a group.
It was 1956. The war hadn't been over too long. I saw many people,
man, with their heads bowed comin' to those concerts. When we
played, you'd see smiles come on their faces. People who'd never
smiled for as long as they could remember. They wanted to shake
our hands, or just get an autograph from us. It meant so much to
them! And, I felt as if I was givin' somethin'. Whenever you can
give joy or anything like that, I think it's a wonderful thing. It's a
medicine in itself. The doctor can give you sweetin' water and tell
you it's medicine, and if you wake up and feel better, then he did
somethin' for you. He did do somethin' for your mind!

◌◌

I am a young man who grew up in New Orleans. A young man fortunate enough to have a good family, and blessed enough to have
good friends. I experienced a kind of musical training that was very
special, because I was taught to see in me a type of heritage which is
critically important. I was fortunate enough to go on to school and
do the work necessary to get out of it what was truth, and to realize
at a very early age something about which way to pursue it. I hope
in the future that I will be able to keep my health, my strength, and
the meaningful purpose in life I now feel.

8

It Does *Matter Who*
Your Folks Were!

Them that's got shall get, Them that's not shall lose;
So the Bible said, and it still is news;
Moma may have, Papa may have, but,
God bless the child that's got his own; That's got his own.

Yes, the strong gets more, while the weak ones fade.
Empty pockets don't ever make the grade;
Moma may have, Papa may have, but
God bless the child that's got his own! That's got his own.

Money, you got lots o' friends, crowdin' 'round the door.
When you're gone, and spendin' ends, they don't come no more.
No. No. No.

Rich relations give, crust of bread and such.
You can help yourself, but don't take too much!
Moma may have, Papa may have, but
God bless the child that's got his own! That's got his own.

"God Bless the Child"
by Arthur Herzog, Jr., and Billy Holiday (LADY DAY)*[1]

Daddy, What's Opportunity Mean?

Lady Day knew. Each time Billie Holiday sang her own "God Bless the Child," she relived her childhood of insecurity and denial. Her story is a jazz legend: discovery, success, growing unhappiness, and the tragedy of narcotics addiction that ended with her being alone and dying in a New York hospital bed. She was alone in a society that still claims to be classless and still maintains that all of us can make it if we will only try.

In reality it just doesn't happen that way. We don't live in a classless society but organize our social relations, as Celia Heller has suggested, within "a system of structured inequality in the things that count."[2] Some people are just "more equal" than others. Certain jobs or activities are considered more important by the members of a group, community, or society and are rewarded accordingly. The Billie Holidays don't get the opportunity to enter the middle section, let alone its upper reaches, for whites have routinely dismissed blacks as candidates for upward mobility from the lower classes. Of course many whites never progress through this system, either, but they start off with only one stereotype working against them—their class. The black man always starts with race as his albatross as well.

Until the recent civil rights legislation, blacks had been prevented from becoming part of a social system that regularly disperses the greatest rewards to people having those roles and occupations that require the highest technical training and education. Blacks have not typically had the free ingress to these qualifying areas that make it possible to move up to the positions of higher value and reward. The nature of Jim Crow tended to stereotype all blacks of varying capacity and performance into a single lower to lower-middle-class mold. Meanwhile, the white majority judged those few blacks who succeeded in sports, entertainment, or education as being some kind of social mutation, certainly not as setting a trend.

Since many American whites have been hesitant to recognize a social-class structure within the general population, it just hasn't occurred to most that one might exist among blacks. But, even the first black men to arrive in America brought a wide array of status differences with them from the villages of Africa and the islands of the Atlantic. The process of capture, transport, and the separation of family members—all with dehumanizing pressure—

didn't wipe out their memories. Once things began to be organized in plantation life and other settings where slaves were utilized, further differences in status emerged. The Negroes considered most attractive by the owners were chosen as house slaves to minister to their master's family's desires. Over time, this brought those chosen higher status and greater privileges. Some were even set free and inherited property.

Benjamin Quarles, writing at length about the non-slave Negro, has commented, "In 1790 non-slave Negroes numbered 59,557, and in 1860, 488,070. . . . Of the nearly half a million non-slave Negroes on the eve of the Civil War, 250,787 were to be found in the South where they were known as free Negroes."[3] The majority of the persons in this group had obvious economic, educational and general social advantages not available to the remaining 90 per cent (roughly) of Negroes in the American population at that time. It's true that the restrictive, segregationist color codes of the postbellum South had a strong inhibiting affect upon all black people in the United States, but those who had been free possessed a chance of more extensive interaction in American affairs. Within black society they became the merchants, bankers, professionals, and educators who made their little enclave a success. Out of this situation was created the first Negro middle and upper class. Within the New Orleans area, the people who inherited the positions of relative power were the Creoles of Color. Quarles, describing this power said, "The free colored people of New Orleans were more advanced than Negroes in any southern city. Numbering 18,000 in 1860, they owned $15,000,-000 in taxable property. These free Negroes left a record of achievement in military affairs, science, and literature."[4] They were, in effect, the vendors to, and stabilizers of, a relatively disillusioned and unorganized collectivity of former plantation blacks. They shared the label "Negro" with the blacks, but not the style of life. While the problems of the two were sometimes common (when dealing with the white man), their general interests often were not. Thus, long before the Civil War, there was a distinct social-class system in operation among New Orleans blacks with vast differences in life chances between its upper and lower levels.

One of the compelling aspects of the indices of social class is the way they became associated with other phenomena to produce this differential in life chances and help to perpetuate it. Higher education is a usual, though not universal, requirement for the more valued and better rewarded occupations of both black and white communities. If you are able to get the necessary education for a prestigious occupation, you usually also have considerable self-confidence and motivation for success. This is called "the achievement motive" by psychologists. But what about those people who start at the bottom, or near it? It has been found that they're unable to break into the "circle of success." It takes at least three things to accomplish this, and often some, or all of them are lacking. The first is opportunity, then motivation, and finally intrinsic ability. We now know that most people have the intrinsic ability to perform at least at the middle levels; still, few in the disadvantaged minorities ever "make it." People in the lower echelons are exposed to the legends of success just like anyone else. Yet, their usual response is, "but not for me." Generations of frustration, discrimination, and heartbreak have eroded their confidence and motivation. Although opportunity for blacks to participate in American society has increased considerably over the past half-century, most of those affected have been in the black middle classes. Lower and lower-middle-class blacks are still mostly outside the reaches of opportunity. In fact, within the past few years, the gap between the black lower and middle classes has widened.

The history of New Orleans' blacks reveals a number of similarities to black groups elsewhere as well as some differences. The similarities lie in the sharing of over two hundred and fifty years of general suppression by the white man. Even today, the most privileged, affluent, successful, and happy New Orleans blacks bear scars of indignities whites never had to experience in this country. There are few areas, if indeed any, in which Crescent City blacks have anywhere near the access to upward mobility enjoyed by white people. The only one that comes to mind is the situation where white tourists demand to see old black men play two-beat jazz. But even this has a patronizing tone to it. Currently, several older musicians have been touring the country with bands featuring traditional jazz and making salaries comparable to those of successful doctors and dentists. Remember, though, this affluence is recent and affects only some of the older musicians. Younger men are not really eligible, because they don't quite fit in the category of nostalgia.

The New Orleans' black experience is different than that of many other American cities. New Orleans was never a typical American city, and several of its peculiarities fostered an antebellum social-class system among blacks unlike that in other places. It was the white majority who created, and even fostered, the Creole of Color group for a long period. With this powerful support, the Creoles became a separate but almost equal society comparable to the upper and middle elements of Crescent City whites. Class distinction existed among the Creoles of Color, with a core of distinguished families making up the leadership. Beneath the Creoles in this social order were the Negroes; as far removed from social equality with them as could be achieved. The melding of the Creoles of Color and the black men into the single category Negro in the postbellum period did very little to change their internal social order. Though life was difficult for all Negroes, the prior educational and occupational training of the Creoles allowed them to fare much better in a world that was swiftly developing all of the technical requisites of an urban—industrial complex. The Creole had an attitude of superiority toward the lower-class Negro, and only when the Creole needed the Negro's support in dealings with the whites did the Creole admit any common bond existed. Time and social change, though, have softened some of the differences between them. Because both groups have experienced over one hundred years of relatively common subjugation to the white world and because new avenues of mobility have opened up (such as sports and entertainment) requiring little formal education, the two groups now have more in common. Though the public education available to all blacks has been inferior, there have been relative gains, and these have permitted limited upward mobility by some of the earlier disadvantaged group among Crescent City Negroes. The matters we have been discussing have affected the entire black community of New Orleans. But, what of the members of Bourbon Street Black?

Makin' It in Bourbon Street Black

The same "system of structured inequality" that Heller speaks of in describing the power relationships by which people in the general community influence each other's lives exists in Bourbon Street Black. Some of the distinctions between people are made on the basis of considerations such as how much education a person has, how important his job is thought to be by others, the size of his income, and whether he lives in a nice house in a good neighborhood. Still, these standard sociological indicators of social class don't tell the whole story of power and style of life in Bourbon Street Black. These indicators worked rather well in the past when the goal was to learn about the general power structure of white communities, but Bourbon Street Black is a specialized black semicommunity.

Certain differences between the relative power of blacks and whites in the United States do make the use of some of the usual indicators open to question. Parker and Kleiner, in a study of the effects of goal striving and stress upon the mental health of black Philadelphians, found they had to make changes in the usual order of measuring social class.[5] When determining whether occupation or education is the most important gauge of a man's status, whites usually give more weight to occupation. Just the reverse seems to be true for blacks, at least at this time. Although both have been difficult for blacks to obtain, educational advancement has been an easier goal to reach than the more prestigious occupations. After all, higher education (high school and college) can be, and has been, segregated. Whites have been able to avoid "contamination" through separate educational facilities, but occupation is another matter. It would have been considerably more difficult and economically impractical for whites to have permitted a parallel occupational system. So the black man was, and is, often educated *beyond* his opportunity to get commensurate employment. Consequently, blacks, in general, feel that the job a man has is considerably less important as a measure of status than is his education. There are exceptions to this pattern. Some occupations entered by blacks have been less threatening to the white majority than others. When there were full parallel educational systems, becoming a teacher in the Negro system was inoffensive to the white system. There was simply no meaningful connection between the two school systems at any point. Other fields were "safe" for different reasons. As nationwide travel and communication became a reality, professional sports, music, and to an extent the theatre arts opened up to the Negro. Here he could become the entertainer and pose no threat. Not everything in these areas was open to him, just those unoccupied by majority whites. Some minority whites, such as Italians and Jews, succeeded in that way too, but special niches were reserved for the black man. In sports it was often those areas where physical risk is high and the long-term job security weak. Theater arts placed him in a position of self-denigration by his playing the buffoon, the "king of fools." Music gave him third-class travel and a kind of gaudy notoriety. It's here in this small selection of occupations that the black man has occasionally been able to realize a kind of prestige that exceeds that derived from higher education. And this usually occurs only in those special kinds of community settings that can provide for their realization and support. Bourbon Street Black is such an instance.

Within their semicommunity, and even in Greater New Orleans, the jazzmen have now reaped considerable prestige. Their role as the direct heirs to jazz, America's only indigenous art form, makes them the keystone to Bourbon Street Black. Their eminence in their semicommunity is not a new phenomenon. The musicians who are "the greatest" with the white tourists today have consistently been at the top of the social order of Bourbon Street Black. There is a range in the social status of the musicians, but it is somewhat narrower than that of the entire black community. Because of the esteem in which their occupation is held locally and their relatively superior education, they range from the lower-middle to upper classes of Crescent City black society. Most are concentrated in the middle and upper-middle groups, while a few have achieved the lower echelons of the upper class.

Over the past two generations, the jazz musician's families have undergone decisive changes that affect life chances. Just at the dawning of the twentieth century, or a short time thereafter, several of the older musicians had their first experience with formal education. The schools of that time were completely segregated, and the Negro system took what was left over from the white operation. Things were bleak, but the musicians were going to go a lot farther in their education than their fathers had. Almost half of their fathers hadn't been able to stay in school beyond the fourth grade;[6] survival had been their guiding principle, not upward mobility. By the time the present generation of musicians had left school, only two per cent had failed to go beyond the fourth grade, and while most of their fathers had not gone beyond the eighth grade, over two-thirds of them had.[7]

Even when the older and middle-aged musicians were "comin' up" their parents had aspirations for their schooling.[8] It seemed the only way out of their present existence. There were the Negro institutes and colleges they could go to if they did well in the lower schools and could get the necessary financial support. The predominant feeling was that it was good to have just as much education as you could get. The particular area of education was not as important as just having it. The parents were not quite so definite about what occupation they would have liked their child to enter.[9] Almost half made no suggestions as to what specific career he should follow. They were realists. They knew there was a slight chance he might be able to go on in school, but that it would be folly to aspire to any of the higher status occupations.

The one occupation they were specific about was musician. Almost one-third encouraged their sons to be musicians. Sometimes when the men did not receive the direct encouragement from their parents, they got it from a relative or friend. Many of the middle-aged musicians were of school age during the great depression of the thirties. Some men dropped out of school early and became involved with "road" bands. The subculture of Bourbon Street Black gave them an occupational opportunity that had not been realized by as great a proportion of the older jazzmen. They were realizing upward mobility without the full credentials of formal education. World War II interrupted their career in civilian music, but most who became involved with the military actually profited by it. They were "naturals" for the service bands, and several became leaders and organizers. This meant increased rise in upward status. With the end of the war came the GI Bill of Rights, a perfect vehicle for further advancement. Some finished high school this way, while others started and finished college. A few went to graduate school.

The trend toward more formal education continues, with the younger musicians generally spending many more years in school than the older ones. Though they had more opportunities than their fathers, the older musicians still had at least two considerations facing them to cut short any extended educational plans. Their families usually needed them as a producer rather than a consumer, and even if they were to obtain higher education, the market for educated Negroes was so limited that the added years in school would not really help them advance that much. So they took the more practical routes. Some, if they were lucky, got into the trades as journeymen. This often wasn't possible, though, be-

cause such skills tended to remain in the families that had a tradition for them. The Creole of Color tended to control the trades
and most "middle" and "upper" occupations. There have only
been minimal changes in this, even now. One of the cats describes how the Creole musicians reacted to darker people from
Uptown about 1900:

There was a thing with it. Downtown musicians were sometimes
clannish. Sometimes the Creoles thought they were more than everybody else, and they would say, "them Uptowners, they don't know
what they're doin'. They play raggedly." In the beginnin' the Creoles
did have higher standin'. That one-square mile area (The Vieux
Carré) even had more halls for them to play in—more work. The
Creoles were in the buildin' trades, and they were lighter skinned.
The lighter you were, the brighter your environment was.

This fact of Creole ethnicity has been operative throughout
much of the history of New Orleans and has affected virtually
every facet of Crescent City Negro interaction. Though the distinctions are considerably muted, their effect is still evident.

When the young jazzmen were in school the major civil rights
legislation was beginning to be felt. Most of the young musicians
became part of new school music programs. They were learning
their profession earlier than had their elders. By this time their
parents had recovered from the effects of the Depression and had
been able to consider things other than survival. An increasing
percentage of men have gone on to college, and several have
graduated with distinguished records. Many of the men now display quiet confidence—a self-assurance that "things will work
out." This new outlook should be understandable. The past two
generations have realized substantial upward mobility in both
education and occupation. Gains in the occupational sphere are
especially dramatic. Exactly one-third of the musicians have
achieved significantly more education than their fathers, but almost two-thirds have more prestigious jobs.[10]

The somewhat atypical leap in occupational mobility is probably due to a combination of factors peculiar to Crescent City. At the beginning of the twentieth century, the music business as the jazzmen know it today really had not yet begun. The Negro musician's employment status as a professional in New Orleans was not well organized. Gigs were played whenever he could get them. There was no Local to act as a clearinghouse. With some exceptions, they were just unable to earn enough money to be full-time musicians. Most of the time the musician had a day job (often menial) which allowed him to do music moonlighting. In our interviews, a number of the jazzmen described their musically trained fathers as longshoremen, mattress makers, and draymen—not as musicians. After the Local was founded in the early twenties, the music scene gradually became more formal, secure, and professionalized. In time, more of the men came to describe themselves as musicians. More became full-time because the market was beginning to open up somewhat for blacks in New Orleans and elsewhere. This new full-time occupation in music can account for some of the upward mobility.[11] Those who are presently part time, with their major emphasis on a day-job, have also had new opportunities for upward mobility. As a result of civil rights advancements, the black jazzmen are now increasing their participation in a job market that used to be reserved for whites.

The chances for getting ahead in Bourbon Street Black are based on the same kinds of factors that operate elsewhere. If you came from a family of relatively high standing in the community, your likelihood of actually achieving the goals to which you aspire is considerably greater than in the situation of someone whose family has less status. If your father has been more highly educated, the chances of your reaching your own educational goals are much greater than if your father has had less.[12] What this shows is that the relative power structure in Bourbon Street Black has not changed all that much over the years. With some minor exceptions, those who had a head start in the days of the postbellum period are still significantly ahead, and most of the upward mobility in Bourbon Street Black has affected primarily the middle and upper-middle classes.[13]

The correlates of social-class position also have an interesting relationship to personality characteristics. Those musicians who have had more formal education tend to have more confidence in their own playing ability and rate themselves as being "among the best."[14] Part of this may be youth speaking out, because the younger jazzmen have had substantially more years in school than the older ones. There are other tendencies in this direction, though. Those who have the higher rated occupations (either full-time musician or day jobs) also look at the reasons for success differently than men whose occupations are lower in the status hierarchy. Those who have "made it" think that ability is the key to success, but those who have not, believe success occurs by chance or fate.[15] It even goes beyond this. We had previously determined that those coming from higher status families had fewer brothers and sisters, i.e., smaller families. When we asked the musicians what in life could make them happier than they are now, those from smaller families (and of higher social status) mentioned nonmaterial things.[16] Also, those who had received help from their families at the beginning of their musical careers and had (comparatively) "made it" believe their success due to ability. Those whose families were unable to help felt that a person becomes successful through getting "the breaks."[17] Since social change has increased the opportunity for affluence (more people are now able to cope than fifty years ago), we often found some of the older jazzmen who were reared in families totally unable to help them acquire the tools to rise socially in an increasingly complex world, philosophically accepting the idea that fate decided whether a person got ahead or failed to do so.

The homes and general physical surroundings of the musicians vary greatly. There are the somewhat subtle differences in housing that tend to accompany degree of affluence; single dwelling vs multiple unit, owner occupied vs rented; size, and general condition of the unit and its contents. There are also the more dramatic indicators such as the neighborhood density and the value of the property. Most of these are frequent correlates of social class in cultures like our own where material success is the goal many of us learn. In walking around the neighborhoods of Bourbon Street Black and visiting its inhabitants, the careful observer can see the musicians and their families are carried along, to an extent, in this race for survival and gain. It would be a mistake, though, to assume they live for success. Beyond their general recognition that success is sometimes a desirable goal, they share through all social-class levels a gentle concern for each other's welfare. Competition goes only so far here. The belief is strong that you should better yourself but not to the extent of cutting down one of the other persons. There are still the Creole of Color–black man differences, but these are insignificant when compared to the patterns of mutual assistance that have grown even stronger since the postbellum restrictive codes. It's still possible today for a lower-class boy, as was the case with the young Louis Armstrong, to walk into the midst of Bourbon Street Black and be noticed, listened to, and responded to—with concern and passion for his individuality. The differences in the usual social-class indicators are there, and they do affect each individual's life chances. But it would be foolhardy to believe that you had found the key to the life-styles of this subcommunity just by applying the formulas of occupation and education so often used elsewhere. Once you are in the place a while, you discover that the social life of these people is bound not by how long they went to school, who their father and mother were, or what kind of house they live in, but a special sort of "glue" that goes beyond these general labels. These men and women, boys and girls are propelled into each other's lives through an ongoing local ideology— Bourbon Street Black—a community that has developed over the years and is dedicated to the production and nurturance of music for people, in general.

Time and social change are beginning to erode some status differences in Bourbon Street Black, but those who become "the greatest" still come more frequently from the middle and upper status groups. This is increasingly the case since, over the years, the Local has brought the bulk of its members into a style of life that is either lower-middle class or above. The realization of opportunity is more likely for the youth who came out of the upper segments of Bourbon Street Black than for those from the general New Orleans black community. There are still the occasional Louis Armstrongs, just as there are Billie Holidays in other settings. The pattern of mutual assistance and the constant effort at maintaining excellence make it possible for the poor boys to come up through the system more than they might elsewhere. Because there is a benevolent Bourbon Street Black, some "make it" up from the lower classes of New Orleans and go on to a lifetime of national fame and financial security. When they go "up" and out of the Crescent City, they know they leave an environment of support, tenderness, and concern. They also know they can come home anytime they want to. Billie Holiday didn't have that option when she "came up" in Baltimore and New York City.

9

Giggin' and Socializin'

In the Fourteenth Century, when gears and wheels added to its efficiency, the clock became the harbinger of progress and gave us the complex social life of urbanization and industrialization. We worked the clock around, and then found time to spare; leisure time. This time to play was new for most, and with it came *the entertainer*—he who works to help others play; sleeps as others work.

Not All Gigs Are Alike

In a world organized for the convenience of day people, the musician is a night person with little choice of his hours of work and leisure. Time gets turned around for him as the clock helps build a barrier between his activities and those of the "nine to five" community. It's true that the musicians of Bourbon Street Black and their day people public sometimes converse at musical performances, but these contacts are brief. There is much charade in this encounter. Both parties see the event as special, a bit of a game between the performer and his audience. The members of the audience have come to be entertained, and they often approach the event in a mood of exhilaration. The success of the musician's performance will depend upon his discovering what is wanted, and then supplying it. In this brief interchange, neither one has a chance to learn much about the other.

As the tourist watches the seemingly casual performance of

Louis Barbarin on a gig. Photographed by Jack V. Buerkle.

the jazzmen of the Vieux Carré, he might well fail to see the care with which they approach their work. Being on the "wrong side" of the clock has given their work the *appearance* of superficiality. Like other popular musicians, they are often considered entertainers and not players of serious music. But the judgment is incorrect. In Bourbon Street Black, work is serious business. Musical performance is seen as requiring a kind of excellence and precision that can be attained by only a few. One of the older cats comments:

It takes a lot of ability, ambition, and ingenuity to be a musician. Just anybody can't be a musician, because a man has to be an advanced thinker to be one. In other words, you're readin' the notes over there, and you're playin' it way back here! So, if you can't see the note over there, and then hear the note before it comes outa the instrument, you're in trouble! You don't just play. You read the note. You see the note. But, your eyes notice only a sign that shows you the degree and pitch the note has to be played in, and the time. It's a silent sign. So, you see the sign with your eye, and you know from practice where the note should be played on the instrument. But, you've read this thing way over there, and you're playin' it over here! And, if you can't think that fast, you can't play music! A slow thinker can't make it playin' music! Then, another thing. You have millions of people in this world that can't memorize anything. And, you have other people who can memorize a book of stuff like this. So, they's no comparison in the two sets of people. And to play music, you gotta know how to memorize. Lots of the music I play, I just look and see what key the thing's written in, and put it in my pocket and go ahead and play!

Jazzmen have a highly professional attitude toward their work. Responses by the musicians showed that satisfaction with the music was their first concern, and money, their second.[1] There is even strong evidence that a number of the men refuse gigs where they believe either the musicians or the music are below their standards. A typical attitude was, "the money don't excite, don't worry me. I'd rather play for a group that make ten dollars a night playing right; something soothing to my ear. I think a whole lot of music!" Because Local 496 has exerted a certain amount of quality control over music performance, and because New Orleans has a long standing reputation for excellence in the music arts, there just isn't that much inferior performing in the town. Occasionally, however, a musician with high standards does feel strong monetary pressures:

I guess the financial thing ought to overpower you if you're gonna be practical and look at life as it is. You can go off into aesthetic things and spiritual unions and become a hermit if you want to. But, I don't want to become a hermit. I want to enjoy life. I feel like if I had to throw in with cats who weren't as good, but were makin' money, I'd do it at times to get me outa the financial fire. Then I can go on my own for a while.

The fact that a musician will occasionally stray from his performance ideals to make money is much less important than the sureness with which he returns to his original commitment. His problem is that people are often much more willing to pay money for repetition of the familiar than they are to witness creativity.

The turnover of gigs in the Crescent City is routine. While some hotels and clubs keep the same groups for long periods of time, sometimes years, most do not. Most proprietors claim that if they are to maintain profits and the interest of the public, they must make frequent changes. This may appear to leave the musicians' employment very tenuous. For the ones on the fringe of the activities of Local 496 it does. Some are infirm and can't work on a regular basis; some have day job conflicts and have difficulty scheduling the gigs they could get; and a few are considered by leaders to be either undependable or relatively incompetent. Since job insecurity has existed for a long time in Bourbon Street Black, many of the jazzmen have developed ways of adjusting to it. Those who are full time often belong to two or more groups, as well as a brass band. Brass band work usually occurs in late morning, afternoon, or early evening. The gigs with the inside bands usually begin during midevening or later. A full-time musician has to hustle to coordinate his activities, but a number seem to be able to do it on a regular basis. The part-time people do similar things, just in less elaborate combinations. The day job, for instance, couples quite well with weekend club work, the jazz halls, parties, or conventions.

In spite of their multiple membership in groups, most of the musicians are quite enthusiastic about the quality and activities of each of their groups.[2] There seem to be very few signs of serious dissension in the bands with which the men are now working. Bourbon Street Black is actually a rather small community where a large proportion of the men are going to spend most of their lives, and they just can't afford extensive conflict with each other. Most have a strong, congenial relationship with their associates, and those who have problems (for example, endemic competition) usually make an effort to get along. "Sooner or later you get in a hang up with musicians. A personality clash. You have to work with 'em, so you don't have a fatal disagreement with 'em. So, you say to yourself, "I'll work with 'em again," but you are sorta careful about how you let go around them after that, because the musicians are always competitors."

The professional popular musician is not only a "night person," set apart from many others by the clock, but he is an entertainer—a performer dependent upon the precise, interlocking, and immediate support of several other persons: the rest of the band. He is unlike a creative writer or a college professor, who don't usually depend upon the immediate help of their colleagues. Creative writers and college professors perform alone; he does not.

When the musicians look back on the engagements they have played, they are often able to focus on one "golden" one. Less than ten per cent mentioned money as the thing they liked most about the event.[3] They felt the greatest rewards were from good working conditions, being treated well by the proprietor, being asked to an honorific event, such as jazz festivals and a gracious audience response. One middle-aged man remembers one special time away from the Crescent City:

There was that gig in Texas. Man, that was somethin' else! We stayed there nine months. Everythin' we did, man, seemed to get over, ya know? It was just like bein' at home, but not *at* home. Every day we worked there, I couldn't wait for nighttime to come so the gig could start.

For those who have traveled extensively and acquired some national and international recognition, singling out an occasion is usually more difficult.

It's hard to say what was my best gig, but one good one was when I helped make the sound track for *The Benny Goodman Story*. They didn't show me in the movie. I was supposed to be in that, but I was workin' in Las Vegas, and I couldn't get away. There were some fine musicians in that: Benny Goodman, Lionel Hampton, and others.

The men had much less difficulty remembering the worst gig they ever played. Over one-fifth said the worst time they could remember was when they didn't get paid. Only one man said his worst gig came from a poor audience response. Most of their trouble, however, centered on problems they had with proprietors. A young musician describes a problem involving racial discrimination that he had in a club outside the New Orleans city limits:

The whole concept of the club was bad. Everythin' about it was false. The cat had pictures of black musicians all over the wall. Musicians like James Brown, The Temptations, everybody. But he wouldn't let black people come in! It was standard that when we finished the set we couldn't mingle with the audience. He made us go back to the dressin' room. He really ticked me off! One night some black people came and tried to buy some tickets. He called the police, and about fifteen carloads came and searched them. The police took them to jail on the charge of disturbin' the peace. I just quit on the spot, and refused to play there any more.

A more frequent kind of complaint from the older musicians centers on poor working conditions (a problem that is much less evident since the rise of the musician's union).

The worst job I ever played was a jitney dance here in town. I worked there two weeks. They wanted me to stay on after that, but it was so bad they couldn't give it to me! They ought to erect a monument for all the fellas who have had to play jitney dances in New Orleans. For this kind of dance in New York, they used to have two bands doin' it. Here one band did it. You went to work at eight o'clock and worked till three or four in the morning, playin' continuous music. It's the worst thing in the world!

And like many persons, the jazzmen often feel they are under-compensated for their talent and originality. One younger musician summed up their feelings this way:

We're not paid enough, in many cases. We're not respected enough, or looked upon as professionals like doctors and lawyers much of the time. We do as much studyin' as the cats in symphony orchestras, but look who gets most of the respect! Much of the time the jazzman is a better musician than the symphony guy. He's just sittin' there, playin' somethin' somebody else wrote down! We create with our own brain every day we play!

We were able to elicit complaints like these from the musicians because we specifically asked them to talk about personal and professional difficulties. But complaining about what they don't have or fighting among themselves is not a significant part of the scene. By living with them, day after day, going on gigs, or just "socializin' and shuckin'," you discover the tone of their life style is a kind of gentle and mutually considerate exuberance. A central normative code that is adhered to strongly is, "don't down another cat—live and let live." The exuberance with their life style touches most of their activities but is most evident in their attitudes toward their work in music. One older cat said:

In music, you are learnin' things everyday. You broaden your vocabulary everyday. You get more knowledge because everyday somebody comes out with somethin' you never heard, and it's educational, in a way. To my idea, the musician never learns everythin'. He always has somethin' new to learn. New song come out—he gotta learn it. You're still in school, in a way of speakin'.

The "Kid Sheik" Band with (left to right) George Colar (Sheik), Chester Jones, Pa
Barnes, Emanuel Sayles, and James Miller. Photographed by Jack V. Buerkle.

Another older musician of considerable international reputation said:

I make contacts. I meet people. If they don't know me already, they might say, "I've read of you, and I think your playin's great," and then I feel like I'm somebody in the world. People compliment me on how I play, and they like it. If they didn't enjoy it, they wouldn't say anythin'. My relatives—they all played. And I enjoy it. I even enjoy practicin'. Even if it doesn't sound like much sometimes!

A middle-aged musician commented:

One of the main good things is playin' for an audience; a good recep-tive audience, and seein' that they enjoy themselves, and knowin' that you're gettin' over to them. To please and satisfy the people, so to speak. For myself, there is no end to the enjoyment I get because, like I said, that's my first love—music. Just to play it.

A younger jazzman said:

I like the complexity. I like to be noticed and liked. You see 'em ravin' when you groove. You don't even know 'em. "Man, I like that!" "I dig that!" I like to do somethin' the audience digs. They say, "man, you made my night better!" I say to myself, man, they made *my* night better! I dig playin' music, period!

These examples of how the members of Bourbon Street Black approach their occupation and the gig are typical. The elements of the stereotyped commercial musician making the gig just for the money involved or of the legendary jazzman, completely alienated from the audience, whom he has to tolerate for eco-nomic survival do not exist. The musicians of Bourbon Street Black try to meet their audiences on even terms, where they give something and also get something, whether it comes from seeing the audience enjoying themselves or just from the sheer joy of being able to play. Each night as the tourists walk back to their hotels satisfied that they have now seen and heard genuine black New Orleans jazzmen perform, they *have* made one accurate assumption about these "night people." The musicians *do* enjoy playing for them, and know they have been appreciated.

Have Horn, Will Travel

The musician has always approached the *road* with mixed emotions. For the young man just beginning in his profession it means adventure, the opportunity to break away from the strictures of home, and a chance to be seen and heard by a wide audience so that he may become famous. Often to the older man it has meant long bus rides, not getting enough sleep, poor food, and loneliness. Time has not made traveling less lonely, but it has muted some of its less attractive features. Jet airplane travel has made it possible to take distant but lucrative gigs and be away from home for only a weekend. Civil rights legislation has opened up the better hotels and restaurants, and some of the older musicians who in the past could only play in them are now their clients. Where in the past traveling often meant being away eleven months and home one, it now usually involves relatively short tours. About the longest any of the jazzmen are away from Bourbon Street Black now is four months, and this occurs with the touring traditional jazz units. These groups often utilize comfortable mobile quarters where there are accommodations for the musicians' wives and provisions for some limited Creole cooking.

Slightly over one-third of the jazz musicians are not presently involved in road traveling. About a quarter of them spend a month or more of each year on the road. Today, the road is seen by many as a kind of pleasant diversion from local gigs, but only to be engaged in occasionally.[4]

Experience on the road is an individual thing; some remember mostly the good times, others the bad. One middle-aged musician remembers it this way:

The worst gigs I ever had was durin' my first experience in travelin'. We was playin' in theaters. They'd run the movie, then clear the place and bring in a new audience as we was to go on with the stage

The Onward Band is off again for another gig on the Strekfus riverboat, *President*. Photographed by Jack V. Buerkle.

show. We used to do five to six shows a day, and usually stayed at
each place one week. The entertainers always got payed first, but
when they got down to the band, they was always short some loot.
Some cat was always there to say that he'd make it up on the next
gig. This went on for months! That's the dues, man! They would
give us just enough to get to the next town, get a room somewhere,
and one meal! By that time, you're hurtin', man, and ready to go
back to work!

Another middle-aged man sees family ties as the main obstacle
to his travel:

I'm still away from home quite a bit. About four months a year. But,
I'd rather play at home now, because I've been on the road. I've
lived there. I have more to live for right here in New Orleans, ya
know. The kids are beginnin' to get big and we don't have that much
more time together.

An older musician remarked:

When I was younger, I played on the road for a couple of years with
quite a few show bands. I like the road sometimes now, but it's too
hard! You see, you don't get enough rest on the road. And, playin'
music is hard at its easiest! Playin' music is as hard on a man as bein'
a carpenter, bricklayer, plasterer, cement finisher, or iron worker.
Only thing, in those trades, you handle more material, but, for
playin' music you handle everythin' a man's got. It's hard! Any other
tradesman can work eight hours a day. A musician can't work over
five hours. If you work a musician eight hours a day, in a few years
he's cashed in. Add this to bein' on the road for a long time, and a
cat's wiped out!

One of the younger men sees it somewhat differently:

I'm away about seven or eight nights a month now. It used to be a
lot more. I enjoy it every now and then, because it's a change. You
see new things and different people. It's nice. I didn't always feel
this way, though. At one time, I was afraid of the road. I'd heard so
many stories. The cats would come home and tell wild stories, but I
figured I really wouldn't know till I went out. I was scared as hell!
But, I found out the road is pretty good if you just take care of busi-

ness. You've got to stay away from some people and just adjust to all
the things that go with bein' in lots of different places—not just act
stupid 'cause you're away from home. I guess it did have a little effect on my family life. My wife and I used to call each other about
three times a week, no matter where I was. Many times I'd send for
her if we were gonna play a location for two weeks or so.

Another viewpoint about traveling comes from a young man
who hasn't traveled extensively:

You get a kinda road fever. You get to playin' in one town too long
and you got to get away from it. I've always felt that I will have to
get out of the South if I'm goin' to make some kinda headway in music. This is because opportunities are limited in the South. Nobody
of importance will see you play here. A lot more things are happenin'
in the North, and on the West Coast.

Some of the older jazz musicians travel occasionally. One who
semi-retired in the Crescent City after years of travel with internationally renowned black bands comments on his new role as a
celebrity at jazz festivals:

Sometimes travelin' is pretty great. It's a prestige thing, like a jazz
festival. Being a musician, you got a little ham in you. So, you always
feel nice if you're invited and contracted to play one of the big festivals like Newport, Monterrey, or various other festivals. You go because it gives you a lift to know that you still have something to offer
the public.

Of those musicians who travel or have done so in the past, over
four-fifths say that their being away has had no serious long-term
negative effects on their family life.[5] The families of Bourbon
Street Black adjust to long absences by the musicians probably
because they understand that travel is a routine part of a musician's life and that the husbands and fathers of this community
have traveled for generations. Family members have understood
that they will be together whenever possible, and give support to
each other by letters and phone calls when they are apart. When
a jazz musician goes on the road, both he and his family have the

emotional and sometimes financial backing of the entire interde-
pendent community. A road musician emanating from Bourbon
Street Black is much less apt to find loneliness in travel than the
jazzman from a less supportive community. The people from
New Orleans know their musician is a night person because he
has to be, and have merged their lives into his side of the clock.

The fact that road travel affects some people's security is realized by the musicians, and a few interpret this to mean that marriage is a precarious situation for people in their occupation.[6]

Women are oriented toward a certain belief—the steady job. They're
security minded. Financial security. There aren't too many women
with an aesthetic sense. They can't see what you see as a musician.
They want to know if the check is gonna be there, and if the rent is
gonna be paid. If a fella is a serious minded musician, he's gotta have
a place and a time to think. 'Cause if he doesn't, he might as well
give up and become a "nine to fiver." There are alimony courts and
child support courts. These are apt to take care of a cat if he doesn't
do what she says.

Still, almost two-thirds believe the musician is better off
married.

A musician has to have a very understanding lady. She has to know
his faults. Because of his position as a musician, she has to be a
strong lady. She deserves a lot of respect.

One of the older musicians sees some of the virtues of a wife in the
physical comforts she makes possible for him:

If he's got a wife, he's looked after better. If a man is single, he
misses a whole lot of meals. Sometimes, he's not particular where he
sleeps, if he's single. If he's got a wife, he's gonna have a better pad
to go to. She's also gonna keep him clean. When you're on your own,
there's a whole lotta things you just don't have time to do. And,
eatin' in restaurants; it's terrible!

Others felt that a musician should be married because of the psychological support he can get and needs:

A musician is better off bein' married. He needs a companion to care for him because the life he leads is not disciplined. He needs someone to come home to. If you lead a bachelor life as a musician, you'll generally find yourself in a hotel room, or roomin' with somebody, and you don't get the things you really need. But, bein' married, you got somebody to show you your shortcomin's and help you with your "longcomin's," if I can put it that way. Somebody to praise what you're doin'.

"A companion to care for him . . . someone to come home to . . . somebody to show you your shortcomin's and help you with your longcomin's . . . somebody to praise what you're doin'"; these words capture the essence of man–woman relationships in Bourbon Street Black. Long before Louis Armstrong joined King Oliver in Chicago, even before Freddie Keppard toured the country with the Original Creole Band, the women of Bourbon Street Black were saying goodbye to their men—men going on the road to "make it" or because that was their way of trying to survive. Just as it became a tradition for the young musician to want to go, so it was for the young woman to be taught that he eventually would. Survival for her in this environment meant she must willingly attach her life to his and then see what happened.

On the Town

Popular musicians share with other entertainers an interesting distinction. Since they work to help others play, and often sleep as others work, their own recreation and leisure activities must be fitted into the remaining time. This time varies according to the specific requirements of the gig, but much of it occurs when the day people are working. The clubs they join are usually small, informal, geared to their hours, and often formed by themselves. They are usually unable to belong to many clubs and fraternal groups, because they are often working when these organizations meet. The jazzmen who are part-time musicians are less affected and sometimes join the regular groups. Those who travel

Working a House Party on the Rue Bourbon during Mardi Gras. Photographed by Jack V. Buerkle.

are least likely to participate in any formal or informal groups that meet on a regular basis.

Danny Barker comments on the history and present status of several Crescent City social organizations, some of which have been patronized by members of Bourbon Street Black:

New Orleans is a good time city. There has always been a strong social life. People want to belong to things. Years ago, they had an abundance of clubs, like the Lions Club (not the national organization), the Bulls Club, the San Jacinto Club, and the Tammany Club. These clubs were organized for social life. There was a tremendous amount of energy that went into organizing these clubs. They would get themselves a piece of land, and build a clubhouse. So many musicians belonged to the building trades here. Plasterers, bricklayers, carpenters, roofers, glazers—so it was a matter of pitchin' in and buildin' a club. Some of these clubs like the Bulls Club, which is now the Elks Club were beautiful big buildings. Uptown, they had the Bulls Club. They were a group of boys who worked in the Cotton Exchange. There were the Bulls and the Bears. Just like the stock exchange! These guys heard the terms used when they worked there, and so they used them when they formed their clubs. Both clubs were Uptown. The Bulls were successful, but the Bears went under.

All these clubs gave affairs. This is one of the reasons there was such an abundance of work for musicians. 'Cause you had—like Fourth of July, all the clubs had their affairs. If they didn't have it on a Sunday, they had it on a Monday. Most of these original clubs aren't around now. The guys who liked that—they were dedicated, man! Gamblin' flourished! They had poker games in the clubs, and a pool hall. It was what the younger generation liked then. But, when the Depression came through, it knocked the pillars from all the places. No money. They couldn't pay their taxes, and the clubs went into the hands of the receivers. These clubs were beginnin' to to be formed around the 1880s and 1890s. These were black people who wanted to belong to somethin'. They wanted to be identified.

There's an abundance of clubs, even now, but they're different. They're Carnival (Mardi Gras) clubs. The Bon Tons, and a number of others. They give fabulous balls durin' the Carnival season. There's a clamor to get an invitation, 'cause they put on tableaux; wonderful things! Between New Years and Mardi Gras, they have all these Carnival balls. Every night there's a ball for about two weeks before Carnival Day. There's an abundance of balls—three or four a night—all kinds of clubs. The Wonderful Boys, the Bon Tons, and many others.

None of the blacks go to the white balls, but the whites are beginnin' to come to the black balls. For instance, at the Creole Fiesta Society and at the Zulu's there have been more whites dancin' on the floor than blacks, lately. They want to see what's happenin' with blacks. They've heard about the ball from the blacks that work for them. The people give their employers invitations; the ones who are not so adament on this racial thing. There's a chance for them to go to a ball, and these balls are on a par with the white balls. Actually, during Carnival, the Zulu King is on a par with the King Rex.

Less than half of the musicians belong to social clubs, but many of those who do share this opinion of a younger man: "I belong to the Wonderful Boys. It's a social club for men. We mostly play pool and things to get away from it all. It's a good thing, 'cause we can just get together, drink beer, and plan dances and things like that. The dances help us raise money when we need it." Usually, women have contact with the clubs only at dances or other such events, but form parallel clubs of their own. The sexually segregated social clubs are relatively common in New Orleans, but the members of Bourbon Street Black spend only a small proportion of their leisure time in them.

Half of the musicians usually take their wives or other members of the family with them when they go out for a night of recreation.[7] About the only time they go to Bourbon Street for recreation is to hear another musician play. For the most part, though, when the jazzmen have spare time, they either stay home with their families, visit with family friends, or take the family out to dinner (outside the Quarter). The tourist areas of the Crescent City are the places where they normally work. When they have recreation time, they want to spend it elsewhere. A middle-aged veteran of traditional bands reflects a common attitude among the musicians: "I don't usually go out. If I want a drink, I can have it here at home. Invite some friends in and listen to records. You know, bein' home is my recreation, be- cause I'm around people all the time at work." Another said: "Sometimes we go out to eat and take the kids with us. We go to a nice restaurant, because I get tired eating at home; a Chinese restaurant, or somethin' like that."

Wherever the popular musician has gone, he has been accom- panied by a persistent legend about what he does with his time between gigs. As fiction, motion pictures, and television often see him, he is a possessed creature, using himself and others with abandon when he is off the job. The jazzman's bacchanal may have occurred in the distant past of Bourbon Street Black, though there is considerable doubt it ever followed the script. Less than half of the musicians go anywhere but home after gigs. Those who do stay out for a time usually go to a restaurant for either a meal or a snack before going to bed. The younger men show no important tendency to stay out later than the older men, but this may not have always been the case. One older man contends:

We don't hang out much no more like we used to. We are older, and the novelty of sittin' around barrooms and gin mills till dawn is gone. We may go to a restaurant for breakfast, but we don't booze. In fact, we don't booze up like we used to when we were younger. When we were younger, we might go to a "good time house" where there was a lotta fictitious action. You wanted to see what was happenin'. Now we *know* what's happenin', and all the people our age are in bed, or they're full of arthritis or other ailments. So, you go home to get your rest. You cool it! In other words, you're over the hill!

During the period between 1900 and 1930, there appears to have been considerable jamming in New Orleans after and even during gigs. But this was gradually discouraged, and finally pro- hibited by the Local. Coupled with this prohibition, there has been a gradual diminution of "action" after 2:00 A.M., the usual quitting time for most of the city's musicians. Part of the reason for this is that the wives of the middle-aged and younger men of Bourbon Street Black have become better educated and conse- quently these women have come to expect "rights" from their

husbands that would have never occurred to their mothers and
certainly not their grandmothers. One of these rights is to have
her husband home soon after the gig. Where their fathers may
have gone out after a little "honest action" after the gig, these
men are not so apt to do so; they are experiencing a new kind of
pressure from their wives. The women are already making a
number of adjustments as a result of their husbands' schedules,
and they resist any additional inconveniences, particularly if they
are likely to be demeaning to them.

Being a night person somewhat limits the popular musician in
his intimate, primary social contacts—his friendship groups. Most
of the musicians he works with are his business associates; only
some are friends. Most people in his neighborhood are working
while he sleeps and are either involved in mealtime activities or
family recreation as he goes to the gig. Of course, he gets to know
some of them, and a few become friends, but their different
schedules limit their social interaction. The jazzmen, therefore,
generally choose their best friends from among family members
and other musicians,[8] and to most of them, friend means something very special. An older man said:

Through the years, people have gotten in touch with me, and I'll remember that this person and I had a good relationship. *But, a friend?
A friend?* You know, I want to analyze that word *friend* sometime;
the depth of it! Because, some of your friends are better to you than
your close relations. They're closer! They'll do more for you, and
you'll do more for them. But, it's all in how you get involved. It's
hard to name them. Especially, for a man who's been in the music
business as long as I have.

Friendships in this context are intense but limited in number.
This does not imply that cordiality is confined to the bounds of
friendship. It's just that the idea of *friend* is usually limited to
especially intense affective relationships. A younger musician
underlines this theme: "Wow! Friends are somethin'! You don't
have many friends; real friends. You know a lot of people, but

you don't have many friends. Friends are lotsa times closer than brothers, I think."

Despite the limited contact the musicians have with some of the more conventional forms of community activity, there are a number of spheres where their civic behavior is evident. Their working hours restrict them from going to meetings of community and neighborhood betterment organizations, but almost one-quarter of them are active in working for civic improvement, most of it with children. They have minimal formal involvement with local or national political organizations, but over three-quarters of them vote regularly in municipal elections. All subscribe to at least one local newspaper, and over a third of them to two. Many take several magazines by subscription, and those most often seen are *Newsweek, Time, Life, Playboy, Downbeat, Ebony, Esquire, Jet,* and the *Musician's Journal.*

What do these people do when they have spare time? They play music for themselves—either instrumentally, or by phonograph. Many of them like to relax by playing jazz at home.[9] Jazz records are most in evidence in their homes, closely followed by classical and light-classical selections. One of the musicians describes his record collection:

If you look at my collection of records—I've got everythin'. I like all kinds of music. You'll even find Western music in there. There are certain times I like certain things. I've got a fair amount of symphony stuff: some Bach, Schoenberg, and even some Mahler. Sometimes I don't feel like listenin' to anything else.

Another man shows some irritation that others have tended to "type" both his playing and listening interests:

I like all kinds of music if it's good and pleasin' to me. That's what I think music is. Rock and Roll is pleasin' if it's good! Sometimes it gets too monotonous, at least some of it. Actually, when it comes to listenin', I like some kinds of chamber music and opera. I'm in the jazz field, but I don't like to play *just* traditional jazz. Sometimes, people think that's all I play, and have bypassed me for other kinds of gigs. If I ask them a question about it, they say, "Well, you don't fit into that category." I like to play music that's good—with good musicians.

Some of the men use their time at home to "expand" the music they play. One young man sees the occasion as an opportunity to develop his own "sound":

The kind of music that I like doesn't have a name yet. It's my own music. Some people call it avant-garde. But it's not really the kind of avant-garde I hear people playin'. Not stuff like Elvin Jones or Charlie Mingus. I'm not really atonal. I can't deal with that. I'm a traditionalist on the one hand, and a progressive revolutionary on the other. There are some things in music you can't change. Like there are the rules and regulations, and when you change this, you got chaos. You gotta have some sorta rules. When you have no rules at all, you have no order. I like order in my music. I really couldn't call it avant garde, or whatever. It's just *my* music. I like what John Coltrane's group did. He was close to what I'm tryin' to do. Not his last group, but before that. Chord changes and real hip harmony with lotsa sevenths and nineths. Flated fifths and flatted nines— things like that. This is the kind of thing I mean. Also, it's gotta swing! If it don't swing, it don't make it! When it really comes down to it, it's gotta swing!
I used to like the West Coast style when I started out. Some of the other guys liked rhythm and blues, and some liked East Coast jazz. Some of the cats used to put me down 'cause I dug the West Coast sound. They'd say, "Man, them cats ain't with it. How the hell can you listen to that crap?" I just felt—so what! I don't have my own thing together yet to put *anybody* down! I feel that way now. Until I get my own thing completely together, I don't have *no* room to put nobody down! I'm not judge and jury!

What the young man was complaining about in his altercation with other young musicians some years back was their criticism of his liking a jazz style that had become identified with whites— West Coast jazz. Although the style was strongly influenced by Miles Davis, it was rather quickly dominated by Californians like Dave Brubeck and graduates of the Stan Kenton and Woody Herman bands. Such criticisms of differing music styles and forms are rare in Bourbon Street Black. About the only occasions where such caustic attitudes about somebody else's music occur is when youth are groping for a style they want to settle in, and they sometimes adopt temporary hard line positions about one form or another. Usually when a musician doesn't feel enthusiastic about a particular style of music, he sees it as a deficiency in his own ability:

There was one kinda music I couldn't get into for a long time. When I was a kid, we tried to play a funeral, and I just couldn't make it. It was a school band. Some fella died outa town, and Victor (the school band leader) had taken us there to play this funeral. Man, I just couldn't get with it! I don't know if he had it goin' right himself, 'cause, man, ya know Victor wasn't up on funerals. Not to my knowledge, ya know. But, he had us guys tryin' to walk the right way in the procession. Man, (laugh) we couldn't even do that! Man, it was a disaster!

I stayed away from that scene until about eight or nine years ago. A cat came to my house and told me he wanted me to play for the funeral of somebody my daddy knew, so I tried to play it. We was marchin' along and I was lookin' down readin' the part. When I looked up, the damned band was almost a half a block ahead of me! I couldn't get used to readin' the music and keepin' up. I had to run like hell to catch up! At that time, I was about the youngest cat in the group, and I just hadn't done it to speak of. After that I didn't have no trouble.

Being a musician is not *just* having an occupation; a job to go to, for the jazz musicians of Bourbon Street Black. It becomes the excuse—the center—for all other things as they adjust to the exigencies of the clock. Because they so love their work, recreation and leisure time take on an uncommon meaning. In a very real sense, for many of them, to work is to play.

꒰ꆤ꒱

After the midsixties, Paul Barbarin and his *Onward Brass Band* were finally allowed to march in the "greatest" of the Carnival parades. This parade had always been a "white" affair, ex-

cept for a few black boys carrying torches and jiving down the
street between the floats and the white bands.

There were new problems associated with the parade this evening in 1969, though. Paul didn't feel well, and besides, the
marshals in the parade were giving him trouble. The parade had
always been a military thing, in terms of cadence. The Onward
Band is a two-beat, swinging, jazz brass band. As Paul told the
marshal. "If you're out there swingin' with two-beat, the cadence
is too slow to keep up with the pace those military marchin' cats
set. They take long steps, while we're bouncin' and takin' short
steps." The marshal said, "I can't worry about that, Paul. You're
holdin' up the parade! You're behind! If you can't play somethin'
fast, you're gonna have to get outa the parade!"

Paul became tense and felt worse. It had taken too many years
to get into the parade; they couldn't let themselves be thrown out
now! So, they snapped into a military cadence with the understanding they would play only after they caught up with the
group in front of them. Paul felt worse, and finally dropped out
with instructions for the band to go on.

When the band finally arrived at the Municipal Auditorium,
they were approached by a policeman. "You know that man in
your band that got sick? He died a few minutes ago. It was an
aneurysm—a clot." They stood silent for a while, then one of
them said, "It meant so much for him to march in that parade."

10

In God's Country

I did a lot of things in my life that I wanted to do and I am quite sure that there is nothing that I would be ashamed of. If I had to live my life over again, I would do the same that I have done again because some things that people probably say was bad, probably seem bad to them, but in a time when something happens and you know that you have done wrong, you sort of take your own judgement and try to get out of it the best way you can. Anyway, I am very happy now and I am living a life pretty easy. And I'll always play music as long as I possibly can. All them crotchets, I'll put them down with my clarinet or my saxophone and I'll play as long as I have breath. I think I did the best I could with my life. I made everybody happy close to me. I had a lot of worries, but now I have decided I have figured that out because I figured the day would come when I'd have to leave here, which everybody does. Nobody lives for a lifetime. I'm not worried about the body. If I didn't do with it what they want, I have used it and it is finished and I am satisfied.

I am an old man now; I can't keep hanging on. I'm even wanting to go; I'm waiting, longing to hear my peace. And all I've been waiting for is the music. All the beauty that there's ever been, it's moving inside that music. Omar's voice, that's there, and the girl's voice, and the voice the wind had in Africa, and the cries from Congo Square, and the fine shouting that came up from Free Day. The blues, and the spirituals, and the remembering, and the waiting, and the suffering, and the looking at the sky watching the dark come down—that's all inside the music.[1]

Joys and Concerns

Sidney Bechet had been away from New Orleans many years
when he spoke of his life in this hauntingly beautiful passage
from *Treat It Gentle*. It had been almost four decades since he
had played in the halls and cabarets of the Crescent City, but his
convictions about life and death still bore the imprint of Bourbon
Street Black. Louis Armstrong, Paul Barbarin, Pops Foster and
George Lewis—also had these same convictions—this understanding and acceptance of self, a kind of "open" approach to happiness that includes a belief in the frailty of mankind and an ac-
knowledgement of the end of one's life on this earth. Woven into
all this is the precept that music—to be able to be near it, hear it,
play it, and love it—is the organizing condition giving everything
else meaning. The music carries within it a people's heritage
which the musicians, in a sense, reconstruct each time they perform. Spirituals, blues, and ragtime, tell many tales of joy and
sadness.

God is always nearby in Bourbon Street Black, for woven into
much of the music is a philosophy of existence strongly affected
by religion. In the late 1800s and early 1900s, the spirituals of
the Negro Protestant Church entered the two-beat rhythms of the
brass and inside bands. This further affirmed the presence of
God and the vulnerability of Man. The hymns and spirituals set
to early jazz rhythms helped verify a message within the Protestant Ethic that saw life on earth as a ceaseless struggle. The belief emphasized, "Don't look to the left or the right but toil un-
complainingly as God would want you to, and in the end you
will be rewarded." In Bourbon Street Black, heaven is a very real
goal for which to strive. Under these circumstances, the problems
of life can be tolerated because the afterlife will bring a perpetual
realization of happiness as you join your loved ones who have
preceded. One of the most common of these "converted" hymns
carries the message:

Oh, when the Saints go marchin' in
Oh, when the Saints go marchin' in
Oh Lord, I want to be there in that number
When the Saints go marchin' in![*2]

Much of the tone of resolution and consequent redemption is realized when a Crescent City two-beat band does the "Saints." Barry Ulanov has said "it is at once delicate and assaulting, satyrical and deeply religious."[3]

The power of the church is still very discernible in Bourbon Street Black and is most frankly displayed in some of the statistics reflecting the religious commitment of the musicians.[4] You might well expect that the men, if for no other reason than the nature of their working hours, would have minimal contact with the church, but this is not true. All but a few still maintain an active membership in some church. The memberships aren't just nominal, either, for almost two-thirds attend services at least twice a month, and more than a third go weekly.[5] Probably some of this regularity grows from the Catholic Church's edict that absence from weekly Mass is a mortal sin. Still, some Catholic musicians do experience problems of attendance.

I don't go to Mass that much. Oftentimes, I just go in the church for a while when I pass it. I stop in and light a candle, and make an offerin'. I pause for a few moments, and then I come out. But, this steady church business of every Sunday; I can't do it. Playin' music makes it difficult to make Mass every week. I just do the best I can, and hope God will forgive me.

Although his problem of conflicting time schedules does make Sunday morning attendance difficult, he is not typical, for most do attend.

Of even more interest are the reasons for disaffiliation given by some of the men who no longer belong to the conventional

---

* "When the Saints Go Marching In" New words and new music arrangement by Paul Cambell TRO. Copyright 1951 Folkways Music Publishers, Inc., New York. Used by permission.

churches of New Orleans. One said, "I was a Catholic, but when
I got out on the road, I just got exposed to different philosophies
and ways of life. This turned me away from the Church. Now,
I just believe in God, worship and give my respect. It's as simple
as that." One of the older men believes the church has moved
away from its original purposes:

Your religious people—if you go over the countries and around the
common people—have been fooled so much by church leaders in the
name of the Bible and God, that it is ridiculous! Now, I don't have
nothin' against religion. I don't have nothin' against the church or
the people who believe in it. But, from what I have seen in the first
war overseas (World War I), in Panama in 1906, and all over this
country that I have been; I think the people that preach it and teach
it should be more to help the little people insteada keepin' 'em in
poverty! Now, you go into Mexico and you see thousands of people
in poverty. Some of the most beautiful work you ever wanta see in
the churches is done by these poor individuals that are so wrapped
up in the church, in Christianity, that they can't get along themselves. Now, the Bible says, "Love thy neighbor as thyself"; not
better than yourself! Now, if a man or a woman don't love themselves, they can't really love the other fella!

While this old man is quite bitter about what he thinks has happened to organized religion, less than one-tenth of the musicians
have dissociated themselves from their churches, and none of
them seem to have adopted a fundamentally different moral outlook. When the break does occur, it is usually the musician con-
tending the church has "let the people down," or that its official
representatives are not following the original intent. Less than
five per cent profess a non-Christian religious belief, but their
moral beliefs and philosophy of Man and existence still reflect
more of the overall teachings of Jesus Christ than of any other
source. However much they might have hoped to develop a "new
and more equitable conception of Man," the residue of the New
Orleans Latin-Catholic, Baptist, and Methodist ideology affects
their beliefs. Prayer is an interesting case in point. Over two-

thirds of the musicians say they have special favorite prayers.[6] Catholic musicians frequently mention making a novena asking for help in their career or in family matters. Protestants often utilize the psalms in their praying; the twenty-third psalm is the most popular.

In Bourbon Street Black, the religious groups live close to each other with scant evidence of conflict. For the most part, there seems to be a calm mutual respect among the men regarding differences in religious persuasion. It is not uncommon to hear Protestant musicians or those without any affiliation mention they prayed to Saint Jude, or that they lit a candle in a Catholic Church when faced with a special problem. Some Catholics describe how they occasionally attend Baptist or Methodist services because they prefer the music there. These somewhat ecumenical religious attitudes are particularly significant in the history of the evolution of early jazz in the Crescent City. Many of the Creoles of Color have a long Catholic tradition where the Church's approach to its religious service and music is relatively formal. Had the Creoles not been forced into contact with the Protestant blacks by the postbellum codes, they quite likely would not have acquired the swinging music style of the Protestants. In the Negro Protestant services they experienced the hip-swinging, clapping, and moving revivalistic style of the spirituals and hymns totally unfamiliar to the Catholic Church. Much of the impetus of this hybrid culture of black New Orleans derives from an experience where the blacks and Creoles of Color literally gave life to each other on several levels. The Creole taught the black man technique on European musical instruments and regained for themselves the loose-knit, free style of soul music. Together they have been able, somehow, to cope.

Funerals and Bars

As Sidney Bechet so eloquently affirmed, music here is as much a part of death as it is of life. While life has been filled with uncertainty and potentiality of day-to-day trouble, certainly Heaven will possess only that which is good, and much of that good will be a perpetual supply of excellent music.

Four centuries ago the Dahomeans and the Yoruba of Western Africa were laying the foundation for one of today's most novel social practices on the North American continent—the jazz funeral. Their secret societies assured individual members of a proper burial at the time of their death. Many of the associations had the features of a cooperative where through pooled resources individuals were able to accomplish what they couldn't by themselves. When black men were brought to America either direct or via the West Indies, one of the things many retained from their past was this belief in secret societies and their benefits. As time passed, some of the basic ideas were applied to lodges and other fraternal organizations, and the burial insurance idea was retained. Within much of the core and on part of the periphery of Bourbon Street Black the practice of having music during funeral proceedings was added to the basic African pattern. The tradition of music at funerals has some of its roots in the French martial music played in funeral processions. Throughout the early history of the Crescent City, both Creoles of Color and blacks had ample opportunity to see such funeral parades.

By the latter part of the nineteenth century, the jazz funeral was beginning to take on many of the facets we see in it today: It is usually organized at the deceased's request through a fraternal society or lodge; it involves several days of "wakin'"; it employs a black brass band; a second line either develops spontaneously or is hired; and, most important, the funeral is seen as a major celebration by the participants. This view is possible since the departed brother or sister are really going to a life of eternal happiness, and thanks are in order for the Grace of God.

Not everyone in Bourbon Street Black believes in jazz funerals —some consider them blasphemy. Danny Barker stated that "it's pretty much of a diehard cult of some of the musicians and a few of their followers who still do this." Barker believes the rejection by a number of persons in Bourbon Street Black and the wider black community is a social-class phenomenon. Those who accept and ask for burial "with music" are secure in their status ambitions and don't feel threatened by doing something labeled as too "earthy" by some insecure persons in the middle and upper-middle classes of the community. Although some middle-class people have a jazz funeral, most of the "believers" come from the most secure persons in the core of Bourbon Street Black and poor people whose primary social contact is with certain neighborhood bars.

A few black neighborhood bars in New Orleans have served as organizing points for many of the jazz funerals. The bars are usually the social clubs of poor people and are crucial factors in maintaining two-beat music in funerals. The bars have become a "second home" for a number of their customers, particularly non-musicians.

The people in these settings who really make things "move" are the bartender owners. They know all their regular patrons well, promote friendship among them, and do some planning of social celebrations. Most of the "characters" who frequent these bars love two-beat music; in fact, in one neighborhood the bar crowd organizes a parade every year employing three or four of the traditional bands. Many of the bar patrons look forward all year to the opportunity to march down the street behind a two-beat band in a brightly colored silk shirt and holding an oversize cigar. The planning for this parade is done at one of the bars.

When one of the regular members dies, the bar membership contributes to his funeral and sees to it that he has music. An older cat remarked about one of these bars:

If you're a member of the local drinkin' community and you hang out at [this] bar, or your brothers do, and your family don't mind you havin' music they'll pass the hat around and try to get ninety to a hundred dollars. Very few people who love this sorta thing will refuse to put some money in the hat to pay the band. The guys passin' the hat'll say, "Well, you knew so and so. We want to have music for his funeral. We know you'd like to put somethin' in the hat." If they get only part of what they need, the bar owners will put in the rest.

An interestin' thing happened not too long ago. There was one boy who hung around one of the bars, and he was very popular. He didn't have any people. So, a neighborhood undertaker took the body to his place because he buries most of the people in that neighborhood. The undertaker has a reputation for bein' a good man and helped this young man even when he didn't have any money. He got the body ready and donated a casket, but didn't have any place for the wake. He has a small place and already had two other bodies there. So, the bar owner told the undertaker, "Give him to me; He can come to my place." So they took his body to the barroom and laid it out there in a little place off the main part of the barroom. It was a shock to some of the people with this young man bein' laid out there, but not to the people he was involved with. He was a swingin' cat, this boy that hung around the bar, and they loved him so. The bar stayed open twenty-four hours a day 'cause there's no curfew, so they just held the wake in there. Thousands of people went to see this man laid out in the bar. It was the talk of the town! He wasn't a jazzman. He was just a neighborhood boy. A young man in his thirties; well-liked, poor, but everybody liked him. He worked. He wasn't no character of no sort. Never got into trouble. Just died. Likeable, and lived alone, and didn't have no immediate relatives, or if he did have them, they couldn't do nothin' for him. So, the bar owner, the undertaker, and the rest of the cats just took over and they put him away in what they felt was their style. Nobody in the neighborhood rebelled.

Certain bars serve as an organizing point for the brass bands playing for the funerals. They are convenient places in which the musicians can stop and have a beer before assembling to march to a nearby funeral home. Once the funeral is over it is to one of these same bars the musicians and some of the second-liners return to talk over old times and listen to stories of events in the life of the deceased.

However, according to several of the musicians the future of the jazz funeral is bleak. They see the neighborhood bar as the main impetus nowadays for these funerals, and hold that the old-fashioned humble neighborhood bars in the Crescent City are dying out. Their demise, they say, will occur because young men no longer hang out in the neighborhood bars. "When you hear somebody speak about a young boy in one of those places, they usually mean a guy in his late thirties or early forties. It didn't used to mean that." The feeling is widespread that within a short period of time it just won't be possible to bring enough people together to plan assistance in the funerals. It appears that about the only way this tendency could be reversed is through formal endorsement by several of the fraternal and social organizations. However, as the general economic and social level of black people in New Orleans continues to rise, the fraternal organizations are becoming much more middle and upper-middle class in their outlook and seem to be moving away from the jazz funeral. Members of some of the groups are saying that "it just isn't dignified." There have been a few instances of whites having jazz funerals, but no increase in their embracing the practice is evident. White musicians have shown little interest in requesting "music" for their own funerals. One celebrity in town has remarked, however, that he intends to stipulate it in his burial instructions.

I Want Music When I Go

The death notice appeared in the *States-Item* and *Times-Picayune* on Monday, and yesterday in the black *Louisiana Weekly*; Another old jazzman is gone. The veteran musician has been "waked" by several hundred of his friends, lodge brothers, and associates for the last four days. He was seventy-nine last Saturday when he died at Charity Hospital. The old man hadn't worked regularly for the last two years, but until the last three weeks he enjoyed jamming, once in a while, with a few of his old friends. For several years he had been telling both his wife and lodge brothers, "when I go, I want music; lots of music." The wish was about to be granted.

Another old jazzman is laid to rest. Photograph courtesy of the New Orleans Museum.

The body is scheduled to be taken from the funeral home to the church in about forty-five minutes. The members of the Onward Brass Band are beginning to arrive here at the neighborhood bar three blocks from the mortuary. They've been coming in pairs and singly. Now they're all here. It's a drizzly, gray day, and they linger as long as they can until Louis Cottrell says, "We gotta go now"! On go the raincoats, and the covers to protect their band caps. Outside, they line up in "two's" and head toward the funeral home to the medium cadence of one of the snare drums.

In less than ten minutes they're there and Cottrell is in talking to the funeral director. Now, he's back outside and says, "pretty soon." By the time Onward has lined up and started the dirge "Just A Closer Walk With Thee," the pall bearers have raised the casket from its stand and are proceeding slowly toward the large black hearse parked out front. Once there, they begin to ease the casket into the hearse as the band moves slowly by to the front of the hearse to become the vanguard of the procession. The dirge continues as members of the family are taken to limousines for the long slow ride to the church and the cemetery. The music has a sad, almost off-key moaning to it as it continues. As the mortician gives the signal, it stops.

Almost immediately, the drums begin a slow, respectful and muffled cadence as the band moves off with the rest of the procession following. The second-liners begin to follow along on the sidewalk, and today their umbrellas are something more than decoration. Everybody's out there! All ages, sizes, and descriptions, they stand watching the procession move off. Some even join the second line; kids no more than six or seven catch a kind of excitement in the situation. The band begins another dirge after about a block. This time it's "The Old Rugged Cross." The trumpet almost wails as the clarinet seems to simulate a crying woman. There are no other sounds quite like a New Orleans black brass band playing a funeral dirge. "Rugged Cross" continues for a couple of choruses and then winds down. At this, the drums pick up the beat, and the cats move along at almost a military beat. Here is the church, finally. The rain has stopped now, but the gray sky seems no brighter than before.

The band, along with an honor guard from the departed brother's lodge, goes to church steps. All form a double file on each side of the steps as the pall bearers get ready to bring the casket into the church where several hundred friends and associates have already gathered. Onward begins to play the dead musician's favorite hymn, "Just A Little While To Stay Here." Slowly, the casket is brought up the steps past the band and the lodge brothers (who have just raised crossed swords). The widow, children, and grandchildren are escorted to their seats. Then the service begins. It drones on for almost an hour longer than usual with eulogies, hymns, and prayers, because the old jazzman had been an official in several important community organizations, including his church. After almost two and one-half hours, the funeral director comes out to Cottrell, and says, "We're ready. OK?" "OK."

While the church service has been proceeding, several hundred people are crowding the sidewalk on both sides of the street. Even a couple of Crescent City tour guides have paused with their limousines to explain to eager tourists about the unique custom. The band commences this time with "Take Your Burden To The Lord" as the casket is brought out of the church and placed in the hearse. In moments, the procession is ready to move off again, this time toward the cemetery. As the band leaves the church, its cadence seems even more dragging, leaden, almost as though they are trying to prolong their last few minutes with the fallen brother. When the dirge is complete, the drums again move the beat faster. The second liners follow on the sidewalk, and there are almost two hundred of them now. The band marches to the drum for about two blocks, then begins "What A Friend I Have In Jesus." Within a block they are through this, and the drummer again picks up the cadence.

Within a few minutes, they are eight blocks from the church and headed toward the cemetery. At this point, Grand Marshal

Danny Barker signals to the funeral director riding in the hearse that the time has arrived. Just as the director acknowledges the signal, the bandsmen continue marching, but move toward the edge of the road as the hearse starts to accelerate. Then, as the hearse passes, Danny gently pats it on the side and shouts, "Turn 'em loose"! The hearse and all the cars behind it gain speed and head toward the cemetery without the band. Nowadays, the bands do not usually accompany the procession to the cemetery because the old cemeteries in the central part of the city are either filled or the aboveground vaults are unusable because today's caskets are too large for them. Most of the cemeteries utilized by black families today are on the outskirts of New Orleans.

The family and friends of the old man have gone about four blocks away from the band when it abruptly swings around and heads back toward town and the bar where they had met earlier. Then it happens! The bass drum resounds like a small cannon with Boom, Boom, Ba, Boom, Boom, Boom! The whole mood has changed as Onward screams happily into "Bourbon Street Parade." The second liners go wild! They laugh, dance with broad gyrating hip-swing movements; dipping and whirling their umbrellas, they sway, strut, and jive. The crowd has grown to over a thousand now as Onward goes blasting down the street. Almost everyone in their path gets caught up in the absolute, released joy and frenzy. As they move along, they go almost immediately from one happy "finger-poppin'" tune to another. Because the departed brother was a "ramblin' man," a "swingin' cat," they do "Didn't He Ramble?" Then it's "The Saints Go Marchin' In" and "The Saint Louis Blues." With all this, the band seems to have come completely back into key as the "happy jazz" bounces and shouts down the street.

Within a half-hour, they are back at the bar—a little wet but happy that they were able to put their old friend away in the style he wanted. The drinks are flowing now, and musicians and non-musicians are happily discussing episodes from his life. He really was a ramblin' man! The cats are happy because they know he has gone to a better life through the Grace of God. As they get up to go to their homes, one says: "He has been redeemed. God will not let him down. God will not let us down"!

૭૧૭

A few months ago a white man died away from here. He had been a New Orleans boy. He was young, and he told his wife as his last request that he wanted a jazz funeral. He was from a long way off. His wife came down here with the body, and he was laid out here in one of the fanciest funeral parlors in town before he was buried, and they hired our brass band to play the funeral. The band met at the cemetery in this case, a good distance from the center of town. We were told to be there for twelve o'clock. We were to give this gentleman the same ceremony that we give the black brothers: the whole procedure. So, we waited out in front of the cemetery. It's a quiet cemetery; a beautiful cemetery; well kept; high classed place.

Finally, the funeral party arrived with the white funeral director and only four limousines, no cars, because it seems like he had been away for a long time and didn't have any relatives here. So, when the procession pulled inside the cemetery, the funeral director gave us the cue and we got in front of the hearse and marched about two blocks into the cemetery to the grave. When we got there we formed just like we do for the black brothers. The family got out of the limousine. They had the limousine drivers and a couple of other guys actin' as pall bearers. So they carried his casket to the grave and laid it out there like they do, with the flowers. I remember those flowers. That's the first time I saw beautiful roses of such a dark color. We went through the services as the priest took charge. It was a real sad scene. There wasn't many people there. Just the widow, a colored woman holdin' the widow's little child, and a couple of friends. The ceremonies were very brief.

When the priest finished, he turned to us in the band and said, "It's a wonderful thing that you fellas came here to pay this man this honor of givin' him his last request, and if we had more like this in this community it would help so much with so many things. I'm proud to be a part of this today." Then he came over and shook our hands. While he was doin' this, I looked over at the white limousine drivers. Man, they were lookin' wild-eyed, because I doubt if they ever participated in a white funeral that followed a black procedure of buryin'! The priest went on to tell us about how he felt so good that day because the dead man's spirit should feel so good. Man, it was really great! It brought tears to my eyes.

So, after it was all over we marched out of the cemetery and started down the street. The widow had sent word sayin', "Would you all play a marchin' tune out for a ways down the street like you do"? We said yes. All the other limousines cut out for town, so it was just her limousine that followed us from the cemetery. We went down the street playin' a light sorta swingin' tune, "Just A Little While To Stay." Kinda soft. We done that for just two blocks. The last thing the widow did was when the guy blowed the car horn and we looked around. The limousine went by us slow and she waved at us and blew us kisses and sayin', "Thank you very much." There were tears come to my eyes again. The guy stepped on the gas and the limousine left. We played about four more bars; stopped, and then walked to our cars.

An Older Jazzman

Diggin' the Squares
and the Hips

The story ends with death. Our Mr. Martin, from the moment he began fooling around with pianos, was riding for a fall. I shouldn't have said fooling, because he wasn't fooling; he meant it. In Rick Martin's music there was, from the first, an element of self-destruction. He expected too much from it and he came to it with too great a need. And what he expected he never quite found. He might have found it in another kind of music, but he had no training or any way of coming to know another kind of music. So he stuck to jazz, and to the nervous, crazy life that goes with it. And, he made a good thing of it; he made an amazing thing of his own playing; he couldn't even keep pace with it himself. He was, in his way, like Tonio Kröger, Mann's inspired and bewildered poet, who "worked not like a man who works that he may live; but as one who is bent on doing nothing but work; having no regard for himself as a human being but only as a creator."[1]

From the prologue *Young Man With a Horn* by Dorothy Baker

The Legend

Dorothy Baker's antihero blasted out of the ashes of the Jazz Age to reinforce a public image of the jazzman begun more than three decades earlier. The pattern is fetchingly tragic: a talented orphan boy with an urge to create discovers the world of jazz musicians and is swept irretrievably toward his doom. Along the way he learns, struggles for recognition, makes love, drinks booze, gets recognition—even fame, but dies alone, young, and forgotten. Almost twenty years later, Andy Silvera's destiny was being framed the same way in Evan Hunter's *Quartet in H.*

Whatever the medium of communication, the jazzman is usually seen to be in desperate combat with conventional society. Possessed by his music, this "outsider" is seen to retreat to small enclaves of "hipdom" to avoid the "squares." Like Martin, he is pictured as a kind of frenetic nomad, living only in and for the world of now. Thoughts of neighborhood, marriage, and family are an anathema to him—a cursed reminder of the urban slum and childhood in a broken family.

In the 1940s and '50s, musicologists, behavioral scientists, and psychiatrists began to comment on the position of the jazzman in society, and, for the most part, they tended to agree with the literary depiction of him as a deviant.[2] Howard S. Becker, a sociologist, wrote:

Every interest of this group emphasized their isolation from the standards and interests of the conventional society. They associated almost exclusively with other musicians and girls who sang and danced in night clubs in the North Clark Street area of Chicago and had little or no contact with the conventional world. They were described politically thus: "They hate this form of government anyway and think it's real bad." They were unremittingly critical of both business and labor, disillusioned with the economic structure, and completely cynical about the political process and contemporary political parties. Religion and marriage were rejected completely, as were American popular and serious culture, and their reading was confined solely to the more esoteric *avant-garde* writers and philosophers. In art and symbolic music they were interested also in only the most esoteric developments. In every case they were quick to point out that their interests were not those of the conventional society and that they were thereby differentiated from it. It is reasonable to assume that the primary function of these interests was to make this differentiation unmistakably clear.[3]

Though Becker saw this as an extreme case, he felt the desire for isolation and self-segregation was "manifested by less deviant

musicians as well." Where there has been a widespread tendency
to see the jazzman as existing in a deviant occupation, there is
considerably less agreement as to *how* and *why* he forges a breach
between himself and conventional society. The novelists and
screenwriters have shrouded his moves in the mysteries of compulsion. The psychoanalysts have sometimes seen it as a clash
between the id (jazz and the jazzman) and the superego (conventional people and their culture). Some sociologists assume the
break between the jazzman and the "square" society grows out of
a series of mutually threatening social interactions. Supposedly,
conflict with parents or some other familial trauma can result in a
rift that causes the youth to seek the emotional support of the
jazz counterculture. Jazz is viewed by the parents as "the Devil's
music" and by the youth as his salvation. He gains psychological
support from other jazzmen who have similarly felt the suppression of the "squares" in their background. The jazzman's contempt
for the outside world is further increased by the realization that society has put him in a position of financial insecurity. Because the
music public demands variety in their entertainment, he is forced
to be a gypsy and go on the road. Moving from employer to employer allows him minimal contractual security and comparatively
poor occupational fringe benefits. He is at the mercy of a fickle
public, unscrupulous club owners, and crooked disc jockeys. In
the midst of all this, he is forced to give the public what *they* want
to hear, no matter how trite, and to stifle his own compulsion for
creativity. The battle between the commercial interests and his
creative ones forces the jazzman to continue to isolate himself emotionally and physically.

We have an egregious lack of information concerning the life
style of all kinds of musicians in the United States—jazz, popular,
classical, rock, country and western. Little is known of the day-
to-day social and psychological behavior of any of these people
within their own peculiar community and familial contexts. The
occupational setting of each has produced allegedly typical models of how each of these people behave. Jazzmen are supposed to

be wild, irresponsible, anti-social; classical musicians are supposed to be disciplined, serious, responsible; and country western performers are viewed as affable, hard-drinking, and "simple people."

Stereotyping is commonly used by novelists in their construction of central characters on the exaggerated, flamboyant, colorful, noticeable, or alarming aspects of the roles people play. This is understandable, and "good" novels often utilize the technique. Rick Martin was possibly a melange of personality high points of the Jazz Age and the years that immediately followed. But was he typical of jazz musicians of that era? The similarity between the characters of a novel and real people is tenuous at best. Even the biographical and autobiographical works about famous musicians can't be seriously considered models for the behavior of those in the profession; they are written from the viewpoint or experiences of a single life and often contain other biases making the report atypical for any time or place.

What of the professional and scholarly studies of musicians? Unfortunately, most of them seem to be no more accurate in describing the range of activities within the occupation than are the novelists and biographers. The psychoanalysts and psychiatrists studying jazzmen have used weak clinical techniques often involving studies of well known (therefore not typical) jazzmen who have usually been interviewed in their work (often a nightclub) setting. A common pattern of results is that the jazzman is said to display aberrant, aggressive behavior brought on by internal conflict; the theoretical reasoning being attached ex post facto.

The sociological studies before the midsixties used two formats: (1) conjectural studies based on prior stereotyped reports, and (2) after-the-fact accounts of vaguely defined interviews with unspecified groups of musicians. Several of the sociologists writing about jazzmen and popular musicians were professional musicians themselves, either before or during graduate school.[4] Regrettably, when they write about either popular musicians or jazzmen, their reports are essentially conjectural and contain personal memories of the music business and the speculative material of others, or they are after-the-fact accounts of musicians they knew and worked with in the 1940s to midfifties. A person reading these reports is given the impression that jazzmen, as a whole, form countercultures, are deviant, and are locked in a kind of combat with the rest of the community.[5] This material, unfortunately, gives no indication of whether the people written about are representative of the general population of musicians.

Do the musicians of Bourbon Street Black conform to this earlier "deviant" stereotyping of the jazzman? Are they of a single mind in their attitudes toward their own groups, and people outside Bourbon Street Black?

Who Needs All Those Squares?

Those who have defined jazzmen as deviant see them as using every opportunity to isolate themselves physically and socially from the "squares." The alienation of the jazzmen is assumed to be so complete that they feel comfortable only at those times when they can fully control their environment. An example of this is the jam session. Observation of the jam session in Bourbon Street Black was not possible for us because a Local 496 edict has forbidden them. Our discussions with the musicians, though, didn't reveal that they were upset at not having them. On the contrary, the musicians believe they can get their "kicks" on the stand and at the same time make the music business economically profitable. In New Orleans, jamming after hours in a club is looked upon as almost the equivalent of scabbing.

Over three-quarters of the musicians have performed on a record, either as a leader or sideman. Many said they enjoyed the experience; still, almost two-thirds said that, if they had to make a choice, they preferred playing for an audience. They reason, "Man, I like the response," or "I like to see that I'm gettin' across to people, and makin' 'em happy." This approach to the audience is in decided contradiction to what some of the sociologists have said, that is, that there exists a conflict between the jazzman desiring to be a creative artist and the audience insisting that he follow their dictates. The musicians of Bourbon Street Black don't see it this way. They feel they have considerable latitude in which to be creative and that this is what their audience expects of them.

What these sociologists have not taken into account is that the relationship between the musician and his audience can be different in different times and places. The public's expectations are not necessarily *always* commercial. When "squares" come to the Crescent City, they often expect to hear jazz and, therefore, the potential for conflict between the musician and his audience need not always exist as an issue. The jazzmen of Bourbon Street Black have also been taught (socialized) from childhood that it is good to play for audiences and that musicians are supposed to please their audiences and thereby derive their own satisfaction. The men differ somewhat in the kinds of audiences for which they like to play, but we found none who didn't like to perform for them. Though there were no important differences between the kinds of audiences the younger and older men liked, some individuals did change their preference as they became older.

I prefer playing for an audience of "over forty" people. It doesn't matter who you play for—black or white or any kind. The object is to communicate with them, and do your job well. That's what really matters. When I was younger I went for the younger audiences, though. They understood what I was doing. For instance, if I played rock to an older group they'd say it was a lot of noise. Understanding really "cures all ills" in that respect.

One of the older jazzmen reveals that this desire to please audiences has a long history in Bourbon Street Black:

We used to play mostly dances when I was younger. We didn't do any concerts, then. At the dances, you had to try to feel the people out, and different audiences would like different tunes and they were popular, and you had to try to feel 'em out and try to play the right tunes so they could get out there and dance. Sometimes they would sit around, and just maybe one or two couples would get out there. Somebody has to start 'em off. A whole lot of 'em would wait for you to play the blues. We played what we called the "low down blues," and then the floor would be crowded with dancers. They'd get out there shakin' and huggin' and stuff like that. Sometimes they would dance for prizes.

Another older musician looks at audiences in terms of their size:

I like a big audience. I don't care whether they're older or younger, colored or white, rich or poor. We played for a millionaires' club in Boston. They were just like anybody else to play for. Once the audience accepts what you're puttin out—you're carryin' the audience—but, if you're playin' to a "dead" audience, and they don't accept what you're playin', that's the hardest night you'll ever want! Big crowds never did upset me!

One of the important considerations to a number of the musicians was that they have "stable" audiences, ones that show promise for a return engagement.

I like the club circuits. Because if you play for the college level, they go on outa school and you never see them anymore, but if you're playin' night clubs, there's always a night club patron or jazz fan who'll continually be your fan. Those college kids are forever movin' outa college, and they forget what happened in college. They might remember they saw you, but playin' in clubs—that's where it's at.

Jazz musicians are assumed to isolate themselves from the people outside their own circles by showing contempt for the public. The term "squares" is used, Howard S. Becker contends, to refer "to the kind of person who is the opposite of all the musician is, or should be, and a way of thinking, feeling, and behaving (with its expression in material objects) which is the opposite of that valued by musicians."[6] Over half of the jazzmen had an opinion about "squares" where they saw them as conservative or uninformed,[7] but only a few came as close to agreeing with the Becker definition as did this older man who has traveled extensively:

Terrible people are squares. A square is somebody who is easily led. A member of the establishment who has been brainwashed not to think for himself. He uses cliché ideas, cliché patterns of life—of living. It's like people who vote for Wallace. Not people who are aware. You can tell them right away. They know what's happenin' and you can spend some time with 'em. Also, when somebody's not square, you can tell by how they speak and how they act. They're interesting! Squares are boresome. Their general make-up is made out of a mold. They're like a gang of Coca Cola bottles lyin' around on the side of the road. Who needs 'em! They don't belong to you. What value do they have? What can you do with an empty Coca Cola bottle? That's a square—nothin'! It's well made—It'll be here a long time—It'll be here when you're gone. It's a round bottle, but it's a square bottle!

Most of the comments of this type were not this eloquent, nor were they as strong. An interesting feature of this response and several others is that the contempt shown for the square does not necessarily specify the nonmusician. The information Becker accumulated reserved the square category for non-jazzmen. Jazz musicians, by definition, were "hip." In some cases, we found Crescent City jazzmen referring to other jazzmen there as square. The definition had many of the characteristics described by Becker, but it was often used to distinguish one complex of behavior from another, not to distinguish jazz musicians from the remainder of the population. One of the older men expressed it thus:

I think it's a guy that don't go for this or that. He usually don't want to go outa his way for anythin'. He don't drink; he don't go anywhere. But, a man that's hip; he's just the opposite. He'll take a chance on anything. He chases the women, gets drunk, fights, and does everythin'.

Almost one-fifth of the men were unable to give any definition of a square, and an even greater percentage said the definition was so variable and personal that no single explanation could be given. One middle-aged musician responded:

Square? That's hard to say. Who ever another cat thinks is square, I might not think he is one. I really wouldn't call anyone square, because I'm not a judge. I don't think anyone knows who a square is.

A younger man commented:

Nobody's all square, but we're all a little bit square. Everybody's hip, to a degree.

Becker's observation that musicians tend to form cliques is borne out in our own situation. It does make sense that the jazzmen would associate primarily with each other. They work the same or similar schedules and generally have the same time free for recreation and leisure. Also, there is considerable clique activity in the hiring procedures. These social groups usually have no more than fifteen or less than six members. Generally, it is within these groups that the phenomenon of rotating leadership takes place. Except when a person is on the road or leaves New Orleans for a protracted period, the composition of each group remains relatively constant for long periods of time, often years. Although the cliques are obviously clannish, they usually profess strong agreement with the conventional moral norms. Some individual musicians see their roles as different from non-musicians, but not better.

Pot and the Hard Stuff

Charles Winick, in writing about drug use among New York jazzmen, made two observations that are important to the understanding of the Bourbon Street Black scene. He first suggested that "the working Negro jazz musician is highly trained, generally enjoys high status and income, and represents a proud group which has given rise to most of the innovations in the whole jazz field."[8] Later on in the same article he said, "In the New Orleans period of jazz, in the early years of the twentieth century, the stimulant most widely used by jazz musicians was alcohol, the use of which was socially acceptable. . . . *This period was one of the few when jazz musicians were an integral and accepted part of their community"*[9] (italics ours). These are particularly perceptive impressions especially since Winick's own research had no direct contact with the New Orleans situation.

Through the years, several elements of the subculture of Bourbon Street Black have kept involvement with narcotics among the musicians to a minimum. The professional competence and pride of the black musician discussed by Winick is evident in Bourbon Street Black. Throughout the book, we have demonstrated how families and the community go to great lengths to assure the development and realization of any musical talent among their young men and women. To become a jazz hero is a standard motivation for the youth as they are growing up. The heroes are very real to them because they can be named, came from the Crescent City, and sometimes come home to be admired. The young musician is taught that only the best make it and that he must do everything to maximize his chances for success. One of the things he is warned to avoid is the use of narcotics. This was true almost from the beginning, as Winick has commented. Even when the musicians were working in Storyville, where many of the whores eventually succumbed to hard drugs, most of the jazz musicians avoided narcotics. There have been a few talented jazz musicians from the Crescent City whose careers were ruined by "junk" during the past seventy-five years. These people have become legends of horror—examples of what to avoid if you want to survive and "make it."

On the other hand, a few jazz musicians have become addicted to alcohol in Bourbon Street Black, but this addiction is not seen as having the fatal consequences of hard drugs. There are strong sanctions dealing with drinking on the gig, but when a musician is not working, the general attitude is "live and let live." In spite of this high level of tolerance, the incidence of alcoholism did not seem any higher here than among the general public. Although we didn't have the opportunity to research this to the degree of

certainty we desire, there are a number of confirming observations. For instance, we have considerable information on the "job
dependability" of the musicians, and believe the jazzmen, as a
whole have excellent records of accountability. One reason for
this, has to do with the nature of their work. When a gig is contracted for, the situation is greatly complicated if someone either
fails to appear for work or shows up and is drunk. The music
group (jazz band, dance band, etc.) involves a series of interde-
pendent performances, and if some persons are missing or not
functioning at an acceptable level, the product (music) suffers.
This is a considerably different operation than is evident in many
other work environments. If a man doesn't appear for work at a
manufacturing plant, some inconvenience occurs, but he can usually be replaced immediately, on a temporary basis. But, music
organizations on a gig are performing. They are before an ex-
pectant public. The men are extremely concerned that everyone
appear on time and ready to play. In this setting, repetitive problems of incapacitation because of alcohol or anything else cannot
be tolerated. From the sideman's point of view, the sanctions are
severe. He is usually not a salaried employee, but a wage worker.
If he doesn't show, he doesn't get paid. Also, because of union
regulations, he can be held accountable to the Local where it is
possible for him to lose his ticket.

In places other than Bourbon Street Black, perhaps some of
these sanctions are missing or are less effective in controlling the
behavior of musicians. But remember that most of these Crescent
City musicians have been reared in a well-organized, intimate,
community—a community that begins to furnish them with their
life-style and goals as they learn to talk and walk.

A number of the older and middle-aged men have worked in
enough situations, both on the road and elsewhere, to have observed the use of narcotics by other musicians.

We used to have a problem back in the '30s with musicians who
didn't drink. They didn't smoke either. But, they smoked pot! That
was a mystery to me. They got a big bang out of it. And, they could

always find one another—these different pot smokers—seemed like they could tell one another. They had a thing goin', and it was that. You couldn't tell 'em nothin'! That's what they wanted, and they was supposed to be puttin' everybody on, and they were wiser than everybody else. They were smart! Hell, they were ignorant! They did those kinds of things and knew it was illegal, and did it behind closed doors, or up on a mountain, or out on an ocean somewheres so they could see what was happenin' and not get caught.

It is interesting to note in this older musician's comments that the marijuana smokers were considered abnormal because they were committing an illegal act and also because they neither drank nor smoked.

About half of the men believe that the use of any stimulant or depressant (other than alcohol off the job) is completely unacceptable for themselves or anyone around them. *All* are completely opposed to the use of hard drugs, but it is clear, that many distinguish between marijuana and all other drugs. About two-fifths of the men say they would not object to others smoking marijuana as long as they don't have to be nearby while it's being done. None would tolerate marijuana on the gig.

The men were not asked directly if they themselves smoked marijuana, but more than three-quarters volunteered that they did not.[10] Our own experience with the musicians tends to bear this out. We did get some feedback from a few of the younger musicians that several of them either have or still smoke marijuana on occasion. When marijuana smoking does occur, it seems to be a phenomenon of youth rather than of the music profession.[11] As far as we can tell, the incidence of marijuana smoking is lower among the younger jazz musicians of New Orleans than that reported to one of the authors by urban college students. This evidence seems to us to be quite substantial because of certain significant differences between the two populations. Where today's college students have come to "intellectualize" differences between marijuana and "harder" drugs, the young jazz musicians of Bourbon Street Black approach the subject from a different vantage point. Throughout the last three generations in the community, there has been a deadly fear of all drugs and their consequences. Though a number of the younger jazz musicians have had college experience and approach such subjects more analytically than some of their older colleagues, they actually preceded the "drug-wise" college generation of the late '60s and the '70s.

The fear component that all drugs engender in these people seems to be relatively high. Part of this fear arises in connection with the belief that any kind of tampering with the nervous system will have a negative effect upon their performance as an instrumentalist.

I don't approve of it (taking drugs). It's no sensation! You gotta be a fool to do somethin' like that, 'cause your music is from your soul and your heart, man! And, that's the way it always will be with me. I don't know what it will be with the rest of them. I love music and it stays with my heart. It comes from my heart! I play it with all my heart!

A middle-aged musician exhibits the same fear of contamination of his performance:

I don't think any musician—any person, any profession, doctor, actor, musician, or anyone—I don't think you need those things to help your talent. If you have talent, and want to do the right thing with it, you have to stay off that stuff. I've never done anything like that in my life. I drink a little bit, sometimes. I may drink a beer or two, but I don't need anything like that. The only thing I need is the band playin' right, and they can inspire me. As far as that other stuff, I recommend that to no one!

Apart from what they believe drugs or alcohol can do to their own bodies, a number of the musicians are tolerant of usage in others, but only up to a point. That point is reached when they believe the other musician could either reduce the total effect of the band's effectiveness or get them in trouble with the Local or the police. The fear of what could happen if he were in the presence of marijuana smoking is expressed by this middle-aged musician:

Well, I'll tell you somethin'. I've played music professionally since I was twelve years old, and I have never used any form of narcotics. I've been on bands with fellas who used them, and I don't have anythin' against them usin' the stuff as long as they don't do it where I can get caught with them. I just don't work with a cat whose doin' it when I'm around.

Another sees it from a business and performance point of view:

A man's personal life is his life. But, if he's workin' with me, he can walk around naked in the daytime, but when he gets on my bandstand, I want him lookin' and actin' like a musician. When he gets on my bandstand, I want him sober, and not high on nothin'. His habits are his business, except when he's workin'. You play well, do your business, that's your thing!

What Other People Think

In writing about jazzmen and some popular musicians, Howard S. Becker has remarked, "In every case they [musicians] were quick to point out that their interests were not those of conventional society and that they were thereby differentiated from it."[12] Accordingly, the people who are important to such musicians are only those other jazzmen who make up their own counterculture or anticonventional group. If a musician cares what a "square" says or does, he is no longer a member of this group, but a "square" himself. No discernible range of opinion is acceptable; either you're in or you're out. From this perspective, whatever the general public is thought to believe about musicians is either considered irrelevant or is vigorously attacked.

Most of the people of Bourbon Street Black find this attitude about non-musicians completely incomprehensible. One of the main reasons they chose a career in music was to derive their own pleasure from pleasing audiences. Sometimes they know very little about the individuals in the audiences for which they play, but their intent is always to please the public—to make them happy. They want the general public to have respect for their music and for them as individuals. The majority of the jazzmen are aware of a segment of the public having mixed or even negative opinions about them and their work, and they find this criticism frustrating.[13] They respond to this by attempting to account for why they are not viewed more accurately. Some believe such differences are mainly caused by the lack of contact between day people and night people.

Well, some people think a musician is just a playboy. Just somebody out there tryin' to make an easy buck. Some people—there are some people who envy musicians. They work hard in the day, and you work at night. They don't know where you're at half the time! But there are some people who really appreciate music. They know what it's all about and the trouble you had to try to learn it. They appreciate it.

Well, the ones that follow us; I think they love us. Some of the other people; I don't know about them. I know some people don't like musicians as a whole. I try to be a good musician, and a decent person. I don't even talk with a lot of people around here. Half the people in this neighborhood don't know what I'm doin' anyway, and I've lived here for years. They see me in the daytime, and I guess they think I'm not workin', 'cause in the daytime I seldom blow my horn without a mute. They know all my kids play, 'cause they've seen them go to school with uniforms on, and with their instruments.

One of the younger jazzmen makes an observation that might well serve as a model for improving our understanding why people, in general, often misjudge others by implicitly believing incomplete information:

It's hard to say. There are different levels. Some people say yes; some people say no. People that don't usually like music are usually the ones that don't like musicians. That's often bothered me. I actually know some people who don't like music. That's amazing! I thought everybody liked music of some sort; something like jazz, spirituals, symphony music, but some kind. There *are* people who don't like music at all. So, they're weird people. Then, there are people who like music, but think musicians are all dope fiends and degenerates. I think these cats believe musicians are ornery people— bad news. I don't think the majority of people feel that way, but it's just lack of information that causes them to feel that way. They really don't know. They just go on hearsay. Most people go on hearsay about a lotta things. If somebody tells them somethin' they just accept it as bein' true. They don't stop to think for themselves if it's really true or not. People are like—the majority of people are like sheep! If one strong statement is made, they'll just accept it. I read a quotation once, and the gist of it was that just because people accept something it doesn't mean that it's true. The majority are ignorant! I don't mean stupid; they just don't know, because they don't bother to find out.

Among the musicians who have traveled extensively, there is a common belief that jazzmen are often held in higher esteem elsewhere than they are here in the United States. A veteran of some of the top jazz units offered this view:

It all depends upon what part of the world you're workin' in. Because, the people in Europe and Asia think more of musicians, jazz musicians, than the people in America. See, the people in America take jazz music for granted, where the people of Europe and the Far East, even the Middle East, worship jazz music. Americans have been hearin' jazz music all the time; they're used to it. But, when these other people hear jazz, it's somethin' new and they notice it has more rhythm than any other kind of music they ever heard.

Becker and others who have written about the popular musician and the jazzman emphasize how as "outsiders" the men feel they are different from and superior to the rest of the population. This may well have been the case in Chicago and New York in the 1940s and '50s (particularly with some white musicians), but the situation in Bourbon Street Black is not, and has not been, that simple. Some of the jazzmen believe the musician leads a fundamentally different existence from the average man, but over two-thirds say there really are no important differences.[14] In response to questions as to whether they looked at life differently from most others, the jazzmen often contended that their working hours are different, but the responsibilities they have and the things they like and dislike are essentially the same. A few responses did indicate that the speaker felt superior because his vantage point as a musician gave him a more thorough understanding of human nature. One younger man used this theme in his reply:

Most musicians have a little edge on the average person. I guess, by bein' in music, you become more introspective. You sorta know yourself a little better than the average person 'cause you take more time to find out who you really are: what you're doin', why, and how. The average person just accepts things. The musician is always lookin' for distinctions; tryin' to find out things. So, his behavior will have to be a little different. He'll discover things the average person won't discover, 'cause they wouldn't even be lookin'.

In the relatively small percentage of cases where jazzmen believed they saw the world differently, the attitude was less one of superiority than a privileged look at some of the details of living that their non-musician friends might envy. An older musician speaks of how he believes his profession has given him a "peephole" into lives of others:

Musicians: They see so much of life. Things that some of my non-musician friends would enjoy and be amazed at, musicians take for granted. They see life in a raw, nitty-gritty sense. They see so much 'cause they're around night people and these people live a different life than day people. Day people don't usually care about night life other than at spurts they go on a bender and have a good time. But, generally, they lead a daytime life which is sunshine. Musicians— they live a night life. They begin to wake up about five or six o'clock in the evenin'. So they see things different. They see intrigue. In night clubs, you sit on the bandstand and see all kinds of happenin's. A real depth of life. You see the underworld. You see all kinds of loose livin' people. 'Cause in the daytime, people are more business-

like; They tend to other things. But, at night, you see people enjoyin' themselves. To a musician, everyday is like a holiday. It's the
good time, and you're playin' for people enjoyin' themselves.

The members of Local 496 have become so identified with
Bourbon Street Black that they usually feel responsive to most of
the moral norms and frequently take the initiative in establishing
them. One of the middle-aged musicians who is admired by many
of the younger men says:

A musician's life isn't supposed to be different than anyone else's.
It doesn't matter if a man is a doctor, lawyer, or musician. You meet
a few guys in music who are way out, sometimes. They don't do
nothin'; they don't give nothin'. Same for any job. I just think people ought to try get along with others. Don't get me wrong. I think
you have to do some things you wanta do. Sometimes you gotta do
your own thing, but you can't be so far out you're in a world by
yourself. I don't want to be so far out that I'm not in this world, and
I'm still here. (laugh)

12

You Can Come Home to New Orleans!

As we sat down to talk, he said,

Man, for as long as I can remember, jazz has been a good thing here! I remember daddy—he was a clarinet man—sayin' that sometimes when he walked through the streets of New Orleans, 'specially at night, he could just feel Buddy Bolden, Papa Joe, and Louis right here with him.

Yesterday

In a way, the old man was summarizing much of what has happened in the Crescent City during the past two hundred and fifty years, and some things even before that time; a heritage that has produced a distinctive way of life. The early part of this heritage is as interesting as it is complex. It begins with black men in Western Africa sharing a commitment to cultural settings where music was a major preoccupation. Ripped from their foundations and thrown westward into chaos and family dissolution, they experienced the further indignities of rape and miscegenation. The peculiarities of this cross-breeding in the antebellum Louisiana Delta region produced the Creole of Color; neither black nor white. An untitled but privileged class of people who became progressively more "white" and "European" in their behavior. For years, they mastered and accumulated many of the technical and intellectual competencies of Western Europe and white America only to be cast downward as "Negro" a short time after the Civil War.

Though disinherited, the Creoles emerged from their almost co-equal status with the elite of New Orleans maintaining a thorough dedication to advancement in the white world. They were completely accepting of capitalism and all that it implied, in spite of their almost overnight consignment to the dregs of Delta society. The Catholic Church had given them a faith in the future, no matter how distant, and they were also not immune to considerable portions of the Protestant Ethic that had diffused into New Orleans over its long history. In short, by the standards of the "majority" culture that surrounded them, they were conventional. Though embittered by their disenfranchisement, those who didn't leave the United States to save their fortunes and way of life chose the alternative of a relatively peaceful coexistence with the whites. To have engaged in open conflict with the majority population would have been unthinkable for them. Apart from their knowledge that it would have been suicidal, they were a disciplined people with great respect for the Napoleonic Code. Then too, the destruction of the vast Creole economic and cultural interests occurred so gradually in a number of instances they were often unaware of the exact sources of difficulty. As they witnessed the dissolution of their material world, they began to adapt themselves within the conventional system into less prestigeful occupations. All the while, they maintained strong ties to the Catholic Church and the legal system.

In his new "world," the Creole of Color became the reluctant confrere of the black man, newly discharged from slavery. Though things have never gone smoothly between them, from the very beginning they had a great deal to give each other. Somehow, with the knowledge that one had of the rules of the white man's game, and the other the ability to survive in a hostile setting, they hesitantly combined skills and were able to cope. Apart from their sharing low status in white New Orleans, the blacks and Creoles had at least one other common element; their love for music. Out of these things, some of them built the semicommunity[1] we have chosen to call Bourbon Street Black. It was not a territorial or physically definable one like we think of when someone mentions Joplin, Missouri, or New Haven, Connecticut. Bourbon Street Black both was, and is, a social psychological semicommunity. True, practically all the events we have discussed have transpired within the territorial limits of New Orleans, and even most either close to or within a few square miles of the Vieux Carré. Still, the geography is only incidental; it's the people who have been important.

Bourbon Street Black was born when a certain group of blacks and Creoles realized they shared some common concerns, and that they had come to depend upon each other for both emotional and physical survival. Their awareness of common interests arose when they first became competitive with each other during the latter third of the nineteenth century. Coming into this relationship, the Creoles had distinct advantages in a social-class system which dispensed privilege and status in proportion of approximation to "whiteness." On the other hand, something was happening to diminish the practical or economical importance of the class differences between the two groups of "Negroes." During the latter half of the nineteenth century, segregation was being enforced at an even greater rate, and the Creole's white clientele was severely diminished. This forced these high caste people into even greater interaction with a new purchasing public: the blacks. The blacks often could pay little, indeed, for their services, but something minimal even like bartering was better than starvation. The highly trained Creole musicians brought to this new public a level of "European type" technical competence far beyond anything they had ever seen. The black audiences were fascinated by these men who could read music and play with such virtuosity.

Other things were beginning to impress the Negro community, too. Relatively inelegant small groups of black musicians were beginning to perform for their picnics, parades, and dances with a kind of exciting music that was different from that of the early Creole bands, but intriguing. More often than not, their musical instruments were either homemade or European ones of low quality or repair. Lack of equipment didn't seem to affect the fervor with which these men made their performances an extension of their own feelings. They were acute observers of their surroundings, and borrowed freely, applying whatever they felt would fit into their format. Later they were to rework a relatively stiff, mechanical ragtime into something that went swinging along the streets of New Orleans as they poured out their own emotions into a music composed of the blues, spirituals, and ragtime!

By this time, the Creoles and blacks were in strong competition for much of the same music market. In some cases, the lower-classed black audiences preferred the "funkier" or more earthy uptown black bands and the higher status Creole listeners employed the more refined Downtown bands, but there was an increasing amount of crossing over and they were hearing each other's music. They remained competitive, but each liked what he heard in the other's work. The blacks began to realize the value of being able to read music (for certain kinds of well-paying gigs), and the Creoles were deeply impressed with how the blacks were making their music swing. During the last years of the nineteenth century and the beginning of the twentieth century, they became "friendly enemies" as their contacts increased. They were learning from each other.

By 1900 Creoles and blacks were playing with each other in greater numbers, and the music was being marketed to a considerably large audience. The men played wherever they could be heard and be paid, though they often played for nothing. Music was now clearly earmarked as an avenue of upward mobility for all talented young Negro men of the community. Storyville and many of the bistros, bars, barrel houses, and whorehouses employed them. By the time Storyville was closed in 1917 many young men were inspired by local heroes, some who were on their way to national prominence. The key roles of the music teacher (most of whom were Creole) were established and, as Danny Barker commented, they were in high demand:

There are currently a group of musicians who are jazz greats who grew up in New Orleans. In the '20s and '30s these men were taking lessons from outstanding teachers here. There were competent teachers all over the city—Uptown, Downtown, and back of town. Teachers like the Tios' who were masters of the clarinet. They also went to Manuel Perez, or Peter Bocage, or Piron. These were people who were the greatest—competent teachers. They knew their instrument; how it's supposed to sound; how it's supposed to play. They could give you the proper technique on the instrument. Legitimate playin'! How to play a clarinet properly. How to blow in it; how to lip it; how to finger it right.

The same thing about the trombone. Good examples of that were Honore Dutrey, Yank Johnson, Buddy Johnson, August Rousseau, and George Fields. These people were masters of the trombone. Some of them were capable of playin' in a symphony orchestra. There was no reason for a young cat not knowin' how to play an instrument by his not havin' the proper trainin'. That's where this term "ham-fat" musician came from. It referred to some guys who, instead of takin' lessons, just picked up their instruments and started playin'. Most of the good men took lessons from these teachers— some didn't. Those who didn't just learned tones, but the good ones at least developed a tone and some technique. If they didn't do that, there were so many critics in town here that would label you as not havin' the proper tone or technique, you just had to quit, 'cause nobody would hire you.

Another thing happened here. We could hear these teachers play in bands outside the lesson time. As kids we got to go to classes where some of the great musicians played. When I started playin' the banjo, I was curious and eager to learn. So, I went every chance I got where one of the bands like Manuel Perez's played. He had Caffrey Daris with him. In the Tuxedo Band and Armand Piron's Band I heard John Marrero. There was Charlie Bocage. These people played the banjo properly. There was also Kimball and Sayles who had taken lessons and were outstanding. I went to the dances so I could watch how these people played. There was no reason to not learn decent time, proper tone and shading; learn the tricks of good banjo playin'.

Once Bourbon Street Black came into existence, the music teachers served the dual function of training a new generation of musicians while serving as heroes or role models for them. Louis Armstrong was the key figure in the hero pantheon, for his great reputation as a jazzman and his international success stood as an example for all young musicians. Louis was proof that hard work and talent might allow you to make it if you got the breaks. Once the "hero system" was firmly established in Bourbon Street Black, much of the early social-class advantage of the Creoles was muted, and several of the heroes were black men. Even before Louis Armstrong became famous, the color of a man's skin or what his father did was much less important than how well he played.

By this time, Bourbon Street Black was a complete and vital semicommunity. They had set central goals which would make them an appropriate and "good" part of conventional society.[2] Whenever these goals of their style of life was threatened, they joined together for mutual defense. The most dramatic instance of this was in the late '20s when they formed Local 496. The Local and its officers became a vital aspect of Bourbon Street Black. The Local not only served to protect their interests both as a group and as individuals, but it was able to mediate business relationships with the outside conventional world in ways not possible for the individual musicians.

Today

Wherever the convention and tourist business is an important concern of a city, musicians are active. New Orleans is no exception. The annual traditional festivals concerned with religious, fraternal, and ethic groups are now dwarfed by the continuous flow of conventions and tourists. Most of the visitors are exposed to live music. Depending upon where they are and the nature of the occasion, it might be rock, ballroom dance music, traditional

Some serious "Groovin'." Photographed by Jack V. Buerkle.

jazz, contemporary jazz, or backup music for dancers. The musicians who play for these different audiences usually reflect age cohorts. The men who were young when traditional jazz was at its peak are now in their 60s, 70s, and 80s. They are now back playing the old two-beat material somewhere in the Vieux Carré. The middle-aged jazzmen are usually employed by big ballroom bands or contemporary jazz units, and the youngest are most often playing rock.

The music teachers continue to be held in high regard in the community, and several have now been absorbed into the public school system. Almost all of them teach in their own or a friend's private music school after classroom hours. They continue to identify and encourage talented children to pursue a career in music. Today they see an even greater chance for upward mobility in music because of the impact of civil rights legislation on employment possibilities. The message hasn't changed, "music is a good thing—it can take you a long ways, if you're good to it."

A new element in the situation is that the youth are now confident that their ability and motivation will get them goals inaccessible to their fathers. The heroes are still there. They don't always play jazz, though. There is Fats Domino, for instance. Fats Domino's earnings are often cited as an example of what hard work and a break can accomplish. Although Louis Armstrong is dead, he is still there, as intense as before. In a real sense, he represents the most pervasive influence we have observed in Bourbon Street Black: warm, genuine, interested in people, and basic in all respects. Not only do the jazz musicians want to "play with soul" like he did, but they want to emulate him in every way possible. Like Louis, they continue to want to please their audiences with their playing. They really couldn't understand doing otherwise.

Tomorrow

The amalgamation of Local 496 with Local 174 during January 1971 might be interpreted as heralding a major change within

Bourbon Street Black. There is little doubt the new dual Local will result in a number of economic and fringe benefit gains for the musicians, but its size and complex organization preclude the kind of friendly and informal atmosphere the jazzmen were accustomed to in 496. In all likelihood, however, the really important things that have held the community together are outside the Union. Bourbon Street Black existed long before Local 496 was founded. It had become an entity through the interdependencies set up between the black and Creole musicians, the music teachers, core families, peripheral families, and certain other persons significant to its operation.[3]

Most of the indicators of the future of this subcommunity of musicians and their compatriots seem to point toward its continuing at a healthy pace and perhaps even growing. The love of music by their people goes on, and with an increasing number of the music teachers becoming associated with the public schools, the possibility of discovering new talent has been greatly increased. The students who can profit by private lessons will probably be encouraged to take them in greater proportion than ever before. Once they are trained, they will have some place to work because the Convention Bureau will probably become even more efficient in attracting tourists and conventions. All this will simply be more proof to the members of Bourbon Street Black that they can continue to pursue their lives within the framework of the conventional moral and economic systems. The 1970s should be especially important in affirming these values to them because of the international attention they will receive during the bicentennial celebration period of the United States. At a time when jazzmen have already made some of the most significant gains of their entire history in the Crescent City, they will be lauded as the heirs and title holders to America's unique contribution to the arts. The idea of heritage has already become important to them within the past few months. An old hall, Dixieland Hall, where many of the older and middle-age musicians have played for the past few years, has just been renamed Heritage Hall. Also, each

nny Barker and the Fairview Baptist Church Christian Band at Congo Square. Photo-
phed by Floyd Levin.

April when thousands come to New Orleans to the new jazz festival, it isn't just a series of jazz concerts they are exposed to, but the Jazz and *Heritage* Festival. At this festival all the young musicians who are just "comin' up" can see their local heroes get billing alongside other jazz personalities from around the world.

Each year, they learn that prominent jazzmen and bands from the Crescent City are invited to be major participants in the Newport, Monterey, and other important jazz festivals. They are aware that the jazz scholar William Russell has documented the life histories of several older traditional musicians. All of these kinds of experiences will continue to "put some fire into these young men" concerning their careers in music.

While the greater part of Bourbon Street Black is being strengthened, some elements of this semicommunity are disappearing. We have discussed the jazz funeral and the reasons it will probably not exist after a few years. There is one other custom that seems to be on the wane—the tradition of the nickname. Colorful ones like Son Do, Whip, Chicken, Boo, Little Cag, and Show Boy appeared in the last directory of Local 496. Presently, almost one-third of the musicians use at least one nickname, and some have two. But such names do not seem to be important to the younger men. Some nicknames were coined for effect or to avoid an unwanted given name. Sometimes they described a common activity or a personality characteristic attributed to the user. The younger men have discarded all this, though. They consider it either demeaning or pointless and only a fraction of them have acquired a nickname. It will be interesting to observe whether some take on the title "Papa" or "Kid" as they inherit one of the old two-beat bands at the death of its leader. Our belief is that they will.

Notes

1
Sportin' Houses and All That Jazz

1. Henry Arnold Krem, "The Music of New Orleans," *The Past as Prelude: New Orleans 1718-1968*, Hodding Carter, ed. (New Orleans: Tulane University Publications, 1968), p. 211.

2. From an unpublished manuscript quoted by Grace King, *New Orleans, The Place and the People* (New York: The MacMillan Company, 1904), pp. 344-45.

3. Rudi Blesh, *Shining Trumpets* (New York: Alfred A. Knopf, 1958), p. 155.

4. Alan Lomax, *Mr. Jelly Roll* (New York: Duell, Sloan and Pearce, 1950), pp. 83-86.

5. George Cable, "The Dance in Place Congo," *Creoles and Cajuns: Stories of Old Louisiana*, Arlin Turner, ed. (Garden City, New York: Doubleday Anchor Book, Doubleday and Company, 1959), pp. 369-78.

6. Nat Shapiro and Nat Hentoff, *Hear Me Talkin' to Ya* (New York: Dover Publications, 1955), pp. 38-39.

7. Lomax, op. cit., p. 73.

8. Whitney Balliett, *Such Sweet Thunder: 49 pieces on Jazz* (Indianapolis: The Bobbs-Merrill Company, 1966), pp. 328-29.

9. Frederic Ramsey, Jr., and Charles Edward Smith, *Jazzmen* (New York: Harcourt, Brace and Company, 1939), p. 24.

10. Martin Williams, *Jazz Masters of New Orleans* (New York: The MacMillan Company, 1967), p. 140.

11. Phil Johnson "Good Time Town," *The Past As Prelude: New Orleans 1718-1968*, Hodding Carter, ed. (New Orleans: Tulane University Publications, 1968), p. 236.

2
Interlude

1. Herbert Asbury, *The French Quarter* (New York: Alfred A. Knopf, Inc., 1936), pp. 451-54.

2. Nat Shapiro and Nat Hentoff, *Hear Me Talkin' To Ya* (New York: Dover Publications, 1966), pp. 66-67.

3. Louis Armstrong, *Satchmo: My Life in New Orleans* (Englewood Cliffs, N.J.: Prentice Hall, 1954), pp. 140-41.

4. Richard A. Peterson, "Market and Moralist Censors of a Rising Art Form: Jazz," *Arts in Society,* IV (1967), pp. 254-55.

3
Who Are These Cats?

1. Though Bourbon Street is the main location of New Orleans traditional jazz bands today, this has not always been true. Only after Rue Bourbon became an entertainment area for American servicemen during World War II did it become known as a place to hear two-beat jazz. Before that time jazz performances were more widely dispersed throughout the city.

2. Ninety per cent were born within the New Orleans metropolitan area.

3. Only 21 per cent of the musicians had no close relatives who played music. In most cases, several members of the family could perform on one or more instruments or sing.

4. The median age is 48 years, and the age range is between 22 and 84.

5. Actually, they fared quite well, comparatively. Six per cent of the members of Bourbon Street Black have a fifth-grade education or less. The 1970 U.S. census reports 5 per cent white adults, and 19 per cent black adults with fifth-grade or less formal education.

6. Over 27 per cent of the New Orleans musicians have some college education or above, as opposed to 26 per cent for whites and 10 per cent for blacks, in general (last two figures, 1970 census). Eight per cent of Bourbon Street Black completed B.A.'s or M.A.'s compared to 5 per cent black males (1970 census), and 15 per cent white males (1970 census).

7. Charles "Cow-Cow" Davenport, *Momma Don't Allow It* (New York: Select Music Publications, 1935).

8. Our analysis indicates only 10 per cent of the present generation of musicians' families are female headed (broken) and only 9 per cent were reared under such conditions. This is in direct contradiction to other re-

ports specifying upwards to one-third of black families in the U.S. were without a male head. In this regard see especially, E. Franklin Frazier, *The Negro in the United States* (New York: MacMillan and Company, 1957), p. 317; and Daniel P. Moynihan, *The Negro Family: The Case For National Action* (The Department of Labor, Washington D.C., 1965).

9. Eighty-two per cent are currently married (living with spouse). The national average for blacks (1967) is 78 per cent. Four per cent of the musicians are currently divorced and not remarried. The national average is 4 per cent.

10. Sixty-one per cent own their own homes, whereas the Bureau of Census (1970) reports U.S. home ownership to be 63 per cent of all occupancies.

11. Almost 60 per cent of the members of Bourbon Street have lived at their present address for over ten years, and of those who have lived at previous addresses, 56 per cent were there over five years. By all national standards, they are a residentially stable population.

4

Second Linin'

1. Paul Barbarin, "The Second Line." Permission granted by Mrs. Paul Barbarin.

2. Twenty-seven per cent began before they were 11, and 4 per cent after age 25.

3. Nat Shapiro and Nat Hentoff, *Hear Me Talkin' To Ya* (New York: Rhinehart and Company, 1955), p. 30.

4. Only 8 per cent of the musicians had no lessons at all; 59 per cent of them had private instruction that they, or someone else paid for. These were primarily lessons with the "professors." A small number (4 per cent) had private lessons for free. The remainder had combinations of the above plus some minimal school group instruction. Only 2 per cent indicated ever receiving any instruction in jazz. They just picked it up from listening to records (later) and groups. Over two-thirds (67 per cent) received instruction in the basics to their instrument. These often included an introduction to the classics. The older men generally started their paid instruction at an older age than did the younger men. The reason for this is that the younger men had money to pay for the lessons at an earlier age. The parents of the younger jazzmen were comparatively more affluent, and money was generally more accessible. Actually, most of the men paid for the lessons themselves. This is true for both the older and younger men. None of the musicians take lessons now, but most see themselves in a continuous process of growth and self-instruction.

5. Over half of the total group (55 per cent) had *no* participating contact with church music groups. Fourteen per cent sang in a choir at one time, and 21 per cent played some kind of instrument accompanying a choir. The remainder (11 per cent) had some kind of musical contact with the church. Danny Barker, for instance, has organized a brass band for youths at the Fairview Baptist Church.

6. Exactly 50 per cent played in a school band during their public or parochial school days, 44 per cent attended schools without bands, and 6 per cent went to schools with bands, but did not join them. These results really reflect some of the comments made by the musicians in the text. It was simply an older–younger thing, i.e., younger musicians were significantly more likely to have played in a school band. School bands are a relatively recent phenomenon. Younger musicians were also more likely to have experienced a school situation where lessons were given.

7. Forty-nine per cent said their parents aspired to "as much (education) as I could get," for them; 26 per cent responded, "left it up to me"; 9 per cent, some college; 13 per cent, college graduate; and 4 per cent, graduate or professional school.

8. Very few wanted their children to pursue work in skilled, semi-skilled, or labor areas (only 8 per cent combined). But almost as many wanted their young to have careers in music (21 per cent) as aspired for their children to have professional careers (23 per cent). We have fairly strong evidence that, in most cases, the aspirations for professional careers were not held strongly by the parent. Very probably such aspirations were lessened by the strong expectation that achievement would not really be possible given the economic situation and other contingencies. Some families might have been able to accomplish it, but not many. Indications of this become evident when we realize that musicians emanating from families of higher socio-economic status had higher educational aspirations than those from families of lower status ($X^2 = 4.3697$, d.f. $= 1$, p. $< .05$). Thus the aspirations were more realistic when controlled for socio-economic factors (occupation and education).

9. 23.4 per cent quit because they wanted to play music and school was interfering.

5

The Local

1. Seventeen per cent said they participate in jam sessions frequently; 28 per cent once in a while; and 14 per cent only rarely.

2. When a test of independence (chi square) was performed running age against knowledge of music business practices, union rules, etc., at

time of entry into the profession, there were no significant differences between the older and younger musicians knowledge.

3. Only 12 per cent said they knew these things as they began, and 5 per
cent said they knew a little.

4. Fifty-five per cent play in one group now, 18 per cent play in two, and
14 per cent play in more than two groups.

6

Of Race and Men

1. H. O. Brunn, *The Story of the Original Dixieland Band* (Baton
Rouge: Louisiana State University Press, 1960), pp. 53-56.

2. All published and copyrighted by Leo Feist and Company. Larry
Shields is listed as co-composer of "At The Jazz Band Ball."

3. Shapiro and Hentoff, op. cit., p. 42.

4. Brunn, op. cit., pp. 53-56.

5. Ralph Ellison, *Invisible Man* (New York: Signet Books, 1953).

6. Stearns, op. cit., p. 124.

7. Leonard Feather, *The Book of Jazz* (New York: Horizon Press, 1965),
pp. 47-49.

8. Nat Hentoff, "Race Prejudice in Jazz: It Works Both Ways," *Harpers*,
218 (June 1959), pp. 72-77. This is an early discussion of one aspect of
the problem. Many others have appeared since, a number appearing in
the jazz fan magazines.

9. LeRoi Jones, *Blue People* (New York: William Morrow and Company, 1963), p. 219.

10. John S. Wilson, "What is Black Music? Cannonball Adderly Ex-
plains," *New York Times*, November 12, 1969, p. 42.

11. Chris Albertson, "Cannonball the Communicator," *Downbeat* (January 8, 1970), p. 13.

12. Mike Bourne, "Defining Black Music: An Interview With David
Baker," *Downbeat*, 36 (September 18, 1969), p. 14.

13. Frank Kofsky, *Black Nationalism and the Revolution in Music* (New
York: Pathfinder Press, 1970).

14. Ibid. This book is a compilation of adulatory interviews with a few
avant-garde musicians, and comments about others. Kofsky was, at the
time of the book's publication, a West Coast history professor. There is
little evidence of historical objectivity, and the book suffers considerably
as the author tries to "glue on" a Marxist rationale to account for the alleged "revolutionary" activities of the avant-garde musicians. There is little doubt that the avant-garde people represent a significant development

in the recent history of jazz, but the Kofsky book does not assist greatly in understanding them. His "interviews" of McCoy Tyner are inept and pathetic, from the vantage points of either historical or sociological objectivity. In these attempts at interviewing, large portions of the exchanges involve Kofsky asking "leading" questions, and then interpreting the responses to be revolutionary on only the slimmest evidence.

15. Several prominent musicians emphasizing the black music theme have dropped the word "jazz" because they see it as an insult to blacks. In a way, their concern is unnecessary, because a large segment of the white population still believes (though incorrectly) jazz to be a white creation. Also, there is fairly strong evidence that the term was first used in connection with a white group in Chicago billed as *Browns Dixieland Jass Band* (1915).

16. It would be a mistake to consider New Orleans "typically southern"; it probably has never been so. Some of the "southern touch" is there, but with a tinge of Latin and European permissiveness.

17. Thirty-eight per cent named a black as playing "the best," whereas 28 per cent chose a white musician, and 34 per cent stated no preference.

18. No difference—52 per cent. Yes, a difference of soul, feeling—26 per cent. Yes, a difference in undisciplined vs formal—13 per cent. Other differences—9 per cent.

19. Sixty-eight per cent said it made no difference to them whether the music was black or white.

20. Paul R. Lentz, "Wallace Davenport: Taking Uncle Tom Out of Dixieland," *Downbeat* (April 1, 1971), pp. 18-19.

7

Who Am I?

1. For relevant theoretical and conceptual material, see George Herbert Mead, *Mind, Self, and Society* (Chicago: The University of Chicago Press, 1934); Erving Goffman, *The Presentation of Self in Everyday Life* (Garden City, New York: Doubleday Anchor Books, Doubleday and Company, 1959). For an important early article dealing with research on self-attitudes, see M. H. Kuhn and T. S. McPartland, "An Empirical Investigation of Self Attitudes," *American Sociological Review,* 19 (1954), pp. 68-78.

2. Sixty-nine per cent felt they would get considerably better than they were at the time of the interview. Only 7 per cent (mostly older men) felt they probably wouldn't improve, whereas 17 per cent saw some improvement was possible. Seven per cent were not sure.

3. Almost 98 per cent said their playing had improved considerably since they began playing professionally.

4. Forty per cent claimed they were better than their friends, whereas 38 per cent said they could play about equally as well. Twenty per cent were unable to make a comparison, and only 2 per cent felt they could not play as well as their friends.

5. Practice was the reason most often given for assuming another's superiority in playing—37 per cent. Twenty-two per cent felt that experience or exposure accounted for the difference, but 38 per cent were unable to account for why another musician might be better. Only an insignificant 3 per cent felt such differences might be due to natural talent.

6. This musician was in a distinct minority, being unable to rate himself. Only 4 per cent were unable to place themselves in this rating. Thirty-six per cent said they "were among the best," 24 per cent were "better than most," 31 per cent were "average," and only 2 per cent contended they were "not as good as most." Three per cent gave some other reason.

7. Seventeen per cent of the musicians viewed success from a materialistic perspective; 59 per cent described it in non-materialistic terms, and 24 per cent saw it as a combination of both materialistic and non-materialistic factors.

8. This was the factor to which the greater proportion (49 per cent) of the musicians attributed success. Thirty-two per cent felt you need both the "breaks" and ability to achieve success, while only 19 per cent saw ability as the major element in realizing success.

9. Eighty per cent of the musicians said they intended to play music for the rest of their lives, if possible. Twenty per cent felt they would not be playing professionally after what they considered retirement age.

10. Ninety-two per cent of the musicians contend they would, or have advised their son to be a professional musician. Four per cent said they would not give such advice, and 4 per cent felt they would be unable to influence him. Also, 87 per cent said they were presently active in encouraging someone to become a musician. Only 13 per cent were not active in this respect.

8

It Does *Matter Who Your Folks Were!*

1. Copyright Edward B. Marks Music Corporation. Used by permission.

2. Celia Heller, *Structured Social Inequality* (New York: Macmillan and Company, 1969), p. 4.

3. Benjamin Quarles, *The Negro in the Making of America,* revised edition (London: Collier Books, Collier Macmillan, Ltd., 1969), p. 8.

4. Ibid., p. 91.

5. Seymour Parker and Robert J. Kleiner, *Mental Illness in the Urban Negro Community* (New York: The Free Press, 1966), pp. 395-400.

6. Forty-five per cent of their fathers received 4 years of formal education or less.

7. Only 26 per cent of musicians' fathers stayed in school beyond the eighth grade, but 67 per cent of the musicians themselves stayed in school beyond that point.

8. Most of their parents (71 per cent) wanted some college or higher for them. Only 29 per cent were not urged to go on to some form of higher education. Clearly, most did not make it, but the parental wish was there.

9. Forty-three per cent stated no preference of occupation for their child.

10. Sixty-seven per cent of the musicians equaled their fathers' educational level, while 33 per cent were significantly above it. None were below. Thirty-nine per cent of the musicians equaled their fathers' occupational level, and 61 per cent were significantly above. Occupation, as we use it here, includes the category full-time musician, and for some, their major other job if they are part-time musicians. The questions we addressed ourselves to here for such men were: "What type of 'day job' is now available to the cat? Do the men hold jobs of higher prestige than those of their fathers?"

11. The Great Depression of the thirties had an inhibiting affect on this professionalization, but it began to pick up again by the '40s.

12. Significantly more musicians who reached their educational goals had fathers whose own education was classified in the *higher* bracket. $X^2 = 4.1344$, d.f. $= 1$, p. $< .05$.

13. For instance, if a musician's education expectations for himself were high, it is likely that his father was in the high educational category, $X^2 = 4.3719$, d.f. $= 1$, p. $< .05$. Another consideration that bears this out is the relationship between the father's education and the education his son actually received. $X^2 = 9.2041$, d.f. $= 1$, p. $< .05$.

14. Musicians with more education more often rate themselves higher in ability than do those with less education, $X^2 = 3.9506$, d.f. $= 1$, p. $< .05$.

15. $X^2 = 4.3006$, d.f. $= 1$, p. $< .05$.

16. Those from the larger and lower-status families mentioned the importance of material things to their happiness, $X^2 = 5.4669$, d.f. $= 1$, p. $< .05$.

17. $X^2 = 9.7383$, d.f. $= 1$, p. $< .05$.

9

Giggin' and Socializin'

1. The musicians were asked, "Would you rather play with a group that plays well, or one not as good that makes more money?" Seventy-two per cent preferred the group that plays well, and 28 per cent said they

would go with the group that makes more money, but with lower standards.

2. Almost three-fourths (74 per cent) felt that the group(s) they were in were better than the average for New Orleans. Eighty-nine per cent believed their group(s) would stay together for at least the near future.

3. Only 10 per cent mentioned money as the factor that made the gig · 1d out as the "best."

Only 21 per cent of the men preferred to stay in the Crescent City all time. Sixty-two per cent like to travel occasionally, and 17 per cent enjoy frequent traveling.

5. Only 17 per cent said that travel had some serious effect on either the marriage or their children.

6. Thirty-five per cent felt that the problems and opportunities of the road were such that the serious musician was better off single. Still, almost two-thirds (65 per cent) saw his career and life, in general, improved by marriage.

7. Seventy-seven per cent of the musicians are married.

8. Only 14 per cent of the musicians said that half or more of their five best friends are non-musicians.

9. Half of the men said they listened to jazz at home. The remainder of the men prefer the following music styles: rock and roll—3 per cent, classical—9 per cent, pop and show tunes—4 per cent, several kinds (including jazz)—30 per cent, none—4 per cent.

10

In God's Country

1. Sidney Bechet, *Treat It Gentle* (New York: Hill and Wang, 1960), pp. 217-18.

2. Copyright Folkways Music Publications, Inc. New words and music arrangement by Paul Campbell. Reprinted by permission.

3. Barry Ulanov, *History of Jazz in America* (New York: The Viking Press, 1952), p. 47.

4. Eighty-eight per cent of the musicians belong to a church. Of these, 35 per cent are Protestants, and 53 per cent are Catholic. The remainder say they are committed to a sect or belief not traditionally a part of the American religious setting, or they profess no religious beliefs. Some believe in a universal religion of their own construction, while others have attached themselves to some of the philosophy of Far Eastern religions. Those in the latter group are often young and middle-aged men.

5. Ten per cent said they attend less than once a year, 14 per cent—three to five times a year, 11 per cent—once a month, 24 per cent—two to three

times a month, 38 per cent—weekly, and 3 per cent—more than once a week.

6. Thirty-three per cent have no special prayers, but 62 per cent usually make use of orthodox or standard prayers, while 5 per cent employ esoteric or non-orthodox praying.

11

Diggin' the Squares and the Hips

1. Dorothy Baker, *Young Man With a Horn* (Boston: Houghton Mifflin Company, 1938).

2. Norman M. Margolis, "A Theory on the Psychology of Jazz," *American Imago,* XI (Fall 1954), p. 276.

3. Howard S. Becker, "The Professional Dance Musician and His Audience," *The American Journal of Sociology,* LVII (September 1951), p. 143. Other sociologists taking similar positions are Alan P. Merriam and Raymond W. Mack, "The Jazz Community," *Social Forces,* 38 (March 1960), pp. 211-22; and William Bruce Cameron, "Sociological Notes on the Jam Session," *Social Forces,* XXXIII (December 1954), pp. 177-82.

4. Howard S. Becker, Raymond W. Mack, and William Bruce Cameron have all worked as professional musicians.

5. The impact of these assumptions has been widespread in American sociology. Becker, a prominent sociologist, has authored a collection of his articles on the sociology of deviance in book form. This book, *Outsiders* (New York: Free Press, 1963), has been one of the more popular books read by sociology students within the last decade.

6. Ibid., p. 85.

7. Fifty-nine per cent of the musicians said that "squares" are those who are either narrowminded, don't like change, or jazz. Twenty-two per cent said, "It's not for me to say who is a square." Nineteen per cent said, "I don't know."

8. Charles Winick, "The Use of Drugs by Jazz Musicians," *Social Problems,* 7 (1960), p. 247.

9. Ibid., p. 252.

10. A check of arrest records through the New Orleans Police Department revealed that less than 1 per cent of them have *ever* been detained on a drug charge. Given the traditional suspicion of the police (and the public) of musicians—particularly black musicians—this finding is truly remarkable.

11. From a statistical point of view, there were no significant differences between the older and younger musicians regarding conservative–liberal

attitudes toward the use of marijuana by themselves or others. The youths *tended* to be somewhat more liberal about marijuana, but not significantly so.

12. Becker, op. cit., p. 143.

13. Twenty-seven per cent of them believe the general public has a "good" opinion of them; 23 per cent—bad; 44 per cent mixed (good and bad); and 6 per cent—no opinion of how the public feels.

14. Those who believe musicians are fundamentally different—32 per cent; those who see no basic differences—68 per cent.

12

You Can Come Home to New Orleans

1. Bourbon Street Black cannot be classified as a complete community. Communities are largely self-sufficient, meeting most of their needs without outside support. A strong case could be made that Bourbon Street Black executes a number of important social and emotional activities but lacks at least some of physical and economic requirements of the people.

2. In sociological terms, Bourbon Street Black is an excellent example of a *status community*. American sociologists have begun to find this approach, conceived by Max Weber and first supported in the United States by Don Martindale, a promising and sensitive one for dealing with the myriad of semicommunities that make up contemporary society. For further information on this concept, see Holger R. Stub (ed.), *Status Communities in Modern Society* (New York: The Dryden Press, 1972); Joseph Bensman, "Status Communities in Urban Societies: The Musical Community," in Stub, Ibid.; Robert A. Stebbins, "Class, Status, and Power Among Jazz and Commercial Musicians," *The Sociological Quarterly,* VII (Spring 1966); Stebbins, "A Theory of the Jazz Community," *The Sociological Quarterly,* IX (Summer 1968).

3. We see Bourbon Street Black as "a *consensual* community, in which the individual chooses to live out his major life interests within a framework of institutions, culture, practices, and social relationships that are consistent with his adherence to a set of values" (Bensman, op. cit.). From this point of view, Bourbon Street Black might be considerably different from other jazz status communities having a different history and basis for consensus. Because of this, it seems pointless to speak of "the jazzman," "the doctor," "the teacher," or any occupational or status group on an inclusive basis. Local history and consensus can make each group quite distinctive. Time, of course, can also change the norms of a status community.

Appendix

Population

Fifty-one musicians, all members of Local 496, American Federation of Musicians, New Orleans, Louisiana, were interviewed as the central subjects of the field study. At the time of the field work, those interviewed comprised approximately one-eighth of the total membership of the Local. Local 496 was a predominantly black Local, but in January 1971 after our interviews it amalgamated with the previously all white Local 174. The new organization is known as the Musician's Mutual Protective Union, Local 174-496. Local 496 was a jazz union with its members predominantly classifying themselves as jazz musicians.

Procedure for the Field Study

Data were obtained from several sources: interviews with the musicians, a complete review and analysis of jazz history, official records, a personality test (the Kuhn-McPartland Twenty Statements Test), social historical analysis, and participant observation. A few union officials and club owners were interviewed.

The basic interview questions were constructed through pilot study efforts to gain information particularly in the areas of demography, human ecology, social organization, sociometry, social psychology, the sociology of religion, and social deviance. The musicians were each asked 153 questions, many of which contained multiple probes. We encouraged full, free comment by the subjects at all times during the interviews. Questions were printed on 3 × 5 cards in preference to the frequently used interview schedule technique. We felt that making notations on an interview schedule would be disruptive of the interview process. All interviews were tape recorded. Forty per cent of the items were precoded. For the remaining materials, codes were derived after the field period and verified through interjudge agreement.

Interviews averaged between 75 minutes and two and one-half hours, and a total of 115 hours of taped interviews were recorded. Extensive ethnographic notes of family and community life were taken and analyzed throughout the entire period of the field study and manuscript preparation.

Wherever we have quoted individual musicians and identified them by name, their permission was obtained for publication of such comments. The bulk of such quotation appears in Chapter 4, "Second Linin'." The decision to include names in this childhood socialization area was based largely on the desire of many of the musicians to be quoted. To avoid compromising individual musician's concerning their present beliefs and behavior, we developed a policy of anonymity for all other subject matters. Though co-author Barker is a subject of this study, he was one of those chosen randomly at its inception, and was interviewed several months before becoming a partner in the book project.

Though most interviews were completed in the musician's homes, some were done in clubs, the union hall, and in neighborhood restaurants. Considerable participant observation took place while on the bandstand and marching with brass bands during parades. While Barker is a full-time resident of New Orleans, Buerkle spent approximately ten weeks there during the thirty month period of the field study and manuscript preparation.

Equipment for the Field Study

Interviews were recorded on Stuzzi Memocord miniature tape recorders using ninety minute cassettes and directional microphones. The interviews were then transferred to seven inch reel tapes for coding and other detailed analysis. Photographs by Buerkle were taken with a Zeiss Ikon Contaflex Super utilizing 50 mm Carl Zeiss f 2.8 Tessar, and 115 mm Carl Zeiss f 4.0 Pro Tessar lenses. Films used were Kodak Tri-X Pan and Kodak Plus-X Pan. Auxilliary lighting, when necessary, was provided by a Bauer E160 Ultrablitz electronic flash unit using both bounce and direct techniques.

Data Analysis

During the coding procedure, those materials to be processed by statistical methods were transferred by keypunch to IBM cards. The information was then moved to a computer tape from which it was processed on a Control Data Corporation model 6400 computer at the Temple University Computer Center. For the most part, the data collected in this project are of nominal character. Chi Square, the phi coefficient, percentages, and a few instances of product-moment correlation make up the battery of procedures used. Two computer programs were utilized for practically all of the statistical work; BMDO2S was used for tests of independence, and SPSS Procedure CODEBOOK produced frequency tables and histograms.

Index